Florida Biology EOC Test Prep 2025

Comprehensive Study Guide with 500+ Practice Questions and in-depth Answer Explanations for the Florida End-of-Course Biology Exam

By Alaric D. Thornwell

Copyright © 2025 by Alaric D. Thornwell All rights reserved.

No part of this book may be reproduced, stored in a retrieval system, or transmitted in any form or by any means, electronic, mechanical, photocopying, recording, or otherwise, without prior written permission of the publisher, except for brief quotations used in a review or scholarly work.

This publication is designed to provide general information for exam preparation purposes only. While every effort has been made to ensure the accuracy of the information provided, **Alaric D. Thornwell** makes no representations or warranties about the completeness, accuracy, or applicability of the content.

This book is not affiliated with, endorsed by, or sponsored by the Florida Department of Education or any official testing body.

The practice questions, explanations, and study content contained in this book are original works created independently by **Alaric D. Thornwell** for educational purposes.

Table Of Contents

Introduction: Your Complete Path to Success — 5
How to Use This Book for Maximum Success — 5
1. Master the Content Review Sections — 5
2. Engage with Practice Questions — 5
3. Learn from Detailed Answer Explanations — 6
Why This Book Works — 6
Ready to Succeed? — 6

Chapter 1: The Nature of Science — 7
1.1 Scientific Inquiry & Methodology — 7
1.2: Scientific Theories and Laws — 13

Chapter 2: Biochemistry – The Chemistry of Life — 23
2.1 The Chemical Basis of Life — 23
2.2: Enzymes and Biochemical Reactions — 28
2.3: Water and pH in Biological Systems — 33

Chapter 3: Cell Biology — 38
3.1: Cell Structure and Function — 38
3.2: Cellular Transport Mechanisms — 43
3.3: Cellular Energy — Photosynthesis & Cellular Respiration — 48
3.4: Cell Growth and Reproduction — 52

Chapter 4: Genetics and Heredity — 57
4.1: Gregor Mendel's Experiments and Principles — The Foundation of Modern Genetics — 57
4.2: Molecular Genetics — The Blueprint of Life — 61
4.3: Genetic Disorders and Biotechnology — 65

Chapter 5: Evolution and Natural Selection — 71
5.1: Darwin's Principles of Natural Selection — How Evolution Works — 71
5:.2: Mechanisms of Evolution — How Populations Change Over Time — 75
5.3: Human Evolution — Understanding Our Origins — 81

Chapter 6: Ecology and Environmental Science — 87
6.1: Ecosystem Structure and Function — 87
6.2: Biogeochemical Cycles — Nature's Recycling Systems — 92

6.3: Population Ecology ... 97
6.4: Conservation Biology ... 98

Chapter 7: Classification and Diversity of Life ... 101
7.1 Taxonomy and Classification Systems ... 101
7.2: Viruses vs. Living Organisms ... 103

Chapter 8: Human Body Systems and Homeostasis ... 107
8.1: Major Organ Systems and Their Functions ... 107
8.2: The Immune System and Disease ... 110

Chapter 9: Data Analysis and Scientific Literacy ... 114
9.1: Interpreting Graphs and Data Tables ... 114
9.2: Experimental Design and Critical Thinking ... 117

Practice Question ... 121
Chapter 1: The Nature of Science ... 121
Chapter 2: Biochemistry – The Chemistry of Life ... 139
Chapter 3: Cell Biology ... 153
Chapter 4: Genetics and Heredity ... 171
Chapter 5: Evolution and Natural Selection ... 185
Chapter 6: Ecology and Environmental Science ... 195
Chapter 7: Classification and Diversity of Life ... 209
Chapter 8: Human Body Systems and Homeostasis ... 218
Chapter 9: Data Analysis and Scientific Literacy ... 227
10: Test-Taking Strategies for the Biology EOC ... 237
Conclusion ... 244

Introduction: Your Complete Path to Success

Welcome to the **ultimate study guide** for the **Florida Biology End-of-Course (EOC) Exam 2025** — designed to help you **master biology concepts, apply knowledge, and succeed on exam day**. Whether you're **learning topics for the first time** or **reviewing before the test**, this book gives you **everything you need in one place**.

Inside, you'll find:

- **Thorough explanations** of all essential topics.
- **Clear diagrams** to visualize key concepts.
- **Practice questions** with **detailed answer explanations** to ensure deep understanding.

This guide does **more than help you memorize facts** — it teaches you to **think like a scientist**, **analyze information**, and **apply biology to real-world situations**, just like you'll be asked to do on the **EOC exam**.

How to Use This Book for Maximum Success

This book is **organized logically** to make studying easier and more effective. Here's how to get the most out of it:

1. Master the Content Review Sections

Each chapter focuses on a **key topic area**, covering everything required for the **Florida EOC Biology Exam**. You will find:

- **Clear explanations** in easy-to-understand language.
- **Important vocabulary terms** defined and explained.
- **Visual diagrams and illustrations** to help you remember and understand concepts.
- **Real-life examples** that connect biology to everyday situations.

2. Engage with Practice Questions

At the end of every chapter, you'll find **multiple practice questions** modeled after real EOC exam questions. These will help you:

- **Test your knowledge and understanding.**
- **Apply what you've learned to new situations.**
- **Build confidence** in answering various types of questions.

3. Learn from Detailed Answer Explanations

Every practice question includes a **detailed explanation**, so you'll know **why** an answer is correct or incorrect. This will help you:

- **Deepen your understanding** — not just memorize facts.
- **Avoid common mistakes.**
- **Develop critical thinking skills** essential for exam success.

Why This Book Works

- **All-in-One Resource**: Complete **content review, practice questions, and explanations** in one guide.
- **Student-Friendly**: Written in **clear language** with **visual support**.
- **Exam-Focused**: Fully aligned with **Florida EOC Biology standards**.
- **Skill-Building**: Focuses on **thinking, analysis, and application**, not just memorization.

Ready to Succeed?

If you **commit** to working through this guide, **practice regularly**, and **review explanations carefully**, you will be **fully prepared to excel** on the **Florida EOC Biology Exam**.

Let's **get started** on the **path to success!**

Chapter 1: The Nature of Science

1.1 Scientific Inquiry & Methodology

I. What is Science?

Definition of Science:

Science is a **systematic and organized approach** to understanding the natural world through **observations, experiments, and evidence-based conclusions**. It aims to explain **how and why things happen in nature** using logical reasoning and verifiable facts.

Science is **not based on opinions, guesses, or beliefs** but is driven by **evidence that can be tested and observed by anyone under the same conditions**.

Science as a Systematic Study:

- **Systematic** means science follows specific procedures and methods.
- Science helps us explain natural phenomena such as **gravity, photosynthesis, evolution, and ecosystems**.
- It is used to develop **new technologies, solve problems, and improve life**.

Scientific Knowledge is:

1. **Testable** – can be examined through experiments and observations.
2. **Replicable** – others can repeat and verify it.
3. **Falsifiable** – can be proven wrong if new evidence arises.
4. **Based on empirical evidence** – data gathered through direct observation and experimentation.

II. The Scientific Method: A Process of Scientific Inquiry

The **scientific method** is a **structured step-by-step process** that scientists use to investigate questions about the natural world.

The Steps of the Scientific Method:

1. Making Observations:

- Using **senses** (sight, touch, hearing) or tools (microscopes, thermometers) to gather information.
- Observations raise **questions** that lead to investigations.

Example: Noticing that some plants grow faster than others in different locations.

2. Asking a Question:

- Based on observations, a **specific, measurable, and testable question** is formed.

Example Question: "Does the amount of sunlight affect plant growth?"

3. Forming a Hypothesis:

- A **hypothesis** is a **testable, educated guess or prediction** explaining what you think will happen in the experiment.
- Often written in "If... then..." format.

Example Hypothesis: "If plants are exposed to more sunlight, then they will grow taller because sunlight is essential for photosynthesis."

4. Designing and Conducting a Controlled Experiment:

A **controlled experiment** is designed to test the hypothesis by changing **only one variable** (independent variable) and keeping all other factors (controlled variables) the same.

Key Components:

- **Independent Variable (IV):** The factor that is changed by the experimenter (cause).
- **Dependent Variable (DV):** The factor that is measured (effect).
- **Controlled Variables:** Factors kept constant to ensure that only the IV affects the DV.
- **Control Group:** A group that does not receive the experimental treatment; used for comparison.

Example Setup:

- **IV:** Amount of sunlight (full sun, partial shade, no sun).
- **DV:** Plant height.
- **Controlled Variables:** Same type of plant, same soil, same water amount, same pot size.
- **Control Group:** Plants not exposed to any extra sunlight.

5. Collecting and Analyzing Data:

Data Collection:

- Gather **accurate and precise measurements** using proper tools.
- **Quantitative data:** Numerical (e.g., height in cm, temperature in °C).
- **Qualitative data:** Descriptive (e.g., leaf color, texture).

Example Data Collection: Measuring plant height every day for 2 weeks.

Data Analysis:

- Organize data into **tables, graphs, charts**.
- Look for patterns, trends, or differences.
- Use **statistics** like mean, median, and standard deviation to analyze the data.

6. Drawing Conclusions:

Based on data analysis:

- Decide if the data **supports or refutes the hypothesis**.
- **Consider sources of error** (e.g., measurement mistakes, environmental changes).

Example Conclusion: "Plants exposed to full sunlight grew 10 cm taller than those in the shade, supporting the hypothesis."

7. Communicating Results:

Scientists share results so others can review, repeat, and build upon them.

Ways to communicate:

- **Scientific reports** with sections: Introduction, Methods, Results, Discussion.
- **Presentations** at conferences.
- **Publishing articles** in scientific journals.

Communication ensures that science is transparent, verifiable, and open to new discoveries.

III. Identifying Variables in Experiments

Understanding variables is essential for **setting up fair tests**:

Type of Variable	Definition	Example from Plant Experiment
Independent Variable (IV)	The factor changed by the experimenter	Amount of sunlight
Dependent Variable (DV)	The factor that is measured	Plant height
Controlled Variables	Factors kept constant to ensure a fair test	Water, soil, type of plant, pot size
Control Group	The standard for comparison	Plants not receiving any extra sunlight

---

IV. Importance of Control Groups and Replication

Control Group:

- Serves as a **baseline** for comparison.
- Helps show what happens **without** the independent variable.

Example: Plants grown in normal light conditions (control) vs. plants in experimental light conditions.

Replication (Repeated Trials):

- Performing the experiment **multiple times** to ensure results are reliable and not due to chance.
- **More replicates = greater confidence** in the conclusion.

Example: Growing 10 plants in each sunlight condition rather than just one.

V. Reducing Bias and Increasing Accuracy in Experiments

Bias in Science:

Bias occurs when **personal opinions or expectations** affect the results of an experiment.

Ways to Reduce Bias:

- **Blind Experiment:** Participants don't know if they are in the control or experimental group.
- **Double-Blind Experiment:** Neither the participants nor the experimenters know who receives the treatment.
- **Randomization:** Randomly assign subjects to groups to avoid bias in selection.

Increasing Accuracy:

- **Calibrate tools** before use (e.g., zeroing scales).
- Use **precise measuring instruments**.
- **Standardize procedures** so every trial is performed the same way.
- **Repeat experiments** and use **large sample sizes** to reduce error.

VI. Statistical Tools in Data Analysis

Common Statistics Used:

- **Mean (average):** Sum of values ÷ number of values.
- **Median:** Middle value in an ordered list.
- **Mode:** Most frequently occurring value.
- **Standard Deviation:** Measure of variability in data.
- **Graphs/Charts:** Line graphs, bar graphs, scatter plots to visualize data trends.

VII. Summary for EOC Success:

Concept	Explanation
Scientific Method	A process to investigate questions using evidence
Hypothesis	A testable, educated guess about a natural phenomenon
Independent Variable (IV)	The factor you change
Dependent Variable (DV)	The factor you measure
Controlled Variables	Factors kept constant for fair testing
Control Group	A baseline for comparison
Replication	Repeating experiments to ensure reliability
Bias Reduction	Avoiding influences that can skew results
Accurate Data Collection & Analysis	Ensuring valid and trustworthy evidence

VIII. Sample EOC Practice Question:

Question:
A student wants to test how fertilizer affects plant growth. What is the **independent variable** in this experiment?
A) Type of plant
B) Amount of sunlight
C) Amount of fertilizer used
D) Height of the plant

Correct Answer: C) Amount of fertilizer used

11

Scientific Method Practice Worksheet

Part 1: Identifying Variables

Instructions: For each experiment described below, identify the **Independent Variable (IV)**, **Dependent Variable (DV)**, **Controlled Variables**, and **Control Group (if any).**

1. A scientist tests the effect of different amounts of sunlight on tomato plant growth.
    - **IV:** _____
    - **DV:** _____
    - **Controlled Variables:** _____
    - **Control Group (if any):** _____
2. A student tests if the amount of water affects how fast sugar dissolves in a glass.
    - **IV:** _____
    - **DV:** _____
    - **Controlled Variables:** _____
    - **Control Group (if any):** _____

Part 2: Forming Hypotheses

Instructions: Write a hypothesis for each question in "If... then..." format.

1. Does fertilizer make plants grow taller?
    - **Hypothesis:** _____
2. Will saltwater affect seed germination?
    - **Hypothesis:** _____

Part 3: Data Interpretation and Analysis

Instructions: Review the data and answer the questions.

Sunlight Exposure	Average Plant Height (cm)
Full sunlight	25
Partial sunlight	15
No sunlight	5

1. What is the independent variable? _____
2. What is the dependent variable? _____
3. What trend do you observe? _____
4. What conclusion can you draw? _____

Experimental Setup Diagram (Example: Sunlight and Plant Growth)

Diagram Description (For Reference or Drawing in Class):

Experimental Setup for Plant Growth

Group 1: Full Sunlight

Group 2: Partial Sunlight

Group 3: No Sunlight (Control)

Same Water | Same Soil | Same Pot Size | Same Plant Type | Measurement: Height

---

Part 4: Bonus — Scientific Method Scenario

Instructions: Complete the steps of the scientific method based on this situation.

Scenario: You observe that bread molds faster in a humid environment than in a dry one.

1. **Observation:** _____
2. **Question:** _____
3. **Hypothesis:** _____
4. **Experiment Design (describe variables & control):** _____
5. **Data Collection (how would you measure?):** _____
6. **Conclusion:** _____

1.2: Scientific Theories and Laws

I. Differences Between Scientific Theories and Scientific Laws

What is a Scientific Theory?

A **scientific theory** is a **well-substantiated, thoroughly tested explanation** of **how or why natural phenomena occur**. It is based on a **large body of evidence** gathered from multiple observations, experiments, and peer-reviewed research.

Key Features of Scientific Theories:

- **Explains WHY and HOW** something happens.
- Supported by **extensive empirical evidence** and experimentation.
- Subject to **modification or refinement** if new evidence emerges.
- **Broad in scope**, connecting many different observations and facts.
- **Not a guess** — very different from the everyday use of the word "theory."

Example of a Theory:

- **Theory of Evolution** explains **how** species change over time through natural selection.

What is a Scientific Law?

A **scientific law** is a **statement that describes a consistent and universal pattern observed in nature**. It tells us **what happens under certain conditions**, but **does not explain why** it happens.

Key Features of Scientific Laws:

- **Describes WHAT happens**, not why.
- Based on **repeated, consistent observations**.
- Often expressed in **mathematical terms**.
- **Does not change** as long as observations remain the same.

Example of a Law:

- **Law of Gravity** describes that **objects with mass attract each other** with a force proportional to their masses and distance — but it doesn't explain *why* gravity exists.

Comparison Chart: Theories vs. Laws

Feature	Scientific Theory	Scientific Law
Purpose	Explains **why and how** phenomena occur	Describes **what** happens in nature
Based on	Extensive **experimental evidence and observations**	Repeated **observations** of consistent patterns
Changeability	Can be **revised or expanded** with new evidence	Generally **fixed** unless disproven by new observations
Scope	Broad, connects many ideas	Specific, describes a single action or pattern
Example	**Theory of Evolution:** Explains species' changes	**Law of Gravity:** Describes gravitational attraction

II. Clarifying How Theories and Laws Work Together

- **Scientific laws** describe **what happens** — they are **summaries** of observed patterns.
- **Scientific theories** explain **why and how those patterns occur** — providing **mechanisms and reasons** behind natural phenomena.

Example:
- **Law of Gravity**: Objects fall toward Earth. (What happens)
- **Theory of General Relativity**: Explains gravity as the warping of space-time by mass. (Why it happens)

III. Examples of Widely Accepted Theories (With Historical Context and Evidence)

1. Cell Theory

Definition: All living organisms are composed of cells, and all cells arise from pre-existing cells.

Key Statements:
- All living things are made of one or more cells.
- Cells are the basic units of structure and function in living organisms.
- All cells come from pre-existing cells.

Historical Context & Evidence:
- **Robert Hooke (1665):** First observed and named "cells" while examining cork.
- **Anton van Leeuwenhoek (1670s):** Discovered microscopic life (bacteria, protozoa).
- **Matthias Schleiden & Theodor Schwann (1838-1839):** Proposed all plants and animals are made of cells.
- **Rudolf Virchow (1855):** "All cells come from cells."

    Evidence: Observations under microscopes, cell reproduction studies.

---

2. Theory of Evolution by Natural Selection

Definition: Species evolve over time due to natural selection, where organisms better adapted to their environment survive and reproduce.

Key Concepts:
- **Variation** exists in all populations.
- More offspring are produced than can survive.
- Individuals with advantageous traits survive and reproduce.
- Over generations, these traits become more common.

Historical Context & Evidence:
- **Charles Darwin (1859):** Published *On the Origin of Species*, outlining natural selection.
- **Evidence from Fossils:** Transitional species showing evolution.
- **Comparative Anatomy:** Homologous structures (e.g., limb bones in humans, whales, bats).
- **Genetics:** Modern DNA evidence supports evolutionary relationships.

---

3. Germ Theory of Disease

Definition: Diseases are caused by microorganisms (bacteria, viruses, fungi).

Key Concepts:

- Microbes are **pathogens** that cause disease.
- Not caused by "bad air" or "miasma" as once thought.

Historical Context & Evidence:

- **Louis Pasteur (1860s):** Disproved spontaneous generation, developed pasteurization.
- **Robert Koch (1876):** Identified specific bacteria causing diseases (e.g., anthrax, tuberculosis).
- **Joseph Lister (1865):** Introduced antiseptic surgery to prevent infection.

Evidence: Microscopic observations, infection transmission experiments.

IV. How Empirical Evidence Supports Scientific Understanding

What is Empirical Evidence?

- **Data and observations gathered through direct experimentation or measurement.**
- Empirical evidence is **objective, measurable, and reproducible**.

How Empirical Evidence Validates Scientific Knowledge:

1. Experiments and Observations:

- Rigorous experiments provide **testable evidence**.
- Observations help identify patterns and relationships.

2. Peer Review:

- Scientists publish findings in **peer-reviewed journals**.
- Other experts **critically evaluate methods and results** to ensure accuracy.

3. Replication:

- Experiments must be **repeated** by different scientists with the same results.
- Ensures **reliability and validity** of scientific claims.

V. Historical Advancements and Paradigm Shifts in Science

A **paradigm shift** occurs when **new evidence overturns existing scientific understanding**.

Examples of Paradigm Shifts:

- **From Geocentric to Heliocentric Model:** Earth was believed to be the center of the universe until Copernicus and Galileo provided evidence for the Sun-centered system.
- **Germ Theory replacing Miasma Theory:** Understanding that diseases are caused by microorganisms, not "bad air."
- **Discovery of DNA as Genetic Material:** Before Watson and Crick (1953), proteins were thought to carry genetic information.

VI. Summary of Key Points for EOC:

Concept	Explanation
Scientific Theory	Explanation of **why** and **how** phenomena occur (e.g., Evolution)
Scientific Law	Description of **what** happens under specific conditions (e.g., Gravity)
Theories Explain, Laws Describe	Theories = why/how; Laws = what
Cell Theory	All living things are made of cells
Theory of Evolution	Species change over time via natural selection
Germ Theory	Microorganisms cause diseases
Empirical Evidence	Data from experiments/observations that support conclusions
Role of Peer Review & Replication	Ensures accuracy and reliability of scientific knowledge
Paradigm Shifts	Major changes in scientific understanding due to new evidence

Sample EOC Practice Question:

Which of the following best describes a scientific theory?
A) A guess about how something works.
B) A statement that describes what always happens under certain conditions.
C) A well-supported explanation of how something in nature works.
D) An untested idea that needs proof.

Correct Answer: C) A well-supported explanation of how something in nature works.

Comparison chart for "Scientific Theory vs. Scientific Law

Customized Comparison: Scientific Theory vs. Scientific Law

Aspect	Scientific Theory	Scientific Law
Definition	A well-substantiated explanation of an asp…	A statement based on repeated experiment…
Purpose	Explains why and how phenomena occur.	Describes what happens under certain con…
Evidence & Testing	Supported by extensive evidence; repeate…	Constantly supported by empirical data fro…
Flexibility	Can be modified or rejected if new eviden…	Usually stable, but can be refined with bet…
Focus	Focuses on explaining mechanisms and re…	Focuses on describing consistent natural pa…
Examples	Cell Theory, Theory of Relativity.	Law of Conservation of Mass, Newton's La…

Scientific Theories and Laws — Student Worksheet

Part 1: Understanding Theories and Laws

Instructions: Answer the following questions in complete sentences.

1. **What is a scientific theory?**

    _____

    _____

2. **What is a scientific law?**

    _____

    _____

3. **How is a theory different from a law?**

    _____

    _____

    _____

Part 2: Identifying Examples

Instructions: For each example below, decide if it is a **Scientific Theory** or a **Scientific Law**, and explain why.

Example	Theory or Law?	Reason Why
Gravity causes objects to fall toward Earth		
All living organisms are made up of one or more cells		
Microorganisms are responsible for causing many diseases		
Planets orbit the sun in elliptical paths		
Species evolve over time through natural selection		

Part 3: Critical Thinking

Instructions: Answer in 2-3 sentences.

1. **Why can a scientific theory change over time, but a scientific law rarely does?**

2. **Why is it important for scientists to repeat experiments and peer-review each other's work before accepting a theory?**

Part 4: Multiple-Choice Practice (EOC-Style)

1. Which statement best describes a scientific law?
   A) A testable explanation for why events happen.
   B) A statement describing a consistent pattern in nature.
   C) An idea that might be true but lacks evidence.
   D) A guess made without scientific testing.

Answer: _____

2. Which of the following is a scientific theory?
   A) The Law of Gravity
   B) The Theory of Evolution
   C) Newton's Laws of Motion
   D) The Law of Conservation of Mass

Answer: _____

3. What is one key difference between a theory and a law?
   A) Laws explain why phenomena occur; theories describe what happens.
   B) Theories describe what happens in nature; laws explain how.
   C) Theories explain why and how; laws describe what happens.
   D) There is no difference.

Answer: _____

Scientific Tools and Measurements — Student Worksheet

Part 1: Identifying Scientific Tools

Instructions: Match each function with the correct tool. Write **Microscope, Graduated Cylinder, Balance, or Thermometer** next to each statement.

1. Used to measure the temperature of a substance. _____
2. Used to observe cells and microscopic life. _____
3. Used to measure liquid volume accurately. _____
4. Used to measure the mass of a leaf or chemical substance. _____

Part 2: Labeling Diagrams (Optional for Printout)

Instructions: Look at the diagram of the microscope, graduated cylinder, balance, and thermometer. Label the following parts:

1. **Microscope:**
- Part you look through: _____
- Platform where the slide goes: _____
- Adjustment knob for fine focusing: _____
- Source of light: _____
2. **Graduated Cylinder:**
- Curve at the surface of the liquid: _____
- Measurement lines: _____
3. **Balance:**
- Where the object is placed: _____
- The part used to adjust and balance: _____
4. **Thermometer:**
- Part holding the liquid inside: _____
- Number scale that shows temperature: _____

Part 3: Short Answer Questions

Answer in complete sentences.

1. **Why is it important to use the metric system (SI Units) in science?**

2. **What are two safety rules you should follow when using a microscope?**

3. **How do you properly read the level of a liquid in a graduated cylinder?**

Part 4: Practice Data Table and Graph

Instructions: Below is a set of data collected from an experiment measuring plant growth over time.

Day	Plant Height (cm)
1	3
3	5
5	7
7	9

Questions:

1. What is the independent variable? _____
2. What is the dependent variable? _____
3. What type of graph would best show the change in plant height over time? (Bar, Line, or Pie) _____
4. Describe the trend shown by the data. _____

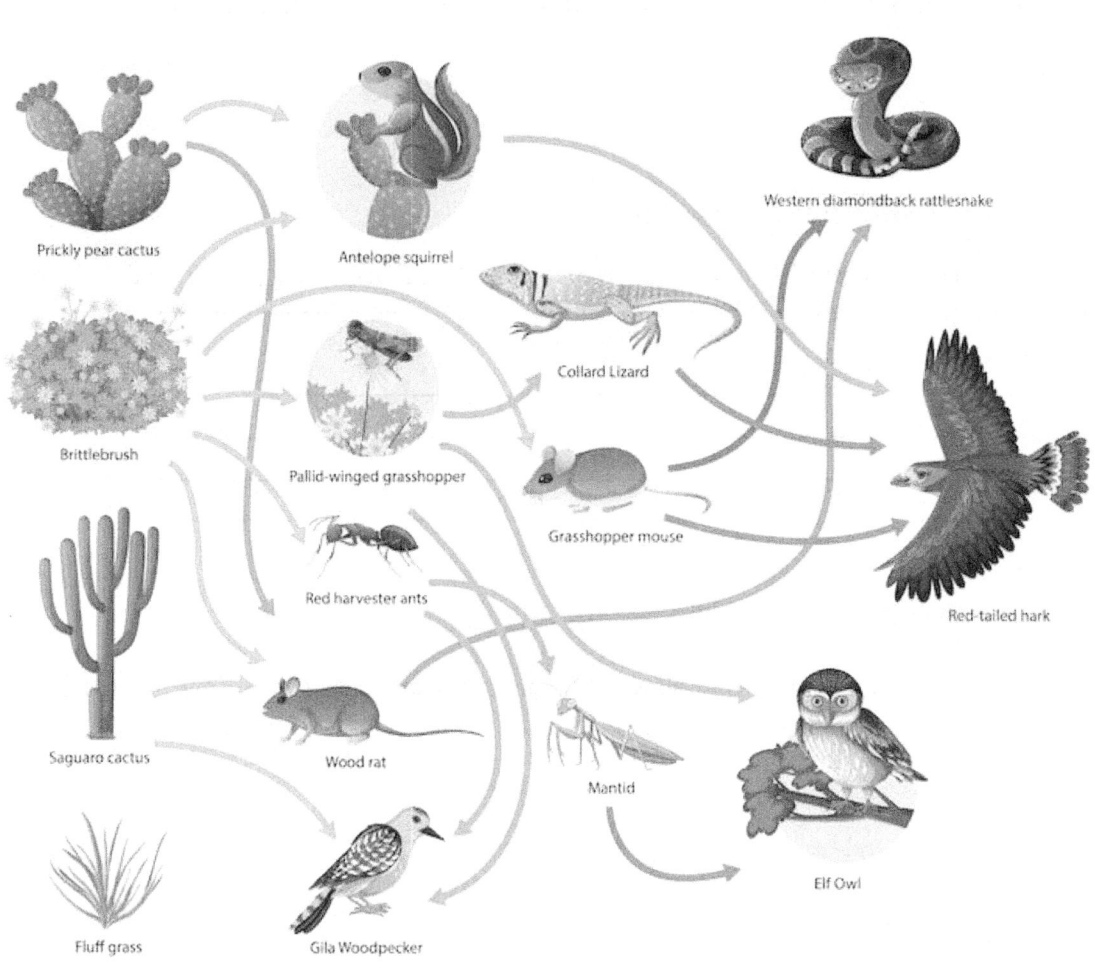

Chapter 2: Biochemistry – The Chemistry of Life

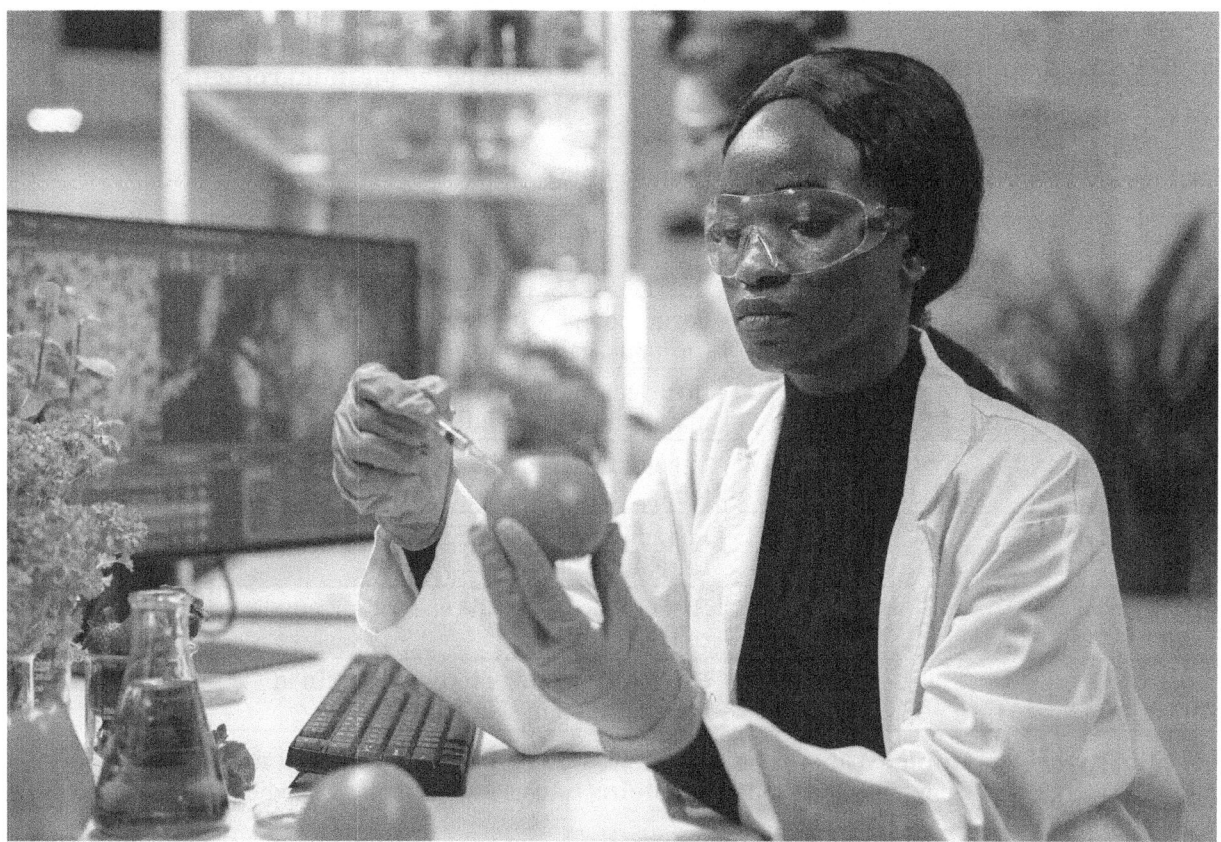

2.1 The Chemical Basis of Life

Why Chemistry Matters in Biology

Have you ever wondered what makes life possible? At its core, **life is chemistry in action**. Every cell, every breath, and every movement relies on countless **chemical reactions**. Understanding the **chemical foundation of life** allows us to see how living things grow, reproduce, and function.

Biochemistry is the bridge between **biology and chemistry**, explaining how molecules like **proteins, carbohydrates, lipids, and nucleic acids** make life work. But before diving into these macromolecules, we must first explore the **elements that make up living organisms** and **why carbon is so special**.

II. Elements Essential for Life

Although the Earth has **118 elements** in the periodic table, only a handful are crucial for life. The **six primary elements** make up about **96% of the human body** and are found in all living things.

The Six Essential Elements for Life:

23

1. **Carbon (C)** – The backbone of all organic molecules.
2. **Hydrogen (H)** – Found in water and almost every biological molecule.
3. **Oxygen (O)** – Necessary for respiration and water.
4. **Nitrogen (N)** – Key part of amino acids (proteins) and nucleotides (DNA & RNA).
5. **Phosphorus (P)** – Important for ATP (energy) and nucleic acids.
6. **Sulfur (S)** – Found in certain amino acids and vitamins.

Think about it: If life were a recipe, these elements would be the **main ingredients**.

What Do These Elements Do?

Each element plays a crucial role in keeping organisms alive.

Element	Why It's Important
Carbon (C)	Forms complex organic molecules (proteins, carbs, fats, DNA).
Hydrogen (H)	Involved in energy transfer and maintaining pH balance.
Oxygen (O)	Used in respiration to release energy from food.
Nitrogen (N)	Found in proteins and nucleic acids (DNA & RNA).
Phosphorus (P)	Essential for ATP (the energy currency of cells) and bones.
Sulfur (S)	Helps form strong proteins (keratin in hair, collagen in skin).

Real-world example: Without phosphorus, we wouldn't have **DNA** or **cell membranes**, and without nitrogen, we couldn't make **proteins** (muscles, enzymes, antibodies).

III. The Unique Role of Carbon: The Element of Life

1. Carbon's Tetravalency: The Secret to Complexity

Carbon is special because it can form **four covalent bonds** at the same time. This means carbon can **bond with itself and other elements**, leading to an **infinite variety** of molecules.

How does carbon's bonding ability shape life?

- It allows for the creation of **long chains, branched molecules, and rings**.
- It can form **single, double, or triple bonds**, leading to even more complexity.
- It enables the formation of **macromolecules**, such as proteins, fats, and DNA.

Analogy: Think of carbon like **Lego blocks** – it can snap together in **endless ways** to create simple or complex structures.

IV. The Four Macromolecules of Life

Living organisms are made up of four main types of macromolecules (large molecules). These molecules **store energy, build structures, carry genetic information, and regulate processes**.

Macromolecule	Elements Present	Building Blocks (Monomers)	Examples	Functions in the Body
Carbohydrates	C, H, O	Monosaccharides (simple sugars)	Glucose, Starch	Quick energy, structural support
Lipids	C, H, O	Fatty acids + Glycerol	Fats, Oils, Phospholipids	Long-term energy, cell membranes
Proteins	C, H, O, N (S)	Amino acids	Enzymes, Hemoglobin, Keratin	Enzymes, muscle structure, transport
Nucleic Acids	C, H, O, N, P	Nucleotides	DNA, RNA	Genetic information storage

1. Carbohydrates: The Energy Source of Life

Carbohydrates are composed of **carbon, hydrogen, and oxygen** in a 1:2:1 ratio (**C:H:O = 1:2:1**). They are used for **quick energy** and **structural components** in plants.

Types of Carbohydrates:

1. **Monosaccharides (simple sugars)** – Examples: Glucose, Fructose.
2. **Disaccharides (two sugars linked)** – Examples: Sucrose (table sugar), Lactose (milk sugar).
3. **Polysaccharides (complex carbs)** – Examples:
    - **Starch** (plants store energy).
    - **Glycogen** (animals store energy in the liver).
    - **Cellulose** (gives plant cell walls strength).

Example: When you eat pasta, your body **breaks down the starch into glucose** for quick energy.

2. Lipids: Long-Term Energy Storage and Cell Membranes

Lipids are **nonpolar**, meaning they **don't mix with water** (hydrophobic). They are essential for **long-term energy storage, insulation, and forming cell membranes**.

Types of Lipids:

1. **Triglycerides (fats and oils)** – Store energy.
2. **Phospholipids** – Make up **cell membranes** (phospholipid bilayer).
3. **Steroids** – Includes hormones like **testosterone, estrogen, and cholesterol**.

Example: The fat in your body keeps you warm and **stores energy for survival**.

3. Proteins: The Workhorses of the Cell

Proteins are made up of **amino acids** linked by **peptide bonds**. They have four levels of structure:

1. **Primary structure:** The sequence of amino acids.

2. **Secondary structure:** Alpha helices and beta sheets.
3. **Tertiary structure:** 3D folding of the entire protein.
4. **Quaternary structure:** Multiple protein chains working together.

Functions of Proteins:

- **Enzymes** (speed up chemical reactions) – Example: Amylase in saliva breaks down food.
- **Transport** – Hemoglobin carries oxygen in blood.
- **Structural support** – Collagen keeps skin and bones strong.
- **Immune system defense** – Antibodies fight infections.

Example: Every time you move, breathe, or digest food, **proteins (enzymes) are at work**.

---

4. Nucleic Acids: The Code of Life

Nucleic acids (DNA & RNA) **store and transmit genetic information**.

Building Blocks:

- **DNA (Deoxyribonucleic Acid):** Double-stranded, stores genetic info.
- **RNA (Ribonucleic Acid):** Single-stranded, helps make proteins.

DNA vs. RNA:

Feature	DNA	RNA
Sugar	Deoxyribose	Ribose
Strands	Double	Single
Bases	A, T, C, G	A, U, C, G

Example: Your DNA determines **your hair color, height, and even your risk for certain diseases**.

V. Summary: Why This Matters?

Understanding biochemistry helps us:
- See how food fuels our body.
- Understand genetic disorders and treatments.
- Develop medicines (insulin, vaccines).
- Solve real-world health and environmental problems.

Biology is chemistry in motion. Life depends on these molecules, and so do we.

Macromolecules Review Worksheet

Part 1: Matching Macromolecules and Functions

Instructions: Match the macromolecule to its primary function. Write the correct letter next to each function.

Macromolecules: A) Carbohydrates
B) Lipids
C) Proteins
D) Nucleic Acids

1. Store and transmit genetic information. _____
2. Provide quick energy for cells. _____

26

3. Form enzymes that speed up chemical reactions. _____
4. Store long-term energy and make up cell membranes. _____

Part 2: Fill in the Table

Instructions: Complete the chart with information about each macromolecule.

Macromolecule	Elements Present	Monomer (Building Block)	Example	Main Function
Carbohydrates			Glucose, Starch	
Lipids			Fats, Oils, Phospholipids	
Proteins			Enzymes, Hemoglobin	
Nucleic Acids			DNA, RNA	

Part 3: Short Answer Questions

1. **What makes carbon so important for forming biological molecules?**

2. **Why are proteins often called the "workhorses" of the cell?**

3. **What is the difference between DNA and RNA in structure and function?**

Part 4: Practice with Diagrams

Instructions: Look at the diagram provided (or the visual above) and answer:

1. **In the carbohydrate diagram, what is the name of the simple sugar unit shown?**

2. **In the protein diagram, label the three parts of the amino acid.**
   - _____ (NH_2 group)
   - _____ (COOH group)
   - _____ (Variable R group)
3. **What is the name of the bond that forms between two amino acids?**

4. **In the nucleic acid diagram, what are the three parts of a nucleotide?**

27

Bonus Question:

If you were asked to build a new cell membrane, which macromolecule would be MOST important and why?

2.2: Enzymes and Biochemical Reactions

"The Protein Machines that Make Life Possible"

I. Function and Structure of Enzymes

1. What Are Enzymes?

Enzymes are **biological catalysts** — **special proteins** that **speed up chemical reactions in living organisms** without being consumed in the process.
Think of enzymes like **tiny machines inside cells** that help build or break molecules **quickly and efficiently**.

> **Example:** Digestive enzymes like **amylase** break down starch into sugar in your saliva — making digestion fast enough to sustain life.

2. Catalytic Role: Lowering Activation Energy

Every chemical reaction needs some **activation energy** to get started — like a spark to light a fire.
Enzymes work by lowering this activation energy, so reactions can happen much faster and at body temperature.

> **Without enzymes**, essential reactions like breaking down food or copying DNA would happen too slowly to keep us alive.

3. Active Site: The "Working Center" of the Enzyme

The **active site** is the **specific region** on an enzyme where the **substrate** (the molecule the enzyme acts on) **binds**.

- The active site has a **unique shape and chemical environment**, perfectly suited for its specific substrate.
- When the substrate binds, it forms an **enzyme-substrate complex**, leading to a chemical reaction.

> **Analogy:** Think of the active site as a **mold** that perfectly fits a specific key (the substrate).

4. Specificity: How Enzymes Know Which Molecule to Work On

Each enzyme is **highly specific** — it only works with **one type of substrate** or a specific group of molecules.

Models Explaining Enzyme-Substrate Interaction:

Model	Explanation	Analogy
Lock-and-Key	The enzyme's active site is perfectly shaped for its substrate.	A key fitting perfectly into a lock.
Induced Fit	The active site **slightly changes shape** to better fit the substrate.	A glove molding around a hand.

Takeaway: Enzymes are **precision tools** designed for specific tasks inside cells.

II. Factors Affecting Enzyme Activity

1. Temperature: The Heat Factor

- **Optimal Temperature**: Every enzyme has a temperature where it works **best**.
- **Too Cold**: Reactions slow down because molecules move less.
- **Too Hot**: Enzymes **denature** — they **lose their shape** and can't function anymore.

Human enzymes usually work best at around **37°C (98.6°F)**, our normal body temperature.
Example: High fevers can **denature enzymes**, which is why very high body temperatures are dangerous.

---

2. pH: The Acid-Base Balance

- **Optimal pH**: Each enzyme works best at a specific pH (acidic, neutral, or basic).
- **Too acidic or too basic**: The enzyme's shape changes, especially at the active site — **enzyme activity drops**.

Examples:

- **Pepsin** (stomach enzyme): Works best at **pH 2** (very acidic).
- **Amylase** (mouth enzyme): Works best around **pH 7** (neutral).

---

3. Substrate Concentration: How Much Substrate is Available

- At low substrate levels, increasing substrate **increases reaction rate**.
- At high substrate levels, enzymes become **saturated** — all active sites are occupied — and the rate **levels off (Vmax)**.

Vmax is the maximum speed of the reaction when enzymes are working as fast as possible.

Takeaway: There's a limit to how fast enzymes can work — no matter how much substrate you add.

Graph Example for Understanding Enzyme Activity:

- **Bell-shaped curve for temperature and pH**: Activity increases to a peak (optimal), then drops as conditions become too extreme.
- **Plateau curve for substrate concentration**: Activity increases with more substrate until it reaches Vmax.

III. Enzyme-Substrate Specificity and Interaction Mechanisms

1. How Do Enzymes Recognize Substrates?

- **Structural complementarity**: The shape of the active site **matches the shape of the substrate**.
- **Chemical interactions**: Specific **charges and bonds** help hold the substrate in place.

   Example: Like how only the right puzzle piece fits into a particular spot.

2. Enzyme Inhibition: Slowing Down or Stopping Enzymes

Sometimes cells need to **regulate** enzymes, turning them **on or off** depending on needs. This is done using **inhibitors**.

Types of Inhibition:

Type of Inhibition	How It Works	Example/Analogy
Competitive Inhibition	**Inhibitor competes with substrate** for the active site — blocks substrate.	Like someone sitting in your chair so you can't sit.
Non-Competitive Inhibition	**Inhibitor binds elsewhere** on the enzyme, changing its shape so the substrate can't bind.	Like bending a key so it no longer fits the lock.

   Real-life Example of Enzyme Inhibition: Some medicines (like antibiotics) **block bacterial enzymes**, stopping the bacteria from surviving.

IV. Summary Table for Enzymes and Reactions

Concept	Explanation	Example/Important Note
Enzymes	Proteins that speed up chemical reactions.	Amylase breaks down starch in saliva.
Catalyst	Substance that lowers activation energy without being used up.	Enzymes are biological catalysts.
Active Site	Region where the substrate binds on an enzyme.	Fits substrate like a lock and key.
Specificity	Enzymes work with only specific substrates.	Lactase only breaks down lactose (milk sugar).

Concept	Explanation	Example/Important Note
Temperature Effect	Enzymes work best at optimal temperature; too high = denatured.	Human enzymes optimal at ~37°C.
pH Effect	Enzymes work best at their specific pH range.	Pepsin in stomach works at pH 2.
Substrate Concentration	More substrate = faster reaction until enzymes are saturated.	Rate levels off at Vmax.
Competitive Inhibitors	Block active site.	Some drugs mimic substrates.
Non-Competitive Inhibitors	Bind elsewhere and change enzyme shape.	Some poisons and toxins.

V. Final Thoughts: Why Enzymes Matter

Without enzymes:

- Life's essential reactions would happen **too slowly to sustain life**.
- Digestion, DNA replication, and even movement would be **impossible**.
- Medicines that target enzymes help **treat diseases and infections**.

Enzymes make life possible — fast, efficient, and beautifully coordinated.

Enzymes and Biochemical Reactions — Student Worksheet

Part 1: Understanding Enzymes

Instructions: Answer each question in a complete sentence.

1. **What is an enzyme, and what does it do in a biological system?**

2. **What is the active site of an enzyme, and why is it important?**

3. **Explain how enzymes lower activation energy in a reaction.**

Part 2: Enzyme Models

Instructions: Match the following descriptions with the correct model (**Lock-and-Key Model** or **Induced Fit Model**).

Description	Model
The enzyme changes shape slightly to fit the substrate perfectly.	
The enzyme's active site is a perfect fit for the substrate without changing shape.	

Part 3: Factors Affecting Enzyme Activity

Instructions: Fill in the blanks with the correct answers (Temperature, pH, Substrate Concentration).

1. When _____ is too high, enzymes can denature and stop working.
2. _____ affects how well the enzyme works, depending on whether the environment is too acidic or too basic.
3. Increasing _____ will speed up the reaction rate until all enzymes are busy (Vmax).

Part 4: Enzyme Inhibition Scenarios

Instructions: Decide if each scenario describes **competitive inhibition** or **non-competitive inhibition**. Write your answer next to each.

1. A molecule resembling the substrate binds to the active site, preventing the real substrate from binding. _____
2. An inhibitor attaches to another part of the enzyme, causing a shape change that prevents the substrate from binding. _____

Part 5: Short Answer (Critical Thinking)

Instructions: Answer in 2-3 sentences.

1. **Why is enzyme specificity important for proper functioning of biological systems?**

2. **How do enzymes contribute to maintaining life processes like digestion or DNA replication?**

Bonus Challenge: Graph Interpretation

Look at the following scenario and answer it:

Scenario: As the temperature increases, enzyme activity rises until a certain point, then drops sharply.

1. **Why does enzyme activity increase with temperature at first?**

2. **Why does enzyme activity drop when the temperature gets too high?**

2.3: Water and pH in Biological Systems

I. Properties of Water — Why Water Makes Life Possible

Water is often called the **"universal solvent of life"**, and for good reason: **all living things depend on water** for survival. The unique properties of water, due to **hydrogen bonding**, make it essential for biological systems. Let's break down these key properties:

1. Cohesion — Water Molecules Stick to Each Other

Definition:
Cohesion is the ability of water molecules to **stick to other water molecules** due to **hydrogen bonds**.

- Water molecules form weak bonds (hydrogen bonds) because of their **polarity** (having a slightly positive and slightly negative side).
- This leads to **surface tension** — a "skin" on the water surface strong enough for insects like water striders to walk on it.

   Real-life example: Drops of water forming beads on a surface, like on a car after rain — that's cohesion in action.

2. Adhesion — Water Molecules Stick to Other Surfaces

Definition:
Adhesion is the ability of water molecules to **stick to other substances** (like glass or plant tissues).

- Adhesion helps **water "climb" structures**, such as plant roots and stems — critical for moving nutrients.

Capillary Action:

Adhesion + Cohesion allow water to **move upward in narrow spaces** against gravity.

   Example: Water traveling from plant roots to leaves (bringing nutrients to every cell).

3. High Specific Heat — Water Resists Temperature Change

Definition:
Specific heat is the amount of energy needed to raise the temperature of a substance.

- Water has a **high specific heat** because hydrogen bonds **absorb a lot of energy before breaking**.
- This helps **regulate temperature** in organisms and environments.

   Why it matters:
- **Humans**: Helps maintain a stable body temperature (homeostasis).
- **Earth**: Oceans and lakes prevent drastic temperature swings, making Earth livable.

   Example: Your body stays at **98.6°F (37°C)** even if it's hot or cold outside — thanks to water!

II. pH and Buffers in Biological Systems — Keeping Balance Inside Us

1. pH Scale — Measuring Acids and Bases

Definition:
The **pH scale** measures the **concentration of hydrogen ions (H^+)** in a solution.

- It ranges from **0 (most acidic) to 14 (most basic/alkaline)**, with **7 being neutral** (like pure water).
- The pH scale is **logarithmic**, meaning each number represents a **10x change** in hydrogen ion concentration.

pH Value	Type	Example
0-6	Acidic	Stomach acid (pH 2), lemon juice (pH 3)
7	Neutral	Pure water
8-14	Basic (Alkaline)	Blood (around pH 7.4), soap (pH 10)

Important: Lower pH = more H^+ ions, higher pH = fewer H^+ ions (more OH^- ions).

---

2. Why pH Matters for Living Things

Enzymes and **metabolic processes** work best within **narrow pH ranges**.

- **Too acidic or too basic** conditions can **denature (damage)** enzymes, **stop reactions**, and even **kill cells**.

Example:

- **Stomach enzymes (like pepsin)** work at pH 2 (acidic).
- **Blood pH** must stay around 7.35–7.45 — even a small change can be life-threatening!

Real-life consequence: If blood pH drops (acidosis) or rises (alkalosis), **organs may fail**.

---

3. Buffers — Keeping pH Stable

Definition:
A **buffer** is a system of molecules that helps **resist changes in pH** by **absorbing excess H^+ or OH^- ions**.

Why Are Buffers Important?

- They help **maintain homeostasis** — the stable internal environment required for life.
- Prevent **harmful pH swings** during chemical reactions.

Example of Buffer System:

Buffer System	Where Found	Function
Bicarbonate Buffer System	Human blood	Keeps blood pH between 7.35 and 7.45
Phosphate Buffer System	Inside cells	Maintains cell pH during metabolic activities

Bicarbonate Buffer in Action:
If blood becomes too acidic (H⁺ increases), **bicarbonate (HCO₃⁻)** binds to H⁺ ions to neutralize them.
If blood becomes too basic (H⁺ decreases), bicarbonate can release H⁺ ions to lower pH.

III. Summary Table — Water Properties, pH, and Buffers

Property/Concept	Explanation	Importance to Life
Cohesion	Water molecules stick to each other.	Surface tension; transport in plants.
Adhesion	Water sticks to other substances.	Capillary action; water movement in plants.
High Specific Heat	Water resists temperature change.	Stable body temperature and environments.
pH Scale	Measures H⁺ concentration; ranges from 0 to 14.	Proper enzyme and metabolic function.
Buffers	Prevent sudden changes in pH.	Maintain homeostasis (e.g., stable blood pH).

IV. Why This Matters in Real Life

- **Water keeps your cells hydrated and functional.**
- **Enzymes work only if pH and temperature are just right** — so your body has built-in systems to **monitor and adjust these conditions**.
- Buffers help **prevent life-threatening conditions** by stabilizing pH.

Without water's special properties and stable pH, life would not exist as we know it.

V. Sample Real-Life Example (Human Body Application):

Example: Running a Marathon

- **Sweating** cools the body because of water's high heat capacity.
- **Blood pH** stays stable (thanks to buffers) despite increased breathing and metabolic waste.
- **Water moves nutrients and oxygen** to muscles through adhesion and cohesion in blood vessels.

Water, pH, and Buffers — Student Worksheet

Part 1: Understanding Water's Properties

Instructions: Answer each question in complete sentences.

1. **What is cohesion, and how does it help water form surface tension?**

35

2. **What is adhesion, and why is it important for plants?**

3. **What is meant by "high specific heat," and how does this property of water help living things?**

Part 2: pH Scale Understanding

Instructions: Fill in the blanks with correct answers.

1. The pH scale ranges from _____ (most acidic) to _____ (most basic).
2. A substance with a pH of 7 is considered _____.
3. Substances with a pH below 7 are _____.
4. Substances with a pH above 7 are _____.
5. Lemon juice, which has a pH of about 3, is an example of an _____.

Part 3: Buffers and Homeostasis

Instructions: Answer the following questions.

1. **What is a buffer, and why are buffers important for living organisms?**

2. **Explain how the bicarbonate buffer system in blood helps maintain pH.**

3. **What could happen if our blood pH became too acidic or too basic?**

Part 4: Critical Thinking and Application

Instructions: Think carefully and answer.

1. **Why does water form droplets on a leaf instead of spreading out evenly? Which water property explains this?**

2. **If a plant could not use capillary action, how would that affect its ability to survive?**

3. **Why might a fever (raising body temperature) affect enzyme activity and overall homeostasis in the body? How does water's high specific heat help in this situation?**

Bonus: Real-World Connection

Challenge Question:
Imagine you are a scientist studying climate change. How might the high specific heat of oceans affect the climate as Earth's atmosphere warms?

Chapter 3: Cell Biology

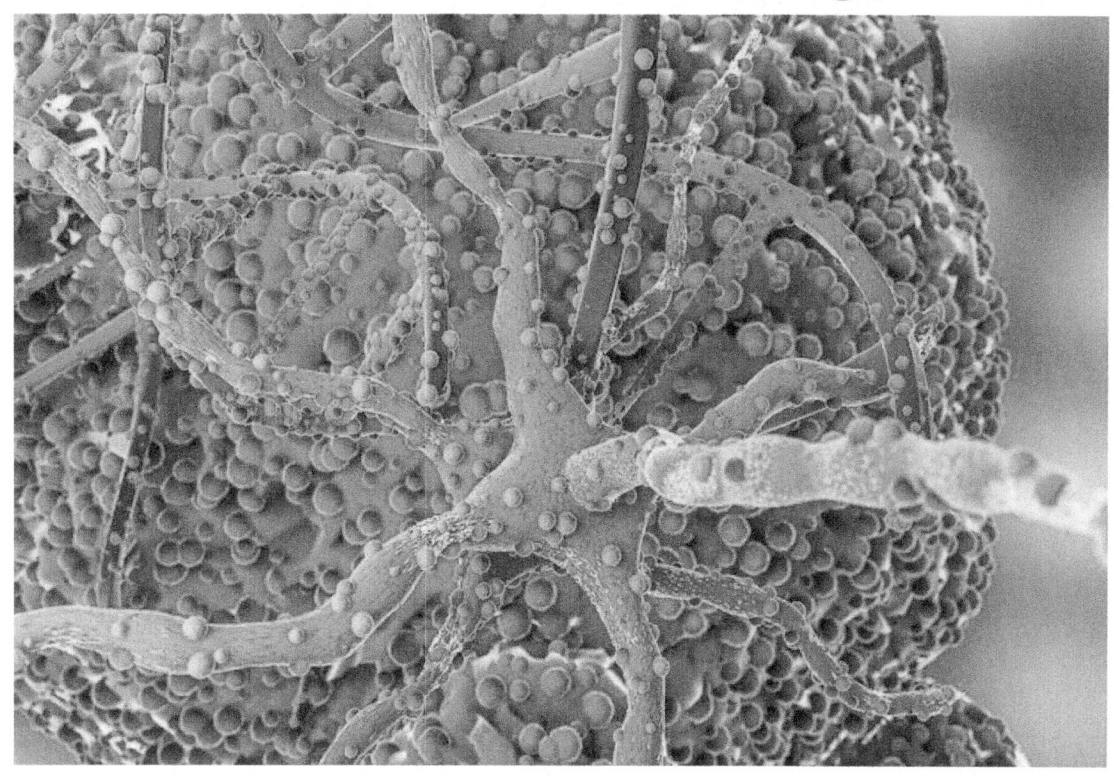

3.1: Cell Structure and Function

I. Prokaryotic vs. Eukaryotic Cells — The Two Main Types of Life's Building Blocks

Every living thing is made up of cells — but not all cells are alike. Life is divided into **two major types of cells: Prokaryotic and Eukaryotic**. Understanding their similarities and differences is essential to understanding how life functions at the microscopic level.

1. What Are Prokaryotic Cells?

Prokaryotic cells are **simpler, smaller cells** without a nucleus or membrane-bound organelles. They include **Bacteria and Archaea**, some of the oldest and most widespread organisms on Earth.

Key Features of Prokaryotic Cells:

- **No nucleus** — their DNA is **circular** and located in a region called the **nucleoid**.
- **No membrane-bound organelles** (like mitochondria or ER).
- Usually **unicellular** (single-celled).
- **Reproduce asexually** by **binary fission** — a simple cell division method.

   Analogy: Imagine a **one-room cabin** — everything the cell needs happens in one space.

---

2. What Are Eukaryotic Cells?

Eukaryotic cells are **larger, more complex cells** that make up **plants, animals, fungi, and protists**. They **do have a nucleus** and many **specialized organelles**.

38

Key Features of Eukaryotic Cells:

- **Nucleus** — a membrane-bound compartment containing **linear DNA**.
- **Organelles** — specialized structures like mitochondria, ER, and Golgi apparatus.
- **Unicellular or multicellular** organisms.
- Reproduce by **mitosis** (for growth/repair) and **meiosis** (for sexual reproduction).

Analogy: Think of a **factory with different departments**, each performing a specific task.

---

3. Prokaryotic vs. Eukaryotic Cell Comparison Table

Feature	**Prokaryotic Cells**	**Eukaryotic Cells**
Size	Small (0.1–5.0 μm)	Larger (10–100 μm)
Nucleus	No nucleus — DNA in nucleoid	Nucleus present
Organelles	No membrane-bound organelles	Many membrane-bound organelles
DNA Structure	Circular DNA	Linear DNA
Examples	Bacteria, Archaea	Plants, animals, fungi, protists
Reproduction	Asexual (binary fission)	Mitosis (asexual), Meiosis (sexual)

II. Organelles and Their Functions — Specialized "Organs" of the Cell

1. Nucleus — The Control Center

- **Structure:** Double membrane (nuclear envelope) with pores.
- **Function:** Stores **DNA** (instructions for making proteins) and controls **cell activities**.

Analogy: The **manager's office** of a factory — holds the blueprints (DNA) for everything the factory makes.

---

2. Mitochondria — The Powerhouse of the Cell

- **Structure:** Double membrane; inner folds called **cristae** for more surface area.
- **Function:** Produces **ATP** (energy) through **aerobic respiration** (using oxygen).

Analogy: Like the **power plant** supplying energy to the city (cell).

---

3. Ribosomes — The Protein Builders

- **Structure:** Made of **RNA and proteins**; found free-floating or on **rough ER**.
- **Function:** Assemble **proteins** based on instructions from DNA.

Analogy: Factories that make products (proteins).

---

4. Endoplasmic Reticulum (ER) — The Manufacturing Plant

Type	Structure	Function
Rough ER	Studded with ribosomes	Makes and processes proteins
Smooth ER	No ribosomes	Makes lipids, detoxifies drugs, stores calcium

Analogy: Assembly lines — rough ER makes products (proteins), smooth ER makes oils and detoxes.

---

5. Golgi Apparatus — The Shipping and Packaging Center

- **Structure:** Stack of flattened membranes.
- **Function: Modifies, packages, and ships** proteins and lipids to where they are needed.

Analogy: Post office of the cell — prepares packages for delivery.

---

6. Lysosomes — The Waste Disposal System

- **Structure:** Membrane-bound sacs filled with **digestive enzymes**.
- **Function:** Break down **waste, old cell parts, and invaders** (like bacteria).

Analogy: Garbage trucks and recycling centers.

---

7. Peroxisomes — Detox Centers

- **Structure:** Small, membrane-bound sacs with **oxidative enzymes**.
- **Function: Break down harmful substances** and **fatty acids**.

---

8. Cytoskeleton — The Cell's Framework

Component	Function
Microfilaments	Support cell shape and help in movement.
Intermediate Filaments	Maintain structure and anchor organelles.
Microtubules	Help move chromosomes during division; form cilia and flagella.

Analogy: The **steel framework** and conveyor belts in a factory.

III. The Plasma Membrane — Guardian of Homeostasis

1. Structure of the Plasma Membrane

- **Phospholipid Bilayer:**
    - **Hydrophilic heads** (water-attracting).
    - **Hydrophobic tails** (water-repelling).

- **Proteins:**
  - **Integral proteins:** Embedded in the bilayer for transport.
  - **Peripheral proteins:** Attached for signaling.
- **Carbohydrates:**
  - Attached to proteins/lipids for **cell recognition** and adhesion.

Analogy: Like a **security gate** with guards and ID scanners.

---

2. Functions of the Plasma Membrane

Function	Description
Selective Permeability	Controls what enters/exits the cell — like a security system.
Communication	Proteins act as **receptors** to receive signals.
Transport	Moves nutrients, waste, and signals via **passive/active transport**.

---

3. Plasma Membrane and Homeostasis

- Regulates **water, nutrients, and ions** inside the cell.
- Helps maintain **stable internal conditions** despite external changes.
- Crucial for **cell signaling** and communication with other cells.

Real-life Example: Helps **white blood cells recognize invaders**, keeps cells healthy and functioning properly.

IV. Summary Table — Major Organelles and Their Roles

Organelle	Main Function
Nucleus	Holds DNA, controls cell activities.
Mitochondria	Produces ATP (energy).
Ribosomes	Protein synthesis.
ER (Rough/Smooth)	Rough: Protein production; Smooth: Lipid synthesis, detox.
Golgi Apparatus	Packages and ships molecules.
Lysosomes	Digests waste and invaders.
Peroxisomes	Detoxifies harmful substances.
Cytoskeleton	Supports cell shape, enables movement.
Plasma Membrane	Controls what enters/exits, maintains homeostasis.

V. Final Thought: Why This Matters?

Cells are the **basic units of life**, and understanding their structure and function is key to understanding **all biological processes** — from how we fight disease to how we grow. Knowing how cells work helps us understand **life itself**.

Cell Structure and Function — Student Worksheet

Part 1: Prokaryotic vs. Eukaryotic Cells

Instructions: Answer the following questions in complete sentences.

1. **What is the main difference between prokaryotic and eukaryotic cells?**

2. **Name two types of organisms made of prokaryotic cells.**

3. **List three organelles or structures found in eukaryotic cells but NOT in prokaryotic cells.**

4. **What is the function of the nucleus in a eukaryotic cell?**

Part 2: Organelles and Functions

Instructions: Match the organelle to its function. Write the correct letter in the blank.

Organelles	Functions
A) Nucleus	1. Breaks down waste and old cell parts
B) Mitochondria	2. Packages and ships proteins and lipids
C) Ribosomes	3. Produces ATP (energy) for the cell
D) Golgi Apparatus	4. Synthesizes proteins
E) Lysosomes	5. Stores DNA and controls cell activities

Part 3: Specialized Structures in Plant and Animal Cells

Instructions: Answer True or False.

1. **Plant cells have a cell wall that provides structure and support.** _____
2. **Animal cells have chloroplasts to perform photosynthesis.** _____
3. **Plant cells contain large central vacuoles for storing water and nutrients.** _____
4. **Both plant and animal cells have mitochondria.** _____

Part 4: Plasma Membrane and Homeostasis

Instructions: Fill in the blanks.

1. The plasma membrane is made of a _____ bilayer.

2. _____ proteins help transport substances across the membrane.
3. The plasma membrane maintains _____, keeping the cell's internal environment stable.

Part 5: Short Answer Questions

1. **Why is the cytoskeleton important for cells?**

2. **How do mitochondria help cells survive and function?**

3. **Explain how the plasma membrane helps regulate what goes in and out of the cell.**

Bonus Question (Challenge):

If you were a scientist designing a new kind of cell for life on Mars, which organelles would be essential for survival and why?

3.2: Cellular Transport Mechanisms

Cells are like busy cities — constantly bringing in what they need (like food and oxygen) and shipping out waste. To do this, cells use **transport mechanisms** to move molecules across the **plasma membrane** — the protective barrier that separates the inside of the cell from its environment.

I. Passive Transport — Moving Without Energy (Like Coasting Downhill)

Passive transport is the movement of molecules **without using cellular energy (ATP)**. It relies on the natural movement of molecules from areas of **high concentration to low concentration**, following a concentration gradient — like rolling a ball downhill.

1. Diffusion — Simple Movement from High to Low Concentration

Definition:
Diffusion is the movement of molecules **from an area of higher concentration to an area of lower concentration**, until equilibrium is reached — where molecules are evenly spread out.

Examples of Diffusion:

- **Oxygen and carbon dioxide gas exchange** in the lungs — oxygen moves from air sacs into blood, CO_2 moves out.
- Perfume scent spreading in a room.

    Analogy: Imagine a crowd leaving a stadium — people move from crowded spaces to emptier areas.

2. Osmosis — The Diffusion of Water

Definition:
Osmosis is the **diffusion of water** across a **selectively permeable membrane**, moving from an area of **lower solute concentration** (more water) to **higher solute concentration** (less water).

Key Terms:

- **Hypotonic:** Lower solute concentration (more water).
- **Hypertonic:** Higher solute concentration (less water).
- **Isotonic:** Equal solute concentration.

Examples of Osmosis:

- **Water absorption in plant roots.**
- Red blood cells swelling or shrinking in different solutions.

    Analogy: Water moving through a sponge, flowing toward the "driest" part.

3. Facilitated Diffusion — Help from Proteins

Definition:
Facilitated diffusion is **passive movement** of molecules across the membrane with the help of **specific transport proteins** — without using energy.

Examples of Facilitated Diffusion:

- **Glucose transport** into cells using **GLUT proteins**.
- Ions like sodium (Na^+) or potassium (K^+) moving through channel proteins.

    Analogy: Like using a revolving door to get into a building — it helps you enter more easily.

Summary Table of Passive Transport

Type	Definition	Example
Diffusion	Movement from high to low concentration.	Oxygen/CO_2 exchange in lungs.
Osmosis	Diffusion of water through a membrane.	Water absorption in plants.
Facilitated Diffusion	Transport via proteins without energy.	Glucose transport into cells.

II. Active Transport — Moving with Energy (Like Climbing Uphill)

Active transport moves molecules **against** the concentration gradient — **from low to high concentration** — and **requires energy (ATP)**.

   Analogy: Like pedaling a bike uphill — it takes work!

1. Pumps — Protein Machines that Use ATP

Definition:
Pumps are **proteins in the membrane** that use **ATP energy** to move molecules **against** their gradient.

Example: Sodium-Potassium Pump

- Pumps **3 sodium ions (Na⁺) out** and **2 potassium ions (K⁺) in** to maintain nerve signals and muscle contractions.

   Key for: Nerve impulses, muscle contractions, and **cell volume regulation**.

---

2. Endocytosis — Taking in Large Substances

Definition:
Endocytosis is the process where cells **engulf external substances** by wrapping them in **vesicles** made from the plasma membrane.

Types of Endocytosis:

Type	Definition	Example
Phagocytosis	"Cell eating" — engulfing large particles/cells.	White blood cells eating bacteria.
Pinocytosis	"Cell drinking" — engulfing liquids and solutes.	Cells taking in extracellular fluid.
Receptor-Mediated Endocytosis	Specific molecules bind to receptors and are engulfed.	Cholesterol uptake into cells.

   Analogy: Like using your arms to grab and pull something inside — but at the microscopic level!

---

3. Exocytosis — Expelling Substances Out of the Cell

Definition:
Exocytosis is the process where vesicles **fuse with the plasma membrane** to **release contents outside** the cell.

Examples of Exocytosis:

- **Secretion of neurotransmitters** from nerve cells into synapses.
- Release of hormones like insulin.

   Analogy: Like sending a package out from a post office — packaged inside, then shipped out.

Summary Table of Active Transport

Process	Definition	Example
Pumps	Protein uses ATP to move molecules against gradient.	Sodium-potassium pump.
Endocytosis (Phagocytosis)	Cell engulfs large particles.	White blood cells consuming bacteria.
Endocytosis (Pinocytosis)	Cell engulfs fluids.	Absorbing extracellular fluid.

45

Process	Definition	Example
Receptor-Mediated Endocytosis	Specific molecule uptake via receptors.	Cholesterol intake.
Exocytosis	Vesicle fuses to membrane to release contents.	Neurotransmitter release.

III. Why Cellular Transport Is Essential for Life

1. Nutrient Uptake:

- Cells need to bring in **nutrients (glucose, amino acids)** for energy and growth.

2. Waste Removal:

- Cells remove **waste products** to avoid toxic buildup.

3. Communication:

- Cells send and receive **signals (neurotransmitters, hormones)** to coordinate body functions.

4. Homeostasis:

- By controlling what enters and exits, cells **maintain a stable internal environment** even when the outside changes.

Without proper transport, cells would starve, poison themselves, and fail to communicate — life would be impossible.

IV. Final Thought: Real-Life Connection

- Every time you **breathe, eat, or move**, your cells are using **diffusion, osmosis, and active transport** to make it possible.
- When you drink water, **osmosis** balances fluids inside and outside your cells.
- When you think or move, **pumps** in your neurons are firing to send signals.
- When your immune system fights infection, **phagocytosis** helps destroy invaders.

Cellular transport is happening every second to keep you alive and functioning.

Cellular Transport Mechanisms — Student Worksheet

Part 1: Passive vs. Active Transport

Instructions: Answer the following questions in complete sentences.

1. **What is the difference between passive and active transport?**

2. **Does passive transport require energy? Why or why not?**

3. **Why does active transport require ATP energy?**

Part 2: Identifying Transport Types

Instructions: Match each transport process with its correct description. Write the letter next to each process.

Descriptions	Processes
A) Water moving through a membrane from low to high solute concentration.	1. Osmosis
B) Molecules moving from high to low concentration without energy.	2. Diffusion
C) Protein channel helping glucose enter the cell.	3. Facilitated Diffusion
D) Sodium and potassium ions moved against gradient using ATP.	4. Sodium-Potassium Pump (Active Transport)
E) Cell engulfing large particles like bacteria.	5. Phagocytosis (Endocytosis)
F) Cell taking in fluids and dissolved substances.	6. Pinocytosis (Endocytosis)
G) Cell releasing substances out via vesicles.	7. Exocytosis

Part 3: Application and Critical Thinking

Instructions: Answer the following in 2–3 sentences.

1. **Why is the sodium-potassium pump important for nerve cells?**

2. **Explain how osmosis helps plants absorb water through their roots.**

3. **Describe how exocytosis helps nerve cells communicate.**

Part 4: True or False

Instructions: Write T (True) or F (False).

1. _____ Passive transport moves substances from low to high concentration.
2. _____ Facilitated diffusion requires a transport protein but no energy.
3. _____ Endocytosis is a form of active transport that requires ATP.
4. _____ Osmosis is the movement of water.
5. _____ Exocytosis removes materials from the cell.

Bonus Challenge Question

Imagine a plant cell is placed in a very salty solution. Predict what will happen to the water inside the plant cell and explain why.

3.3: Cellular Energy — Photosynthesis & Cellular Respiration

I. Photosynthesis — How Plants Make Energy for Life

Overview: What is Photosynthesis?

Photosynthesis is the process by which **green plants, algae, and some bacteria** use **light energy from the sun** to make **glucose (a sugar)** and **oxygen (O_2)** from **carbon dioxide (CO_2)** and **water (H_2O)**.

Formula for Photosynthesis:

$6CO_2 + 6H_2O + light\ energy \rightarrow C_6H_{12}O_6 + 6O_2$

Why it matters: Photosynthesis is how **energy from sunlight** is stored in food and **releases oxygen**, which we breathe to survive.

---

1. Light-Dependent Reactions — Capturing Solar Energy

Where?

- **Thylakoid membranes** inside chloroplasts (stacked discs called grana).

What Happens?

- **Chlorophyll** (green pigment) absorbs light energy.
- **Electrons get excited** (gain energy).
- **Water molecules split** (**photolysis**) to release **oxygen (O_2)**.
- **ATP and NADPH** (energy carriers) are produced to power the next step.

Analogy: Like charging a battery using solar panels — light energy is stored in ATP and NADPH.

---

2. Light-Independent Reactions (Calvin Cycle) — Making Sugar

Where?

- **Stroma** of chloroplasts (fluid-filled space).

What Happens?

- **Carbon dioxide (CO_2)** is "fixed" — turned into an organic molecule.
- Using ATP and NADPH from light-dependent reactions, the plant builds **glucose ($C_6H_{12}O_6$)**.
- Glucose can be used for **energy** or **stored** as starch.

Analogy: Like using stored energy from solar panels to cook food — plants "cook up" glucose!

II. Cellular Respiration — How Cells Unlock Energy

Overview: What is Cellular Respiration?

Cellular respiration is how **cells break down glucose** to make **ATP (energy)** — the "fuel" that powers all cell functions.

Formula for Aerobic Respiration:

$C_6H_{12}O_6 + 6O_2 \rightarrow 6CO_2 + 6H_2O + ATP\ (energy)$

Why it matters: This process **releases stored energy** in food to keep cells alive and working.

---

1. Aerobic Respiration — With Oxygen (Most Efficient)

Where?

- **Starts in the cytoplasm,** continues in **mitochondria** (the powerhouse of the cell).

Stages:

Stage	Location	What Happens
Glycolysis	Cytoplasm	Glucose is broken into 2 pyruvate; makes 2 ATP and NADH.
Pyruvate Oxidation	Mitochondria (matrix)	Pyruvate is turned into acetyl-CoA; CO_2 and NADH released.
Citric Acid Cycle (Krebs)	Mitochondrial matrix	Acetyl-CoA enters cycle; produces ATP, NADH, $FADH_2$, CO_2.
Electron Transport Chain (ETC)	Inner mitochondrial membrane	NADH & $FADH_2$ donate electrons; create proton gradient; **oxygen** is final electron acceptor, forming water. Makes **up to 32-34 ATP**.

Total ATP Yield:

About **36-38 ATP per glucose**.

Analogy: Like burning fuel in a power plant to generate electricity — glucose is "burned" for ATP.

---

2. Anaerobic Respiration (Fermentation) — Without Oxygen (Less Efficient)

When **oxygen is not available**, cells perform **anaerobic respiration (fermentation)** to make small amounts of ATP quickly.

Types of Fermentation:

Type	What Happens	Example/Organism
Lactic Acid Fermentation	Pyruvate turns into **lactic acid**.	Muscle cells under intense exercise.
Alcoholic Fermentation	Pyruvate turns into **ethanol and CO_2**.	Yeast in bread and alcohol production.

ATP Yield:

Only **2 ATP per glucose**.

> **Analogy:** Like using a backup generator — not as efficient but keeps things running when oxygen is low.

III. Comparing Photosynthesis and Cellular Respiration — The Cycle of Life

Feature	Photosynthesis	Cellular Respiration
Purpose	Store energy in glucose.	Release energy from glucose to make ATP.
Organisms	Plants, algae, some bacteria.	All living organisms (plants & animals).
Reactants (Inputs)	CO_2, H_2O, sunlight.	Glucose ($C_6H_{12}O_6$), O_2.
Products (Outputs)	Glucose, O_2.	CO_2, H_2O, ATP.
Location	Chloroplasts.	Cytoplasm (glycolysis), mitochondria.

Relationship and Energy Flow:

- **Photosynthesis stores energy** by making glucose.
- **Cellular respiration releases energy** by breaking down glucose.
- The **oxygen produced** by photosynthesis is used in cellular respiration.
- The **carbon dioxide released** by respiration is used in photosynthesis.

Cycle of Life: Plants make food and oxygen — animals use that food and oxygen and give off CO_2 for plants!

IV. Final Thought: Why This Matters in Real Life

- **Every breath you take** uses oxygen produced by plants.
- **Every bite of food** contains energy originally captured by photosynthesis.
- **Every movement and thought** is powered by ATP made in respiration.
- Even when you exercise and run out of oxygen, **fermentation** lets your muscles keep going for a little while longer.

Photosynthesis and respiration are opposite sides of the same coin — both necessary for life on Earth.

Photosynthesis & Cellular Respiration — Student Worksheet

Part 1: Understanding Photosynthesis

Instructions: Answer each question in complete sentences.

1. **What is the main purpose of photosynthesis?**

2. **What two products are made in the light-dependent reactions?**

50

3. What is the role of carbon dioxide in the Calvin cycle?

Part 2: Understanding Cellular Respiration

Instructions: Answer each question clearly.

1. **What is the main goal of cellular respiration?**

2. **Where does glycolysis take place in the cell?**

3. **What are the final products of aerobic respiration?**

4. **Why is oxygen important for the electron transport chain?**

Part 3: Comparing Photosynthesis and Cellular Respiration

Instructions: Fill in the table comparing these two processes.

Feature	Photosynthesis	Cellular Respiration
Main Purpose		
Reactants (Inputs)		
Products (Outputs)		
Organelle where it occurs		
Type of organisms that perform it		

Part 4: Critical Thinking and Connection

Instructions: Answer in 2–3 sentences.

1. **Explain how photosynthesis and cellular respiration form a cycle that supports life on Earth.**

2. **What would happen to life on Earth if photosynthesis stopped?**

51

Bonus Challenge Question:

If a plant is kept in a dark room for a week, what would happen to its ability to produce glucose? How would this affect an animal that eats this plant?

_____

_____

_____

3.4: Cell Growth and Reproduction

I. The Cell Cycle and Mitosis — How Cells Grow and Divide

Cells must **grow, copy their DNA, and divide** to form new cells for **growth, repair, and replacement**. This orderly process is called the **cell cycle**, and it includes **interphase** and **mitotic (M) phase**.

1. Interphase — Preparing for Division (Most of a Cell's Life)

Interphase is when a cell **grows, performs its normal functions**, and **prepares to divide**. It includes **three phases**:

Phase	What Happens
G_1 Phase	Cell grows; makes proteins needed for DNA replication.
S Phase	**DNA is replicated** — each chromosome makes a copy (sister chromatids).
G_2 Phase	Cell grows more; makes microtubules and proteins for mitosis.

Analogy: Like a bakery preparing to make a cake — gathering ingredients, mixing, and getting ready to bake.

_____

2. Mitotic (M) Phase — Cell Division

The **M phase** is when the cell **divides its nucleus and cytoplasm** to form **two identical daughter cells**.

Stages of Mitosis:

Stage	What Happens
Prophase	Chromatin condenses into chromosomes; nuclear envelope breaks down; spindle fibers form.
Metaphase	Chromosomes align in the middle (metaphase plate); spindle fibers attach to centromeres.
Anaphase	**Sister chromatids are pulled apart** to opposite sides of the cell.
Telophase	Chromosomes decondense into chromatin; new nuclear envelopes form.

Stage	What Happens
Cytokinesis	**Cytoplasm divides**, forming **two identical daughter cells**.

Analogy: Like copying a document and splitting it into two folders — both identical!

II. Meiosis — Making Gametes and Creating Diversity

Meiosis is a special type of cell division that produces **gametes (sperm and egg cells)** for sexual reproduction. Unlike mitosis, meiosis **reduces chromosome number by half** and **increases genetic diversity**.

1. Purpose of Meiosis:

- To produce **haploid gametes** (with half the number of chromosomes).
- To introduce **genetic variation**, making each offspring unique.

2. Phases of Meiosis (Two Divisions)

Meiosis I — Homologous Chromosomes Separate

Stage	What Happens
Prophase I	**Homologous chromosomes pair** (synapsis) and **cross over** (exchange DNA).
Metaphase I	Homologous pairs line up at the metaphase plate.
Anaphase I	Homologous chromosomes separate and move to opposite poles.
Telophase I & Cytokinesis	Two haploid cells form (each with half the number of chromosomes).

Key Event: Crossing over happens here — exchanging genetic material for diversity.

Meiosis II — Sister Chromatids Separate (Like Mitosis)

Stage	What Happens
Prophase II	New spindle forms in each haploid cell.
Metaphase II	Chromosomes align individually at the center.
Anaphase II	**Sister chromatids pulled apart** to opposite sides.
Telophase II & Cytokinesis	Four unique haploid cells form.

3. Genetic Variation Mechanisms in Meiosis

Mechanism	When It Happens	What It Does
Crossing Over	Prophase I	Swaps DNA between homologous chromosomes — new combinations of genes.
Independent Assortment	Metaphase I	Random alignment of chromosome pairs — many possible combinations.
Random Fertilization	After meiosis (during fertilization)	Random egg and sperm unite — trillions of combinations.

Result: No two gametes (or people) are genetically identical — diversity is built-in!

III. Comparing Mitosis and Meiosis — What's the Difference?

Feature	Mitosis	Meiosis
Purpose	Growth, repair, asexual reproduction.	Sexual reproduction (gametes), genetic diversity.
Number of Divisions	1	2 (Meiosis I & II)
Number of Daughter Cells	2	4
Genetic Identity	Identical to parent cell.	Genetically diverse.
Chromosome Number	Same as parent (diploid, 2n).	Half of parent (haploid, n).
Where It Occurs	Somatic (body) cells.	Germ (sex) cells — sperm and eggs.
Crossing Over	No	Yes, in Prophase I.
Homologous Chromosomes Pair	No	Yes, in Prophase I.

Key Idea:
- Mitosis makes clones (identical copies).
- Meiosis makes variety (unique gametes).

IV. Final Thought: Why This Matters?
- **Mitosis** lets us **grow, heal, and replace cells** — like healing a cut.
- **Meiosis** makes sure each new generation is **genetically diverse** — ensuring evolution and adaptation.
- **Without mitosis**, we couldn't grow or heal.
- **Without meiosis**, reproduction would not create unique individuals — and populations would lack diversity.

Mitosis and Meiosis — Student Worksheet

Part 1: Understanding the Cell Cycle and Mitosis

Instructions: Answer each question in complete sentences.

1. **What is the purpose of mitosis in multicellular organisms?**

2. **During which phase of interphase does DNA replicate?**

3. **What happens to sister chromatids during anaphase of mitosis?**

4. **What is the result of cytokinesis in mitosis?**

Part 2: Understanding Meiosis and Genetic Variation

Instructions: Answer each question clearly.

1. **What is the purpose of meiosis?**

2. **During which phase of meiosis does crossing over occur?**

3. **How many cells are produced at the end of meiosis, and are they genetically identical or different?**

Part 3: Comparing Mitosis and Meiosis

Instructions: Complete the table to compare mitosis and meiosis.

Feature	Mitosis	Meiosis
Number of divisions		
Number of daughter cells		
Genetic identity of daughter cells		
Purpose		
Crossing over occurs?		
Chromosome number in daughter cells		

Part 4: Multiple Choice Questions

Circle the correct answer.

1. Which process creates gametes?
   A) Mitosis
   B) Meiosis

2. Which process results in genetically identical cells?
   A) Mitosis
   B) Meiosis

3. During which phase do chromosomes line up in the middle of the cell?
   A) Prophase
   B) Metaphase
   C) Anaphase

4. What is the main goal of meiosis?
   A) Growth
   B) Repair
   C) Genetic diversity

Part 5: Critical Thinking and Application

Instructions: Answer in 2–3 sentences.

1. **Why is genetic variation important in sexual reproduction?**

2. **If mitosis did not happen, what would be the consequence for an organism?**

Chapter 4: Genetics and Heredity

4.1: Gregor Mendel's Experiments and Principles — The Foundation of Modern Genetics

1. Who Was Gregor Mendel?

Gregor Mendel, an **Austrian monk and scientist**, is known as the **"Father of Modern Genetics."** In the **mid-1800s**, Mendel conducted experiments on **pea plants** to understand **how traits are passed from one generation to the next** — long before DNA was discovered!

Why Pea Plants?
- Pea plants have **easily observable traits** (like flower color and seed shape).
- They can **self-pollinate** or **cross-pollinate**, allowing controlled breeding.

---

2. Mendel's Experiments: Simple but Groundbreaking

- **Monohybrid Crosses**: Mendel focused on **one trait at a time**, like flower color (purple or white).
- He **cross-pollinated** plants with opposite traits and observed the **patterns in offspring** over generations.

Key Observation:

- Traits **disappeared in one generation** but **reappeared** in the next — leading to his famous **laws of inheritance**.

---

3. Mendel's Principles (The Laws of Inheritance)

Law	What It Says	Example
Law of Segregation	Each individual has **two alleles** for each trait. These **separate (segregate)** during gamete formation, so each gamete gets **one allele**.	A plant with alleles Aa produces gametes with either A or a.
Law of Independent Assortment	**Alleles for different genes** assort independently during gamete formation.	A plant's seed color and seed shape are inherited independently.

Result: Genetic **variation** in offspring!

II. Dominant vs. Recessive Alleles — The Language of Traits

1. What Are Alleles?

Alleles are **different forms of a gene** for a specific trait.

- **Example:** Gene for flower color — one allele for purple (P), one for white (p).

---

2. Dominant Alleles (Uppercase Letter, e.g., 'A')

- **Expressed** if **at least one copy** is present.
- **Masks** recessive alleles.
- **Example:** If **A** is dominant, both **AA and Aa** show the dominant trait.

---

3. Recessive Alleles (Lowercase Letter, e.g., 'a')

- **Only expressed** if **two copies** are present.
- **Example:** Only **aa** will show the recessive trait.

   Real-life analogy: Think of dominant alleles as a loud voice in a group — you always hear it unless everyone else is quiet (recessive).

---

4. Phenotype vs. Genotype

Term	Definition	Example
Genotype	The **genetic makeup** — combination of alleles.	AA, Aa, or aa.
Phenotype	The **physical appearance** or trait.	Purple flowers or white flowers.

Key Idea: Genotype **determines** phenotype!

III. Punnett Squares — Predicting Inheritance

What Is a Punnett Square?

A **Punnett square** is a diagram that **shows all possible combinations of alleles** in offspring from a genetic cross.

Step-by-Step Guide to Building a Punnett Square:

1. **Determine Parental Genotypes:**

    o   Example: Aa x Aa (heterozygous parents for flower color).

2. **Set Up the Grid:**

    o   **Gametes from each parent** are listed along the top and side.
    o   Example:

	A	a
A		
a		

3. **Fill in the Squares:**
    o   Combine alleles from each parent.

	A	a
A	AA	Aa
a	Aa	aa

How to Interpret the Results:

Genotypic Ratio:

- Count **genetic combinations**:
    o   1 AA : 2 Aa : 1 aa.

Phenotypic Ratio:

- Count **observable traits**:
    o   If **A (dominant)** shows purple flowers and **a (recessive)** shows white:
    o   **3 purple : 1 white.**

IV. Probability in Genetics — Predicting the Chance of Traits

- **Probability** helps predict **how likely** certain traits will appear in offspring.
- **Calculated using Punnett squares** and expressed as a **percentage or fraction**.

Example:

- If Aa x Aa:
    o   Probability of aa (white flowers) = **1 out of 4 = 25%**.
    o   Probability of purple flowers (AA or Aa) = **3 out of 4 = 75%**.

    Key Concept: Although Punnett squares predict chances, **actual offspring outcomes** can vary — probability is about **likelihood**, not certainty.

V. Summary Table — Mendelian Genetics

Concept	Explanation/Example
Law of Segregation	Each parent passes one allele for each trait (Aa → A or a).
Law of Independent Assortment	Genes for different traits (e.g., height and color) separate independently.
Dominant Allele	Expressed if present (A = purple flower).
Recessive Allele	Only shown when no dominant allele is present (aa = white flower).
Genotype	Genetic makeup (AA, Aa, or aa).
Phenotype	Observable trait (purple or white flower).
Punnett Square	Diagram to predict genetic outcomes.
Genotypic Ratio	1:2:1 (AA:Aa:aa).
Phenotypic Ratio	3:1 (dominant:recessive).

VI. Final Thought: Why Mendel's Work Still Matters

- Mendel's discoveries explain **why siblings can look different** and **how traits pass through families**.
- Understanding genetics helps in **medicine (genetic diseases)**, **agriculture (breeding plants and animals)**, and **conservation biology (protecting species)**.

Genetics is at the heart of understanding life and inheritance — thanks to Mendel's simple but powerful pea plant experiments.

Mendelian Genetics — Student Worksheet

Part 1: Mendel's Experiments and Laws

Instructions: Answer in complete sentences.

1. **Who was Gregor Mendel, and why is he important in biology?**

2. **What plant did Mendel study, and why did he choose this plant?**

3. **What is Mendel's Law of Segregation?**

4. **What is Mendel's Law of Independent Assortment?**

Part 2: Dominant and Recessive Alleles

Instructions: Fill in the blanks.

1. Alleles are _____ forms of a gene.
2. A _____ allele is expressed even if only one copy is present.

3. A _____ allele is only expressed when two copies are present.
4. Use **A** for dominant and **a** for recessive: What genotype would show the recessive trait? _____

Part 3: Using Punnett Squares

Instructions: Complete the Punnett square for a cross between two heterozygous parents (Aa x Aa).

	A	a
A		
a		

Questions:

1. **List the possible genotypes and how many of each.**

2. **What is the genotypic ratio?**

3. **What is the phenotypic ratio if A = purple flowers and a = white flowers?**

Part 4: Probability and Genetics

Instructions: Answer the following questions.

1. **What is the probability of an offspring showing the dominant trait (purple flowers)?**

2. **What is the probability of an offspring showing the recessive trait (white flowers)?**

Part 5: Challenge Question — Critical Thinking

If two pea plants are crossed and all the offspring have purple flowers, what can you conclude about the parents' genotypes? Explain.

4.2: Molecular Genetics — The Blueprint of Life

I. Structure and Function of DNA and RNA

1. DNA (Deoxyribonucleic Acid) — The Instruction Manual of Life

Structure:

- **Shape**: Double helix (twisted ladder).
- **Building blocks**: **Nucleotides**, each made of:
  - **Deoxyribose sugar**
  - **Phosphate group**
  - **Nitrogenous base**:
    - **Adenine (A)**
    - **Thymine (T)**
    - **Cytosine (C)**
    - **Guanine (G)**

Base Pairing Rule:

- **A pairs with T**, and **C pairs with G** — held together by hydrogen bonds.

Analogy: Like a zipper where specific teeth (bases) only fit with their partner.

Function of DNA:

- **Stores genetic information** — instructions for making all proteins and running cellular activities.
- **Hereditary material** — passed from parents to offspring.

---

2. RNA (Ribonucleic Acid) — The Worker of Genetic Information

Structure:

- **Single-stranded**.
- Made of **nucleotides**:
  - **Ribose sugar** (instead of deoxyribose).
  - **Phosphate group**.
  - Bases: **Adenine (A), Uracil (U) (replaces Thymine), Cytosine (C), Guanine (G)**.

---

3. Types of RNA and Their Functions:

RNA Type	Function
mRNA (Messenger RNA)	Carries genetic code from DNA to ribosomes for protein synthesis.
tRNA (Transfer RNA)	Brings amino acids to ribosomes to build proteins.
rRNA (Ribosomal RNA)	Combines with proteins to form ribosomes — the site of protein synthesis.

Analogy: If DNA is a recipe book, **mRNA is a copy of the recipe, tRNA are the chefs bringing ingredients**, and **rRNA is the kitchen where cooking happens**.

II. DNA Replication — Copying the Blueprint

Purpose:

- To ensure **each new cell** gets an **exact copy of DNA** during cell division.

Step-by-Step Process of DNA Replication:

Step	What Happens
Initiation	Replication starts at **origins of replication**.
Unwinding	**Helicase** enzyme unzips the double helix, creating **replication forks**.
Primer Binding	**Primase** adds **RNA primers** to give starting points.
Elongation (Leading Strand)	**DNA Polymerase** adds complementary nucleotides **continuously** (5' to 3').
Elongation (Lagging Strand)	DNA Polymerase synthesizes **Okazaki fragments discontinuously**, later joined by **DNA Ligase**.
Termination	RNA primers are removed, gaps filled, replication completes.

Semi-Conservative Nature:

- Each new DNA molecule has **one old strand + one new strand**.

Analogy: Like copying a book and keeping one page from the original in each new copy!

III. Transcription and Translation — How Proteins Are Made

---

1. Transcription — From DNA to mRNA (Making the Message)

Purpose:

- **Create mRNA** from a DNA template to carry the genetic message out of the nucleus.

Steps of Transcription:

Step	What Happens
Initiation	**RNA polymerase** binds to promoter on DNA.
Elongation	RNA polymerase adds **complementary RNA nucleotides**.
Termination	RNA polymerase reaches a stop sequence; mRNA strand is complete.

Outcome: A strand of **mRNA** that carries the genetic code to the ribosome.

---

2. Translation — From mRNA to Protein (Building the Product)

Purpose:

- **Translate** mRNA code into a **polypeptide chain (protein)**.

Step-by-Step Process of Translation:

Step	What Happens
Initiation	Ribosome binds to mRNA at the **start codon (AUG)**. **tRNA** brings methionine.
Elongation	**tRNA molecules** bring specific amino acids. Ribosome **links amino acids** with peptide bonds.
Movement	Ribosome moves along mRNA **codon by codon**.
Termination	Ribosome reaches a **stop codon (UAA, UAG, UGA)** — protein is released.

Outcome:

- A **polypeptide chain** that will fold into a **functional protein**, vital for life functions (enzymes, hormones, structures).

Codons and Anticodons:

- **Codons**: 3-letter sequences on mRNA (e.g., AUG, UUU).
- **Anticodons**: Complementary 3-letter sequences on tRNA.

Example:
mRNA codon: **AUG**
tRNA anticodon: **UAC**

IV. Summary Table — Molecular Genetics Processes

Process	Purpose	Key Molecules Involved	Product
DNA Replication	Copy DNA for cell division.	DNA, DNA polymerase, helicase, ligase.	Two identical DNA molecules.
Transcription	Make mRNA from DNA template.	DNA, RNA polymerase.	mRNA strand.
Translation	Make proteins from mRNA code.	mRNA, tRNA, rRNA (ribosome), amino acids.	Functional protein (polypeptide).

V. Final Thought: Why It Matters?

- **DNA holds the instructions, RNA delivers them, and proteins do the work.**
- Understanding this process explains **how traits are expressed, how enzymes function**, and **how genetic disorders occur**.
- All life — from bacteria to humans — follows this **universal code** for building proteins.

Without DNA, RNA, and protein synthesis, life as we know it would not exist.

4.3: Genetic Disorders and Biotechnology

I. Causes of Genetic Mutations — **How DNA Gets Altered**

1. What Are Mutations?

- A **mutation** is a **change in the DNA sequence**.
- Mutations can be **harmless, beneficial, or harmful**, depending on their effect on gene function.

2. Types of Mutations:

Type	Cause/Explanation	Example/Effect
Spontaneous Mutations	Occur naturally during **DNA replication** — copying errors.	Mispairing nucleotides, strand slippage.
Induced Mutations	Caused by external agents (**mutagens**).	See below.

3. Induced Mutations:

Mutagen Type	Explanation	Example
Chemical Mutagens	Chemicals that modify DNA bases.	**Base analogs**, chemicals causing base modification.
Physical Mutagens	Radiation that damages DNA.	**UV light** causing thymine dimers; **X-rays**.
Biological Agents	Viruses that insert their genes into host DNA.	**HPV** (human papillomavirus).

4. Consequences of Mutations:

Mutation Type	Effect on Protein	Outcome
Silent Mutation	No change in amino acid.	No effect.
Missense Mutation	One amino acid substituted.	Possible change in protein function.
Nonsense Mutation	Early stop codon introduced.	Truncated (incomplete) protein.
Frameshift Mutation	Insertion or deletion shifts reading frame.	Entire protein sequence altered.

Note: Mutations in germ cells (egg/sperm) can be **inherited**, while somatic cell mutations affect only the individual.

II. Genetic Engineering and CRISPR — Editing Life's Code

1. What is Genetic Engineering?

Genetic engineering is the **direct manipulation of DNA** to change an organism's traits.

Applications of Genetic Engineering:

Field	Application
Agriculture	Crops resistant to pests, herbicides; enhanced nutrition.
Medicine	Producing **insulin**, vaccines, and **gene therapies**.
Research	Model organisms to study diseases and gene function.

2. CRISPR-Cas9 — A Revolutionary Gene-Editing Tool

CRISPR-Cas9 is a **precise genome-editing tool**, based on a bacterial defense mechanism.

How CRISPR Works:

1. **Guide RNA (gRNA)** is designed to target specific DNA sequence.
2. **Cas9 enzyme** cuts the DNA at the target location.
3. **Cell repairs DNA**, allowing **insertion or deletion** of genes.

Analogy: Like a **molecular scissor**, cutting and editing genetic code exactly where needed.

3. Applications of CRISPR:

Field	Use
Gene Therapy	Correct defective genes in humans.
Agriculture	Modify plants for drought resistance, yield.
Functional Genomics	Study gene roles by creating mutations.

III. Ethical Considerations in Biotechnology — Balancing Promise and Responsibility

1. Human Genetic Modification:

Type	Definition	Ethical Concerns
Germline Editing	Changing DNA in **sperm, eggs, embryos** (heritable).	Risk of unknown effects on future generations; consent; social inequality.
Somatic Cell Editing	Changing DNA in **body cells**, not inherited.	Safety, access to therapy, enhancement misuse.

2. Genetically Modified Organisms (GMOs):

66

Issue	Explanation/Concern
Environmental Impact	Cross-breeding with wild species; ecosystem effects.
Biodiversity	GMOs outcompeting natural species.
Food Safety	Allergies, long-term health concerns.
Labeling and Consumer Choice	Should GMO products be labeled?

3. Intellectual Property and Farmers' Rights:

Concern	Explanation
Patenting	Biotech companies patent GM seeds, limiting farmers' rights to save seeds.
Economic Access	Small farmers may struggle to afford patented seeds.

4. Privacy and Genetic Information:

Issue	Concern
Data Security	Protecting personal genetic data.
Discrimination Risks	Preventing misuse of genetic data in jobs, insurance.

5. Bioterrorism and Dual-Use Research:

Issue	Concern
Weaponization	Risk of biotech being used for biological weapons.
Regulation	Need for oversight to prevent misuse.

6. Animal Welfare in Biotech Research:

Concern	Explanation
Testing Protocols	Humane treatment of animals in research.
Alternatives	Use non-animal methods when possible.

7. Environmental and Ecological Concerns:

Issue	Concern
Ecosystem Balance	Unintended consequences of biotech on nature.
Sustainability	Long-term impacts of biotech interventions.

IV. Summary Table — Genetic Mutations and Biotechnology

Category	Key Points
Genetic Mutations	Can be spontaneous or induced; may cause diseases or diversity.
Types of Mutations	Silent, missense, nonsense, frameshift.
Genetic Engineering	Direct DNA manipulation for crops, medicine, research.
CRISPR	Precise gene editing; revolutionizing genetics.
Ethical Concerns	Human editing, GMOs, data privacy, environmental impact.

V. Why This Matters?

- **Understanding mutations** helps in diagnosing and treating genetic diseases.
- **CRISPR and genetic engineering** offer hope for curing diseases but raise serious **ethical questions**.
- **GMO technology** can help feed the world but must be managed responsibly.
- **Public discussion and education** are critical to making informed decisions about biotechnology.

Science and ethics must go hand in hand to ensure that biotechnology benefits humanity and the environment safely.

Genetic Mutations and Biotechnology Worksheet with Answers

Part 1: Understanding Mutations

1. **What is a genetic mutation, and what causes mutations to occur?**
   A genetic mutation is a change in the DNA sequence. Mutations can occur spontaneously during DNA replication or be caused by environmental factors called mutagens, such as chemicals, radiation, or viruses.

2. **List and briefly describe the four types of genetic mutations:**

   - **Silent Mutation:** A change in DNA that does not affect the amino acid sequence of a protein.
   - **Missense Mutation:** A change that results in one amino acid being substituted for another in a protein.
   - **Nonsense Mutation:** A mutation that changes a codon into a stop codon, causing the protein to be shortened.
   - **Frameshift Mutation:** Caused by insertion or deletion of nucleotides, shifting the reading frame and altering the entire protein sequence after the mutation.

3. **What are the potential consequences of a frameshift mutation?**
   Frameshift mutations often result in a completely altered and nonfunctional protein, potentially leading to serious diseases or developmental issues.

4. **How can a mutation in a germ cell (egg or sperm) affect future generations?**
   Mutations in germ cells can be passed on to offspring, affecting every cell in their body and possibly leading to inherited genetic disorders.

Part 2: CRISPR and Gene Editing

1. **What is CRISPR, and how does it function as a gene-editing tool?**
   CRISPR is a precise gene-editing technology that allows scientists to cut and modify specific DNA sequences. It uses a guide RNA to direct the Cas9 enzyme to the target DNA, where Cas9 makes a cut so that genes can be added, removed, or altered.

2. **Describe the role of guide RNA and Cas9 in the CRISPR system.**
   Guide RNA (gRNA) guides Cas9 to the specific DNA sequence to be edited. Cas9 acts as molecular scissors that cut the DNA at the precise location targeted by the guide RNA.

3. **Name two potential applications of CRISPR technology.**

- Correcting genetic defects to treat diseases (gene therapy).
- Creating genetically modified crops that are pest-resistant or drought-tolerant.

4. **Why is CRISPR considered more precise than older methods of genetic engineering?**
   CRISPR targets specific DNA sequences using guide RNA, allowing for precise editing without affecting other parts of the genome, reducing unwanted changes (off-target effects).

Part 3: Applications of Biotechnology

1. **How has biotechnology been used in agriculture? Provide one example.**
   Biotechnology has been used to create genetically modified (GM) crops that are resistant to pests, such as Bt corn, which produces a natural pesticide to protect itself from insects.

2. **What are some medical benefits of genetic engineering?**
   Genetic engineering allows for the production of important medicines like insulin, vaccines, and treatments for genetic diseases using gene therapy.

3. **Why might scientists create genetically modified bacteria to produce human insulin?**
   Scientists use bacteria to produce human insulin efficiently and in large amounts, making insulin available for people with diabetes.

4. **How can biotechnology be used in gene therapy?**
   Biotechnology allows doctors to replace faulty genes with functional ones in a patient's cells to treat genetic disorders like cystic fibrosis or muscular dystrophy.

Part 4: Ethical Issues in Biotechnology

1. **What are some ethical concerns about modifying human DNA?**
   There are concerns about unintended consequences, long-term effects on future generations, consent for germline editing, and potential use for non-medical enhancements (designer babies).

2. **Should genetically modified foods be labeled for consumers? Why or why not?**
   Some argue GM foods should be labeled to give consumers informed choices and address allergy concerns. Others argue that if GM foods are proven safe, labeling may cause unnecessary fear.

3. **What could be potential environmental risks of releasing genetically modified organisms (GMOs)?**
   GMOs might cross-breed with wild species, disrupting ecosystems, reducing biodiversity, or creating "superweeds" resistant to herbicides.

4. **Why is protecting genetic data privacy important when using biotechnology?**
   Genetic information is personal and sensitive; if exposed, it could lead to discrimination in employment, insurance, or stigmatization. Privacy ensures ethical use and protects individuals' rights.

Part 5: Bonus — Critical Thinking

Challenge Question: *If you were in charge of regulating CRISPR technology, what rules or guidelines would you create to ensure it is used safely and ethically? Explain your reasoning.*

Sample Answer (Accept Reasoned Responses):
I would create strict regulations to ensure CRISPR is only used for curing serious genetic diseases, not for non-medical enhancements. I would require thorough testing for safety, informed consent for all treatments, and ban germline editing until more is known about long-term effects. Ethical review boards should oversee all projects to ensure fairness and safety.

Chapter 5: Evolution and Natural Selection

5.1: Darwin's Principles of Natural Selection — How Evolution Works

1. Who Was Charles Darwin?

Charles Darwin was a **British naturalist** who proposed **the theory of evolution by natural selection** in his groundbreaking book **"On the Origin of Species" (1859)**. His ideas forever changed how we understand life and its diversity.

> **Key Idea:** Evolution explains **how living organisms change over time** and **how new species arise**.

2. Five Key Principles of Natural Selection

Principle	Explanation	Example
Variation	Individuals in a population show differences in traits.	Some birds have longer beaks; others have shorter ones.
Inheritance	Some variations are passed from parents to offspring.	Offspring may inherit long beaks if parents have them.
Overproduction	Organisms produce more offspring than the environment can support.	A fish may lay thousands of eggs, but only a few survive.

Principle	Explanation	Example
Differential Survival and Reproduction (Survival of the Fittest)	Individuals with favorable traits are more likely to survive and reproduce.	Birds with longer beaks may get more food and survive better.
Accumulation of Favorable Traits	Beneficial traits become more common in the population over generations.	Over time, most birds in the population may have long beaks.

Analogy: Imagine a "competition" — the best-adapted individuals "win" by surviving and passing their traits to the next generation.

II. Evidence of Evolution — How We Know Evolution Happens

---

1. Fossil Record — Clues from Ancient Life

Fossils are remains or traces of ancient organisms found in rock layers. The fossil record **shows a timeline of life on Earth**, revealing changes over millions of years.

Key Fossil Evidence:

- **Transitional Fossils**: Show intermediate forms between groups, linking ancestors and descendants.

  Example: Tiktaalik — a "fishapod" with features of both fish and land animals, bridging water and land vertebrates.

- **Chronological Order**: Fossils appear in a **consistent sequence**, from simpler life forms (like bacteria) to more complex organisms (like mammals).

  Conclusion: Fossils **document evolutionary change over time** and **how species are related**.

---

2. Comparative Anatomy — Body Structure Comparisons

By comparing body parts of different species, scientists find **evidence of common ancestry**.

Types of Anatomical Evidence:

Structure	Definition	Example
Homologous Structures	Similar structures with different functions; indicate shared ancestry.	Forelimbs of humans, bats, whales, and cats — same bones, different uses.
Vestigial Structures	Structures reduced in size/function; remnants from ancestors.	Human appendix, whale pelvic bones.

Key Idea: Similar structures in different animals **point to common evolutionary origins**.

---

3. DNA Evidence — Genetic Proof of Evolution

Modern genetics provides strong evidence for evolution through **similarities in DNA sequences**.

72

Key DNA-Based Evidence:

Evidence Type	Explanation	Example
Genetic Similarities	Closely related species share more DNA sequences.	Humans and chimpanzees share ~98% of DNA.
Molecular Clocks	DNA mutations accumulate at constant rates, helping estimate divergence times.	Humans and gorillas diverged ~10 million years ago.

Conclusion: DNA shows **how closely species are related** and **traces their evolutionary history**.

III. Summary Table — Darwin's Theory and Evolutionary Evidence

Concept	Explanation/Example
Variation	Individual differences within a population.
Inheritance	Passing traits from parents to offspring.
Overproduction	More offspring produced than can survive.
Differential Survival	Better-adapted individuals survive and reproduce more.
Accumulation of Traits	Helpful traits become common over generations.
Fossil Record	Shows life forms changing over time; transitional fossils.
Homologous Structures	Similar bones across species (e.g., human and whale arms).
Vestigial Structures	Leftover body parts (e.g., human tailbone).
DNA Similarities	More similar DNA = closer evolutionary relationship.
Molecular Clocks	DNA changes used to estimate when species diverged.

IV. Why This Matters?

- **Explains Biodiversity**: Evolution explains why we have such a wide variety of species on Earth.
- **Connects All Life**: Shows that all living things share a **common ancestor**.
- **Helps Medicine and Science**: Understanding evolution helps fight diseases (like evolving viruses) and conserve endangered species.

Final Thought: Evolution is the key to understanding life's diversity and our connection to all living things.

Evolution and Natural Selection — Student Worksheet with Answers

Part 1: Understanding Natural Selection

1. Who was Charles Darwin, and what is his contribution to biology?
Charles Darwin was a British naturalist who developed the **theory of evolution by natural selection**. He explained how species change over time and adapt to their environments through the survival and reproduction of individuals with advantageous traits.

---

2. What is natural selection?
Natural selection is the process by which **organisms with traits better suited to their environment survive and reproduce more successfully**, passing those traits to the next generation. Over time, these beneficial traits become more common in the population.

---

3. List and explain the five key principles of natural selection.

- **Variation:** Individuals in a population have **differences in traits**, like size, color, or behavior.
- **Inheritance:** Some traits are **heritable** — passed from parents to offspring.
- **Overproduction:** More offspring are produced than can survive, leading to **competition for resources**.
- **Differential Survival and Reproduction (Survival of the Fittest):** Individuals with **favorable traits survive longer and have more offspring**.
- **Accumulation of Favorable Traits:** Over time, **helpful traits become more common** in the population.

Part 2: Evidence of Evolution

1. What is a transitional fossil? Provide an example.
A transitional fossil shows **intermediate traits between an ancestral species and its descendants**, showing how species change over time.
Example: Tiktaalik, which has both fish and amphibian features, shows the transition from water to land animals.

---

2. What do homologous structures suggest about different species?
Homologous structures, like the similar bone arrangement in the arms of humans, bats, and whales, suggest that these species share a **common ancestor**, even if the structures now have different functions.

---

3. Give two examples of vestigial structures in humans or other animals.

- The **human appendix** (no longer used for digestion).
- The **pelvic bones in whales**, remnants from when their ancestors walked on land.

---

4. How does DNA provide evidence for evolution?
DNA shows **genetic similarities between species**. The more closely related two species are, the more similar their DNA sequences. For example, humans and chimpanzees share about **98% of their DNA**, indicating a recent common ancestor.

Part 3: Applying Evolutionary Concepts

1. If a population of birds lives on an island where only deep flowers grow, what kind of beak would be favored by natural selection? Explain why.
Birds with **longer, thinner beaks** would be favored because they can reach nectar inside deep flowers. These birds would survive better and reproduce more, passing on their long-beak traits.

2. How can overproduction of offspring lead to natural selection?
Since more offspring are produced than the environment can support, **not all will survive**. Those with **advantageous traits** (like better camouflage or stronger limbs) are more likely to survive and reproduce, causing these traits to spread in the population.

3. What does it mean when we say "survival of the fittest" in nature?
It means that **the individuals best adapted to their environment** are more likely to survive, reproduce, and pass on their genes. "Fitness" refers to the ability to survive and leave offspring, **not necessarily strength**.

Part 4: Multiple Choice Questions (with answers)

1. Which of the following is NOT part of Darwin's theory of natural selection?
B) Individuals pass on acquired traits.

2. A structure that has lost its original function is called:
B) Vestigial structure.

3. Which evidence best supports that humans and chimpanzees share a recent common ancestor?
B) They share nearly identical DNA sequences.

4. What is a key reason for variation within a population?
B) Mutation and genetic recombination.

Part 5: Bonus — Critical Thinking

Challenge Question:
Imagine a sudden change in climate makes an area much colder. How might natural selection affect the animal population over generations?

Sample Answer:
Animals with traits that help them survive cold, like **thicker fur or fat layers**, would be more likely to survive and reproduce. Over generations, these cold-adapted traits would become more common in the population, and animals with less protection from cold would decrease.

5:.2: Mechanisms of Evolution — How Populations Change Over Time

I. Genetic Drift — Evolution by Chance

1. What is Genetic Drift?

Genetic drift is the **random change in allele frequencies** (versions of genes) within a population over time. Unlike natural selection, which is driven by fitness, **genetic drift is completely random** and can have a **stronger effect in small populations**.

> **Key Idea: By chance alone**, some alleles (traits) become more common or disappear entirely.

---

2. Effects of Genetic Drift:

Effect	Description	Example
Bottleneck Effect	A sudden **reduction in population size** due to natural disasters, diseases, or human activities, leading to **loss of genetic diversity**.	After a natural disaster, only a few individuals survive — their genes shape the future population.
Founder Effect	When a **small group** from a population **starts a new colony**, the gene pool may be limited to only a few alleles, reducing genetic variation.	A few birds blown to a new island form a new population, carrying only some of the original genetic diversity.

> **Result:** Genetic drift **reduces genetic variation** and can **fix harmful or neutral alleles** in the population by chance.

II. Gene Flow — Sharing Genes Between Populations

1. What is Gene Flow?

Gene flow (also called **migration**) is the **movement of individuals, gametes (like pollen), or alleles between populations**, causing an exchange of genes.

---

2. Impact of Gene Flow:

Effect	Description	Example
Homogenization	Gene flow makes **populations more genetically similar**, reducing differences.	Two populations of deer mixing and sharing genes.
Prevention of Speciation	By mixing gene pools, gene flow can **prevent populations from becoming separate species.**	If fish in two lakes interbreed, they may not become distinct species.

> **Key Point:** Gene flow can **increase genetic diversity** in a population and **prevent or slow down divergence**.

III. Mutations — Source of New Genetic Variations

1. What Are Mutations?

A **mutation** is a **change in DNA sequence** that creates **new alleles**, introducing **genetic variation** — the raw material for evolution.

2. Role in Evolution:

Role/Effect	Explanation	Example
Source of Variation	**Primary source** of all new genetic variation in populations.	Mutation leads to a new coloration in moths.
Types of Mutations	Can be **beneficial** (helpful), **neutral** (no effect), or **deleterious** (harmful).	Sickle cell allele offers malaria resistance (beneficial); others may cause genetic disorders.
Fuel for Natural Selection	**Natural selection acts on mutations** that provide advantages or disadvantages.	Dark-colored mice survive better on dark rocks.

Note: Without mutations, evolution would **have no new traits to select**.

IV. Speciation — The Formation of New Species

1. What Is Speciation?

Speciation is the process by which **new species** arise from existing ones, often due to **reproductive isolation**.

Species: A group of organisms that can breed and produce fertile offspring.

2. Mechanisms of Speciation:

Type of Speciation	Explanation	Example
Allopatric Speciation	Occurs when a **physical barrier** (mountains, rivers, etc.) **separates populations**, preventing gene flow.	Squirrels separated by the Grand Canyon evolving differently.
Sympatric Speciation	Occurs **without physical barriers** — often due to **genetic changes, mutations, or behavioral shifts** within a population.	New plant species formed by polyploidy (extra chromosome sets).

Key Idea: Isolation leads to **independent evolution**, and over time, populations become different enough to be new species.

V. Adaptive Radiation — Evolution Exploding into Diversity

1. What is Adaptive Radiation?

Adaptive radiation is a rapid evolutionary process in which a **single ancestral species diversifies into many different species, adapted to different environments or niches**.

---

2. Examples of Adaptive Radiation:

Example	Description
Darwin's Finches	On the Galápagos Islands, finches evolved into multiple species, each with different beak shapes suited for different foods.
Hawaiian Honeycreepers	Birds on Hawaiian islands evolved diverse beak shapes for nectar, insects, and seeds.

Why It Happens: When species **enter a new environment with many available niches** and little competition, they quickly evolve to fill those roles.

VI. Summary Table — Mechanisms of Evolution

Mechanism	Explanation	Effect on Population
Genetic Drift	Random change in allele frequencies, stronger in small populations.	Reduces genetic variation, may fix harmful alleles.
Gene Flow	Movement of genes between populations.	Increases genetic diversity; reduces differences between populations.
Mutations	Changes in DNA that create new alleles.	Source of new genetic variation; essential for evolution.
Speciation	Formation of new species.	Increases biodiversity.
Adaptive Radiation	Rapid evolution of diverse species from a common ancestor.	Many new species adapted to different environments.

VII. Why This Matters?

- These mechanisms explain **how populations change, how new species arise**, and **why biodiversity exists**.
- Understanding them helps us **protect endangered species**, manage ecosystems, and understand **disease evolution** (like rapidly changing viruses).

Final Thought: Evolution is a dynamic, ongoing process, constantly shaping life on Earth.

Mechanisms of Evolution — Worksheet with Answers

Part 1: Understanding Genetic Drift

1. What is genetic drift?
Genetic drift is a **random change in allele frequencies** within a population, especially impactful in **small populations**.

2. Explain the bottleneck effect and give an example.
The bottleneck effect happens when a **large population is drastically reduced** due to a disaster (like a natural catastrophe or human activity), causing **loss of genetic diversity**.
Example: A disease kills most of a cheetah population, leaving only a few individuals to repopulate, limiting genetic variety.

3. Explain the founder effect and give an example.
The founder effect occurs when a **small group of individuals** starts a **new population**, and their genes shape the gene pool of that population, often reducing genetic variation.
Example: A few birds colonize a new island and create a population that may look and behave differently from the original population.

Part 2: Gene Flow and Mutations

1. What is gene flow, and how does it affect populations?
Gene flow is the **movement of genes between populations**, typically caused by migration of individuals or gametes. It **increases genetic diversity** and makes populations more genetically similar.

2. How does gene flow prevent speciation?
Gene flow prevents speciation by **continuously mixing genes between populations**, keeping them from becoming genetically distinct enough to form new species.

3. What is a mutation, and why are mutations important for evolution?
A mutation is a **change in the DNA sequence** that creates new alleles. Mutations are **the primary source of genetic variation**, providing the raw material for evolution and natural selection to act on.

4. List two possible effects a mutation can have on an organism.

- **Beneficial mutation**: Helps the organism survive (e.g., antibiotic resistance in bacteria).
- **Harmful mutation**: Causes disease or reduces fitness (e.g., genetic disorders).
- **Neutral mutation**: Has no effect on the organism's survival.

Part 3: Speciation and Adaptive Radiation

1. What is speciation?
Speciation is the **formation of new species** from existing ones, typically when populations become reproductively isolated.

2. What is allopatric speciation? Give an example.
Allopatric speciation occurs when **geographic barriers separate populations**, preventing gene flow, and leading to the formation of new species.
Example: A river splits a population of squirrels, and over time, they evolve into two different species.

3. What is sympatric speciation? Give an example.
Sympatric speciation occurs **without physical separation**, often due to genetic mutations, behavioral changes, or ecological differences.
Example: Insects feeding on different plants in the same area may evolve into separate species.

4. What is adaptive radiation?
Adaptive radiation is when a **single species evolves into many different species** adapted to different environments or niches, often rapidly.

5. Describe an example of adaptive radiation from nature.
Darwin's finches on the Galápagos Islands evolved into many species with different beak shapes and sizes, each adapted to eating different types of food.

Part 4: Application and Critical Thinking

1. If a small group of birds is blown to a new island and starts a new population, which evolutionary mechanism is occurring? Explain why.
Founder effect — because a **small group starts a new population**, and only some of the original genetic diversity is present.

2. If a population of deer becomes separated by a mountain range and evolves into two different species, what mechanism of evolution is this?
Allopatric speciation — geographic isolation prevents gene flow and leads to divergence into two species.

3. Why is genetic diversity important for a population's survival?
Genetic diversity increases the **population's ability to adapt** to changing environments and **resist diseases**, improving survival chances.

Part 5: Multiple Choice Questions (Answers Highlighted)

1. Which of the following describes a random change in allele frequencies?
   C) Genetic drift

2. The movement of genes from one population to another is called:
   B) Gene flow

3. A sudden drop in population size that reduces genetic diversity is known as:
   C) Bottleneck effect

4. Which process creates new genetic variations in a population?
   A) Mutation

Part 6: Bonus — Critical Thinking

Challenge Question:
Imagine a species of insects is divided by a new river, preventing them from mating. Over thousands of years, they evolve into two separate species. Which mechanism of evolution is this?

Answer:
This is an example of **allopatric speciation** because the river acts as a **geographical barrier**, causing the two groups to evolve separately until they become different species.

5.3: Human Evolution — Understanding Our Origins

I. Fossil Evidence for Human Ancestry

1. What Are Hominins?

Hominins are the group of species that includes **modern humans (Homo sapiens)** and their **extinct ancestors and relatives**. Studying their fossils helps scientists trace human evolution over millions of years.

---

2. Important Hominin Fossils:

Species	Key Characteristics	Time Period
Australopithecus afarensis	Early bipedal hominin. Famous fossil "Lucy" shows upright walking but with small brain size.	~3.2 million years ago.
Homo erectus	Larger brain, advanced tool use, and evidence of fire use. First to migrate out of Africa.	~1.9 million years ago.

Key Point: Fossils show a **gradual change in anatomy and behavior**, revealing the path from ancient ancestors to modern humans.

---

3. Recent Discoveries:

- **"Pink" Fossil (Spain):**
  A fossil found in Spain with **human facial bones**, dating **1.1 to 1.4 million years old**, is the **oldest human fossil in Western Europe**.

  Why It Matters: This suggests **early human ancestors migrated to Europe** much earlier than previously thought, changing our understanding of human migration patterns.

II. The Impact of Evolution on Human Biology

1. Genetic Adaptations — DNA Shaped by Evolution

Trait	Explanation	Example/Reason
Lactose Tolerance	Some humans can digest milk sugar (lactose) into adulthood.	Evolved in populations with dairy farming traditions.
Disease Resistance	Some genetic traits protect against diseases but have trade-offs.	**Sickle cell trait** provides **malaria resistance** but can cause sickle cell anemia when inherited from both parents.

Key Idea: Genes change over time to help humans survive specific environments.

---

2. Anatomical Changes — Evolving Body Structures

Adaptation	Explanation	Why It Matters
Bipedalism	Walking on two legs; changes in spine, pelvis, and legs.	Frees hands for tool use, better field of view, energy-efficient movement.
Brain Development	Larger and more complex brains in humans compared to other primates.	Allows advanced thinking, problem-solving, language, and culture.

Result: These changes separate humans from other primates like chimpanzees and gorillas.

III. Ongoing Human Evolution — Evolution Never Stops

1. Genetic Studies — Learning from Ancient DNA

Modern technology allows scientists to **analyze ancient DNA** from fossils and compare it to modern human DNA, revealing surprising connections:

Discovery	Significance
Interbreeding with Neanderthals and Denisovans	Modern humans carry **small amounts of DNA** from these extinct relatives, showing **interbreeding**.

Discovery	Significance
Genetic Contributions to Traits	Some genes inherited from Neanderthals affect **immune responses** and **skin/hair adaptations**.

Conclusion: Modern humans are a **blend of different ancient human relatives**!

---

2. Recent Adaptations — Humans Still Evolving

Humans continue to evolve as they adapt to **new environments, diets, diseases, and lifestyles**:

Modern Adaptations	Examples
Disease resistance	Genes for resistance to diseases like HIV and malaria.
Environmental adaptation	Populations living in high altitudes have evolved to use oxygen more efficiently (e.g., Tibetan people).
Dietary adaptations	Amylase gene variation in populations with high-starch diets.

Key Point: Evolution is ongoing — human populations continue to adapt and change even today.

IV. Summary Table — Human Evolution Highlights

Aspect	Key Points and Examples
Fossil Evidence	"Lucy" (Australopithecus), Homo erectus, "Pink" fossil in Spain.
Genetic Adaptations	Lactose tolerance, sickle cell trait for malaria resistance.
Anatomical Adaptations	Bipedalism, larger brains for thinking and communication.
Ongoing Evolution	Ancient DNA shows interbreeding; recent adaptations to diseases, diets, environments.

V. Why This Matters?

- **Explains Our Origins**: Fossil and genetic evidence show **where we came from** and how we've changed over time.
- **Connects Us to Other Species**: Humans share ancestors with other primates — showing the unity of life.
- **Ongoing Process**: Human evolution is **still happening**, influenced by our environment, diseases, and culture.
- **Informs Medicine**: Understanding evolution helps in **genetics, medicine, and disease treatment**.

Final Thought: Studying human evolution **helps us understand ourselves**, where we came from, and where we are going as a species.

Human Evolution — Worksheet with Answers

Part 1: Fossil Evidence for Human Ancestry

1. Who was "Lucy," and why is she important to the study of human evolution?
Lucy is the famous fossil of *Australopithecus afarensis*, an early human ancestor who lived about **3.2 million years ago**. She is important because she shows evidence of **bipedalism** (walking upright) and provides insight into early human evolution.

---

2. What are two important traits of *Homo erectus*?

- **Increased brain size** compared to earlier hominins.
- **Use of tools** and evidence of controlled fire use.

---

3. What is the significance of the "Pink" fossil found in Spain?
The "Pink" fossil is the **oldest known human facial bone fossil in Western Europe**, dating between **1.1 and 1.4 million years ago**. It shows that **early humans migrated to Europe** much earlier than previously believed.

Part 2: Genetic and Anatomical Adaptations in Humans

1. What is lactose tolerance, and why did it evolve in some populations?
Lactose tolerance is the ability to **digest lactose (milk sugar) into adulthood**. It evolved in populations that practiced **dairy farming**, providing a nutritional advantage.

---

2. How does the sickle cell trait illustrate an adaptation for disease resistance?
The **sickle cell trait** provides **resistance to malaria**, a deadly disease. People with one copy of the sickle cell allele are less likely to get severe malaria, which is an advantage in regions where malaria is common.

---

3. What anatomical changes are associated with bipedalism in humans?

- **Pelvis became shorter and broader** to support upright walking.
- **Spine developed an S-curve** for balance and support.
- **Leg bones and muscles adapted** for walking on two legs.

---

4. How has brain development contributed to human evolution?
Humans evolved **larger and more complex brains**, allowing for **advanced thinking, problem-solving, language, and culture**, distinguishing humans from other primates.

Part 3: Ongoing Human Evolution and Genetic Evidence

1. What do studies of ancient DNA tell us about human evolution?
Ancient DNA studies show that **modern humans interbred with Neanderthals and Denisovans,**

contributing **small amounts of their DNA** to today's human populations, especially in Europe and Asia.

2. Give two examples of recent human adaptations.

- **High-altitude adaptation**: People living in the Himalayas or Andes have evolved to use oxygen more efficiently.
- **Increased resistance to diseases**, like HIV resistance in some populations due to specific genetic mutations.

Part 4: Application and Critical Thinking

1. How did bipedalism benefit early human ancestors?
Bipedalism freed up hands for **tool use**, helped with **carrying objects**, and allowed for **better visibility** over grasslands to spot predators and prey.

2. Why is brain size important in human evolution?
A larger brain enabled **complex social behaviors, communication, use of tools**, and **cultural development**, giving humans a survival advantage.

3. How does interbreeding with Neanderthals affect modern humans?
Modern humans carry **Neanderthal genes** that influence traits such as **immune system function and skin adaptation**, showing how interbreeding contributed to human diversity.

Part 5: Multiple Choice Questions (Answers Highlighted)

1. What does bipedalism allow humans to do?
   C) Walk upright on two legs

2. Which species is "Lucy" classified under?
   B) Australopithecus afarensis

3. What adaptation allows some adults to drink milk?
   A) Lactose tolerance

4. What does the "Pink" fossil suggest?
   D) Early humans migrated to Europe earlier than thought

5. What do humans share with Neanderthals and Denisovans?
   B) Some shared DNA from interbreeding

Part 6: Bonus — Critical Thinking Challenge

Question:
If humans continue to evolve, what are some possible traits that might change in the future and why?

Sample Answer:
Humans might evolve **greater disease resistance** as new illnesses appear. Traits like **better adaptation to pollution or climate change** may also evolve. If humans travel to space or colonize other planets, **bone density, muscle mass, and other physical traits** might change to adapt to different gravity.

Chapter 6: Ecology and Environmental Science

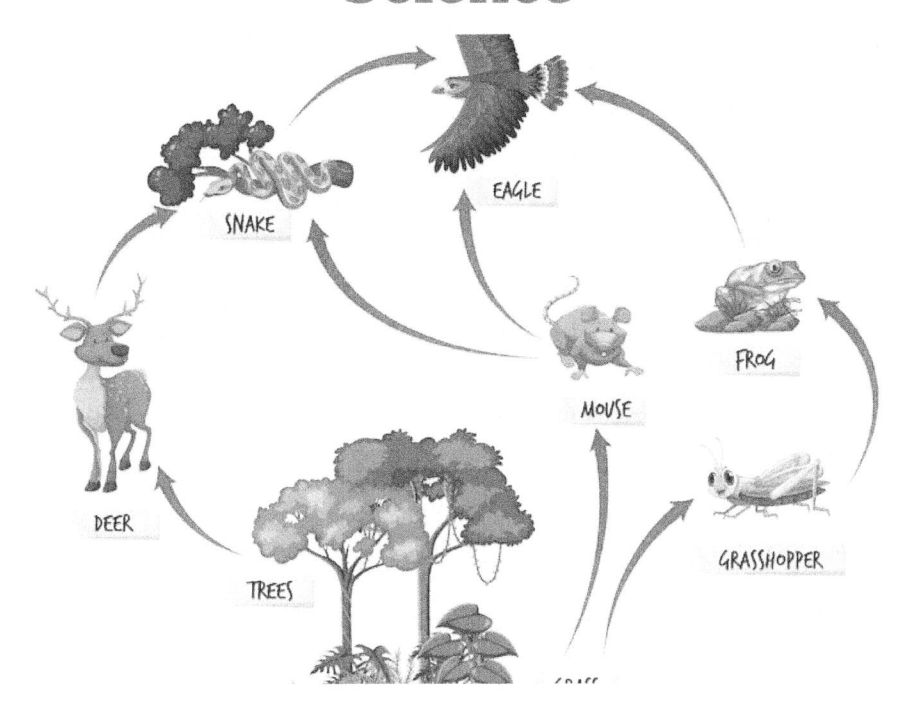

6.1: Ecosystem Structure and Function

4.1: Food Chains, Food Webs, and Energy Pyramids — Understanding Energy Flow in Ecosystems

1. What is a Food Chain?

A **food chain** is a **linear sequence of organisms** that shows **how energy and nutrients flow** from one organism to another in an ecosystem.

Each organism in a food chain belongs to a **trophic level** — the position it holds in the food chain:

Trophic Level	Example
Primary Producers (Autotrophs)	Plants, algae — make their own food using sunlight (photosynthesis).
Primary Consumers (Herbivores)	Grasshoppers, rabbits — eat plants.
Secondary Consumers (Carnivores)	Frogs, snakes — eat herbivores.
Tertiary Consumers (Top Carnivores)	Hawks, lions — eat other carnivores.
Decomposers (Detritivores)	Fungi, bacteria — break down dead organisms and recycle nutrients.

Example Food Chain:
Grass (Producer) → Rabbit (Primary Consumer) → Snake (Secondary Consumer) → Hawk (Tertiary Consumer)

---

2. What is a Food Web?

A **food web** is a **complex network of interconnected food chains**, showing all the **possible feeding relationships** in an ecosystem.

Key Idea: Unlike simple food chains, food webs reflect **real ecosystems**, where most organisms eat and are eaten by **multiple species**.

Example: In a pond, a fish may eat insects and smaller fish, while being eaten by birds and larger fish — all part of a food web!

---

3. What is an Energy Pyramid?

An **energy pyramid** is a **graphical model** that shows how **energy decreases** as it moves up trophic levels in an ecosystem.

Trophic Level	Energy Available (%)
Producers	100%
Primary Consumers	~10% (only 10% of energy is passed up)
Secondary Consumers	~1%
Tertiary Consumers	~0.1%

Key Point: Energy is lost at each level, mostly as **heat**, so **less energy is available** to higher-level consumers.

Rule of Thumb: Only about **10% of energy** from one trophic level is transferred to the next level — this is called the **10% Rule**.

II. Biotic vs. Abiotic Factors in Ecosystems — What Shapes Life?

1. What Are Biotic Factors?

Biotic factors are the **living components** of an ecosystem — all organisms and their interactions.

Biotic Factors	Examples
Plants	Trees, grasses, algae (producers).
Animals	Herbivores, carnivores, omnivores.
Fungi	Decomposers that break down dead matter.
Bacteria & Microorganisms	Important decomposers and nitrogen fixers.

Interactions:

- **Predation:** Lion eats zebra.
- **Competition:** Plants compete for sunlight.
- **Symbiosis:** Bees pollinate flowers (mutualism).

---

2. What Are Abiotic Factors?

Abiotic factors are the **non-living physical and chemical elements** of an ecosystem. These factors **directly affect survival and reproduction** of organisms.

Abiotic Factors	Examples
Sunlight	Provides energy for photosynthesis.
Temperature	Influences metabolism and growth rates.
Water	Essential for all life processes.
Soil	Provides nutrients and structure for plants.
Air (Gases like O_2, CO_2)	Necessary for respiration and photosynthesis.
Nutrients	Nitrogen, phosphorus — critical for growth.

Key Idea: Abiotic factors **set the stage** for which species can survive in an ecosystem (e.g., only cactus can survive in desert temperatures).

III. Summary Table — Ecosystem Structure and Function

Concept	Definition	Example
Food Chain	Linear path of energy flow.	Grass → Rabbit → Snake → Hawk
Food Web	Network of interconnected food chains.	Pond ecosystem with fish, insects, birds.
Energy Pyramid	Graphical representation of energy loss at trophic levels.	Only 10% energy passed to the next level.
Biotic Factors	Living parts of the ecosystem.	Animals, plants, fungi, bacteria.
Abiotic Factors	Non-living parts influencing life.	Sunlight, temperature, water, soil, air.

IV. Why This Matters?

- **Ecosystem health** depends on a balance of **biotic and abiotic factors**.
- **Energy flow** and **nutrient cycling** sustain life and determine how many organisms can survive at each trophic level.
- Understanding food webs helps us **protect endangered species** and manage **human impacts on ecosystems**.

Final Thought: By studying ecosystems, we learn how **everything is connected** — when one part is affected, the whole system can change.

Ecosystem Structure and Function — Worksheet with Answers

Part 1: Food Chains, Food Webs, and Energy Pyramids

1. What is a food chain? Provide an example.

A **food chain** is a **linear sequence** that shows how **energy and nutrients flow** from one organism to another in an ecosystem.

Example:
Grass (Producer) → Rabbit (Primary Consumer) → Snake (Secondary Consumer) → Hawk (Tertiary Consumer)

---

2. What is a food web? How is it different from a food chain?

A **food web** is a **complex network of interconnected food chains**, showing **all possible feeding relationships** in an ecosystem.

Difference: A food chain is a **single path**, while a food web shows **many possible paths** of energy flow because organisms often eat and are eaten by multiple species.

---

3. What is an energy pyramid, and what does it illustrate?

An **energy pyramid** is a **graphical model** showing how **energy decreases** as it moves up trophic levels.
It illustrates that **energy is lost (as heat)** at each level, and only about **10% of energy** is passed to the next trophic level.

---

4. Why is less energy available to higher-level consumers?

Because **energy is used for life processes** (movement, growth, reproduction) and lost as **heat**, so only a small portion is transferred to the next level.

Part 2: Biotic vs. Abiotic Factors in Ecosystems

1. What are biotic factors? Give three examples.

Biotic factors are the **living parts** of an ecosystem.
Examples:

- Plants
- Animals
- Fungi (decomposers)

---

2. What are abiotic factors? Give three examples.

Abiotic factors are the **non-living components** of an ecosystem.
Examples:

- Sunlight
- Water
- Temperature

---

3. How do abiotic factors influence the living organisms in an ecosystem?

Abiotic factors affect **where and how organisms live** — for example:

- Sunlight is needed for **photosynthesis** in plants.

- Temperature affects **metabolism and reproduction**.
- Water availability affects **growth and survival**.

4. Explain how biotic and abiotic factors work together in an ecosystem.

Biotic (living) and abiotic (non-living) factors interact to shape the ecosystem.
For example, plants (biotic) need sunlight, water, and soil nutrients (abiotic) to grow. Animals depend on plants for food and shelter.

Part 3: Applying Concepts

1. In a pond ecosystem, what would happen if all producers (plants, algae) died?

If producers died, **herbivores (like insects and small fish) would have no food and die**, leading to **collapse of higher trophic levels (carnivores, decomposers)** because the energy flow would stop.

2. If a rabbit population grows very large, what could happen to the food chain?

- **Producers (plants) would be overgrazed and reduced.**
- **Predators (like snakes, hawks) might increase** due to more available food.
- **Eventually, rabbit numbers might decline** if plants become too scarce to sustain them.

3. How would a drought (lack of water) affect both biotic and abiotic factors in an ecosystem?

- **Abiotic:** Less water available.
- **Biotic:** Plants would die or stop growing, reducing food for herbivores, causing a decline in herbivores and then carnivores.
  The entire food web would be affected.

Part 4: Multiple Choice Questions (Answers Highlighted)

1. Which of the following is a producer?
B) Grass

2. What is a decomposer's role in an ecosystem?
C) Break down dead organisms and recycle nutrients

3. Which of the following is an abiotic factor?
A) Temperature

4. In a food chain, energy flows from:
B) Producers to consumers

5. Which of these shows the correct order of a food chain?
C) Grass → Rabbit → Fox

Part 5: Bonus — Critical Thinking Challenge

Challenge Question:
Imagine a forest ecosystem. If a disease wiped out all the top predators (e.g., wolves), what would likely happen to the rest of the food web?

Sample Answer:
If top predators like wolves are gone, **herbivore populations (like deer) would increase too much** because nothing would control their numbers. This would lead to **overgrazing and destruction of plant life**, affecting other animals and causing **ecosystem imbalance**.

6.2: Biogeochemical Cycles — Nature's Recycling Systems

I. The Water Cycle (Hydrologic Cycle) — Earth's Circulatory System

Key Processes in the Water Cycle:

Process	Description
Evaporation	The **sun heats water** in oceans, rivers, lakes, and it turns into **water vapor** and rises into the atmosphere.
Condensation	**Water vapor cools** in the atmosphere and changes back into **liquid droplets**, forming clouds.
Precipitation	Water droplets **combine and fall** to Earth as **rain, snow, sleet, or hail**.
Infiltration	Some water **seeps into the ground**, replenishing **groundwater supplies**.
Runoff	Water flows over land back to rivers, lakes, and oceans.

Importance of the Water Cycle:

- **Distributes freshwater** to ecosystems and organisms.
- Helps **regulate Earth's climate** and temperature.
- **Supports life processes**, from plant growth to animal hydration.

II. The Carbon Cycle — The Cycle of Life and Climate Regulation

Key Processes in the Carbon Cycle:

Process	Description
Photosynthesis	Plants and autotrophs use CO_2 **and sunlight** to produce **glucose ($C_6H_{12}O_6$)** and release oxygen.
Respiration	Organisms (plants, animals, decomposers) **break down glucose** for

Process	Description
	energy and release CO_2 back to the atmosphere.
Decomposition	**Decomposers** (bacteria, fungi) break down dead organisms, returning **carbon to the soil** and releasing CO_2.
Combustion	Burning of **fossil fuels** and **biomass** releases **stored carbon as CO_2** into the atmosphere.

Importance of the Carbon Cycle:

- **Regulates Earth's climate** by controlling atmospheric CO_2.
- Provides carbon for **building organic molecules** (proteins, carbohydrates, lipids, DNA).
- **Maintains balance** of gases in the atmosphere essential for life.

III. The Nitrogen Cycle — The Fertilizer of Life

Key Processes in the Nitrogen Cycle:

Process	Description
Nitrogen Fixation	Special bacteria convert N_2 **gas** from the atmosphere into **ammonia (NH_3)**, a usable form for plants.
Nitrification	Other bacteria convert ammonia into **nitrites (NO_2)** and then **nitrates (NO_3)**, which plants absorb.
Assimilation	Plants **absorb nitrates** from the soil and use them to make proteins and nucleic acids.
Ammonification	**Decomposers** break down organic nitrogen in dead organisms, returning **ammonia (NH_3)** to the soil.
Denitrification	**Denitrifying bacteria** convert nitrates back into N_2 **gas**, returning nitrogen to the atmosphere.

Importance of the Nitrogen Cycle:

- Provides **essential nitrogen** for **amino acids, proteins, and DNA** — building blocks of life.
- Keeps nitrogen moving through the environment, **supporting plant and animal growth**.
- Maintains **ecosystem productivity** by recycling nitrogen compounds.

IV. Summary Table — Biogeochemical Cycles

Cycle	Key Processes	Importance to Life
Water Cycle	Evaporation, Condensation, Precipitation, Infiltration, Runoff	Distributes water, supports life, regulates climate.
Carbon Cycle	Photosynthesis, Respiration, Decomposition, Combustion	Provides carbon for life molecules, regulates climate.
Nitrogen Cycle	Nitrogen Fixation, Nitrification, Assimilation, Ammonification, Denitrification	Supplies nitrogen for proteins/DNA, sustains ecosystems.

V. Why Biogeochemical Cycles Matter:

- These cycles **recycle essential elements** (water, carbon, nitrogen) that all living things need to survive.
- They **connect living organisms with the non-living environment**, showing how life and Earth work together.
- **Disruptions** (like pollution or deforestation) can **harm these cycles**, leading to problems like **climate change, water shortages, and soil infertility**.

Final Thought: Understanding biogeochemical cycles helps us **protect Earth's resources** and **live sustainably**.

Biogeochemical Cycles — Worksheet with Answers

Part 1: The Water Cycle (Hydrologic Cycle)

1. List and describe three main processes of the water cycle.

Answer:

- **Evaporation:** The process where water changes from liquid to vapor due to heat from the sun.
- **Condensation:** Water vapor cools and changes back into liquid droplets, forming clouds.
- **Precipitation:** Water falls from clouds to the Earth as rain, snow, sleet, or hail.

2. What is infiltration, and why is it important?

Answer:
Infiltration is when water seeps into the ground to become groundwater. It is important because it **replenishes underground water supplies**, which are critical for plants, animals, and human use.

3. Explain how runoff connects land and water in ecosystems.

Answer:
Runoff is water that flows over land and returns to rivers, lakes, and oceans, connecting the land and water parts of ecosystems and transporting nutrients and minerals.

Part 2: The Carbon Cycle

1. Describe the role of photosynthesis in the carbon cycle.

Answer:
In **photosynthesis**, plants take in **carbon dioxide (CO$_2$)** from the atmosphere and, using sunlight, convert it into **glucose (sugar)** and release **oxygen**.

2. How does respiration return carbon to the atmosphere?

Answer:
Respiration is when organisms break down food (glucose) to release energy, and in doing so, they release **CO$_2$ back into the atmosphere**.

3. What is the role of decomposition in the carbon cycle?

Answer:
Decomposers like bacteria and fungi break down dead organisms, returning carbon in the form of **CO$_2$** to the atmosphere and **organic matter** to the soil.

4. How does combustion add carbon to the atmosphere?

Answer:
Combustion (burning) of fossil fuels and biomass releases **stored carbon as CO$_2$** into the atmosphere, increasing greenhouse gases.

Part 3: The Nitrogen Cycle

1. Why is nitrogen important to living things?

Answer:
Nitrogen is essential for making **proteins and DNA**, which are necessary for growth, repair, and genetic information in all living things.

2. What is nitrogen fixation, and how does it occur?

Answer:
Nitrogen fixation is when bacteria convert **nitrogen gas (N$_2$)** from the atmosphere into **ammonia (NH$_3$)** or **nitrates (NO$_3$)** that plants can absorb and use.

3. Explain nitrification and its role in the nitrogen cycle.

Answer:
Nitrification is a process where bacteria convert ammonia (NH$_3$) into **nitrites (NO$_2$)** and then into **nitrates (NO$_3$)**, making nitrogen available for plant absorption.

4. What is assimilation in the nitrogen cycle?

Answer:
Assimilation is when plants absorb nitrates from the soil and use them to make **proteins and other nitrogen-containing molecules**.

5. What is ammonification?

Answer:
Ammonification occurs when decomposers break down dead organisms and waste, releasing **ammonia (NH$_3$)** back into the soil.

6. How does denitrification complete the nitrogen cycle?

Answer:
Denitrifying bacteria convert nitrates (NO$_3$) back into **nitrogen gas (N$_2$)**, returning it to the atmosphere and completing the cycle.

Part 4: Applying What You Know

1. What might happen to an ecosystem if plants could not absorb nitrogen?

Answer:
If plants couldn't absorb nitrogen, they **couldn't make proteins or DNA**, which would **disrupt growth** and **affect the entire food web**, since herbivores and predators depend on plants.

2. How does human activity affect the carbon cycle?

Answer:
Human activities like **burning fossil fuels and deforestation** add extra **CO$_2$ to the atmosphere**, contributing to **climate change** and disrupting the balance of the carbon cycle.

3. Why is the water cycle important for all living things?

Answer:
The water cycle provides **freshwater** needed for **drinking, growing food, and supporting ecosystems**. It also helps regulate Earth's temperature.

Part 5: Multiple Choice (Answers Highlighted)

1. What process in the water cycle forms clouds?
   C) Condensation

2. What process in the carbon cycle removes carbon dioxide from the atmosphere?
   B) Photosynthesis

3. Which organism helps return nitrogen to the atmosphere?
   D) Denitrifying bacteria

4. What process breaks down dead organisms to release nutrients?
   A) Decomposition

5. Which is an example of nitrogen fixation?
   C) Bacteria converting nitrogen gas into ammonia

Part 6: Bonus — Critical Thinking Challenge

Question:
How might cutting down large forests affect the carbon and water cycles?

Sample Answer:
Cutting down forests would **reduce the number of plants available for photosynthesis**, so **less CO_2 would be absorbed**, increasing carbon in the atmosphere and contributing to **climate change**. Also, fewer trees would mean **less transpiration**, affecting rainfall patterns and the **water cycle** — possibly leading to **droughts and ecosystem damage**.

6.3: Population Ecology

I. Factors Affecting Population Growth

Populations of organisms do not grow indefinitely. Instead, their size is controlled by a combination of **environmental factors**, **resource availability**, and **interactions between species**. Understanding these factors helps scientists predict population changes and manage ecosystems effectively.

---

1. Carrying Capacity — The Maximum Limit for a Population

What is Carrying Capacity?

Carrying capacity is the **largest number of individuals** of a particular species that an ecosystem can **support indefinitely** without causing long-term environmental damage.

- It depends on **available resources** (food, water, shelter) and **environmental conditions** (climate, competition, disease).
- If a population **exceeds carrying capacity**, resources become limited, leading to **increased competition, starvation, or migration**.
- If a population is **below carrying capacity**, resources are more abundant, allowing the population to **grow**.

Example:
A lake with **limited food supply and space** may support only **500 fish**. If the fish population grows to **800**, competition for resources increases, leading to starvation and death, eventually bringing the population back to **500 or lower**.

---

2. Limiting Factors — What Controls Population Growth?

Limiting factors are environmental factors that **slow down or stop population growth**. These factors ensure that populations **do not grow infinitely** but instead **remain stable over time**.

Type of Limiting Factor	Definition	Examples
Density-Dependent Factors	Factors whose effects **increase as population size increases**.	Competition for food, predation, disease, parasitism.
Density-Independent Factors	Factors that affect populations **regardless of size**.	Natural disasters (wildfires, hurricanes), pollution, climate change.

Key Differences:

- **Density-dependent factors** are strongest in **crowded populations** (e.g., more wolves mean higher competition for prey).
- **Density-independent factors** occur **regardless of population size** (e.g., a wildfire affects both small and large populations equally).

II. Human Impact on Ecosystems

Human activities significantly impact ecosystems and population dynamics. The three main human-driven ecological threats are **deforestation, pollution, and climate change**.

Human Activity	Effect on Ecosystem
Deforestation	Large-scale **forest removal** for agriculture, logging, and urban development **destroys habitats, reduces biodiversity, and alters the carbon and water cycles**.
Pollution	The release of harmful substances into air, water, and soil causes **health problems in wildlife and humans** and disrupts ecological balance.
Climate Change	The accumulation of **greenhouse gases (CO_2, methane)** causes **global warming, extreme weather, habitat shifts, and species extinctions**.

Example:
Deforestation in the Amazon rainforest reduces habitat for **jaguars, monkeys, and thousands of bird species**, leading to population declines and ecosystem imbalances.

6.4: Conservation Biology

I. Biodiversity and Endangered Species

Biodiversity refers to the **variety of life on Earth**, including **different species, genes, and ecosystems**. It is **essential for ecosystem health, productivity, and resilience**.

Why is biodiversity important?

- Ensures **ecosystem stability** by allowing species to **support each other** (e.g., bees pollinate plants, which provide food for herbivores).

- Provides **medicinal resources**, as many modern medicines come from plants and animals.
- Helps ecosystems recover from disturbances **(droughts, diseases, natural disasters).**

1. What Causes Species to Become Endangered?

A species is classified as **endangered** when it faces a high risk of **extinction** in the near future. The **main threats** to endangered species include:

Threat	Impact on Species
Habitat Loss	Deforestation, urbanization, and agriculture destroy natural habitats.
Pollution	Toxic chemicals, plastics, and oil spills harm wildlife and disrupt ecosystems.
Overexploitation	Hunting, fishing, and poaching reduce populations (e.g., rhinos killed for their horns).
Invasive Species	Non-native species compete with or prey on local wildlife, reducing biodiversity.

Example:
The **Amur Leopard** has fewer than **100 individuals left in the wild** due to **poaching and habitat destruction**.

II. Sustainable Practices and Conservation Efforts

Sustainable practices focus on **using natural resources responsibly** to ensure they remain available for future generations. Conservation efforts aim to **protect species and ecosystems** from harm.

1. Sustainable Practices — How We Can Protect the Planet

Category	Examples	Benefits
Responsible Consumption	Reducing waste, avoiding single-use plastics, **recycling materials**.	Decreases pollution and overuse of resources.
Sustainable Agriculture	**Organic farming, crop rotation, soil restoration.**	Protects soil and prevents chemical pollution.
Energy Efficiency	Using **solar, wind, hydroelectric power, energy-efficient appliances.**	Reduces reliance on fossil fuels, lowering greenhouse gas emissions.
Water Conservation	Using **water-saving technology**, reducing **chemical runoff.**	Protects freshwater resources and reduces waste.

Example:
Costa Rica produces **99% of its electricity** from **renewable sources**, making it one of the world's leading examples of **sustainable energy use**.

2. Conservation Efforts — How We Save Nature

Type of Effort	Description	Examples
Community-Led Conservation	Indigenous and local communities **protect natural habitats.**	Kenya's **wildlife conservancies** support local communities while conserving wildlife.
Policy and Legislation	Governments **enforce laws** to protect endangered species.	**Endangered Species Act (USA), CITES treaty (international wildlife protection).**
Ecosystem Restoration	Restoring damaged habitats like **forests, wetlands, and coral reefs.**	**The UN Decade on Ecosystem Restoration (2021–2030).**
Species Reintroduction	Returning species to areas where they have disappeared.	**Wolves reintroduced to Yellowstone National Park, balancing the ecosystem.**

III. Why Conservation Matters?

1. **Protects biodiversity** — ensuring life's variety and resilience.
2. **Maintains healthy ecosystems** — providing clean air, water, and food.
3. **Supports sustainable economies** — through ecotourism and sustainable agriculture.
4. **Preserves nature for future generations** — ensuring ecosystems remain intact.

Final Thought: The survival of human civilization is deeply connected to **protecting nature and maintaining ecological balance.**

Summary Table — Population Ecology & Conservation

Topic	Key Concepts
Carrying Capacity	The maximum number of individuals an ecosystem can sustain.
Limiting Factors	Density-dependent (competition, disease) vs. density-independent (climate, disasters).
Human Impacts	Deforestation, pollution, climate change.
Biodiversity	Variety of life, crucial for ecosystem balance.
Endangered Species	Species at risk due to human activity and habitat destruction.
Sustainable Practices	Responsible resource use, renewable energy, eco-friendly agriculture.
Conservation Efforts	Laws, restoration projects, species reintroduction.

Chapter 7: Classification and Diversity of Life

7.1 Taxonomy and Classification Systems

I. Linnaean Classification and Binomial Nomenclature

1. What is Taxonomy?

Taxonomy is the **scientific discipline** of classifying and naming organisms. It helps organize living things into groups based on **shared characteristics** and evolutionary history.

2. Linnaean Classification System — An Organized Hierarchy

Developed by **Carl Linnaeus** in the 18th century, this system arranges organisms in **a series of nested categories**, from broad to specific.

Hierarchical Levels of Classification (from broadest to most specific):

Rank	Description	Example (Human)
Domain	**Largest group**, based on major genetic differences.	Eukarya

Rank	Description	Example (Human)
Kingdom	Broad categories like plants, animals, fungi.	Animalia
Phylum	Groups based on body plan/organization.	Chordata
Class	Further division of phylum.	Mammalia
Order	Groups of related families.	Primates
Family	Groups of related genera.	Hominidae
Genus	Closely related species.	Homo
Species	Most specific, organisms that can interbreed.	Homo sapiens

Tip for remembering the order:
"Dear King Philip Came Over For Good Soup" (Domain, Kingdom, Phylum, Class, Order, Family, Genus, Species).

---

3. Binomial Nomenclature — Scientific Naming of Organisms

Definition: A system for **naming species** using two names: **Genus + species**.

Format:

- **Genus name is capitalized**, species name is lowercase.
- Both are **italicized** or underlined (if handwritten).

Example:

- **Homo sapiens** (humans)
- **Panthera leo** (lion)

Purpose:

- Provides a **universal name** recognized globally, avoiding confusion from common names (e.g., "cougar," "puma," "mountain lion" = **Puma concolor**).

II. Characteristics of the Six Kingdoms of Life

Organisms are classified into **six kingdoms** based on **cell type, structure, nutrition, and reproduction**.

Kingdom	Cell Type	Cell Wall	Organization	Nutrition	Reproduction
Archaebacteria	Prokaryotic	Unique lipids (no peptidoglycan)	Unicellular	Mostly autotroph or heterotroph	Asexual (binary fission)
Eubacteria	Prokaryotic	Peptidoglycan	Unicellular	Autotroph or heterotroph	Asexual (binary fission)

Kingdom	Cell Type	Cell Wall	Organization	Nutrition	Reproduction
Protista	Eukaryotic	Some have cell walls (varied)	Mostly unicellular, some multicellular	Autotrophs (algae), heterotrophs (protozoa)	Asexual and sexual
Fungi	Eukaryotic	Chitin	Mostly multicellular (some unicellular, like yeast)	Heterotroph (absorption)	Asexual (spores) and sexual
Plantae	Eukaryotic	Cellulose	Multicellular	Autotroph (photosynthesis)	Asexual (vegetative), sexual
Animalia	Eukaryotic	None	Multicellular	Heterotroph (ingestion)	Mostly sexual

7.2: Viruses vs. Living Organisms

I. Structure and Replication of Viruses

1. What is a Virus?

A **virus** is a **non-living infectious agent** that can replicate **only inside a living host cell**. Although viruses can **reproduce and evolve**, they **lack the cellular structure and metabolism** found in living organisms.

2. Structure of a Virus

Component	Description	Example
Genetic Material	Either **DNA or RNA**, but **never both**. Carries instructions for making new viruses.	HIV (RNA virus), Herpes (DNA virus).
Capsid	**Protein shell** that encases and protects the viral genetic material.	Icosahedral capsid in adenoviruses.
Envelope (Optional)	**Lipid membrane** taken from host cell's membrane, embedded with viral proteins for infection.	Influenza virus has an envelope.

Note: Not all viruses have an envelope — **"naked" viruses** like Norovirus lack one and are often more resistant to harsh environments.

3. Replication Cycles of Viruses

Viruses cannot reproduce on their own; instead, they **hijack host cells** to make copies. There are **two main viral replication cycles**:

A. Lytic Cycle (Fast-acting and destructive)

Stage	Description
Attachment	Virus binds to specific **receptors on the host cell** surface.
Penetration	Viral genetic material is **injected into the host cell**.
Uncoating	Viral capsid is **removed**, releasing viral genome into the host.
Replication	Host cell machinery is **hijacked to replicate viral genome and proteins**.
Assembly	**New viral particles** (virions) are put together.
Release	Host cell **bursts (lysis)**, releasing new viruses to infect other cells.

Example: The **common cold (rhinovirus)** and **bacteriophages** use the lytic cycle.

B. Lysogenic Cycle (Hidden and long-term)

Stage	Description
Integration	Viral DNA becomes part of **host cell's DNA** (called a **provirus** or prophage).
Dormancy	Viral genome remains **dormant** and is copied with the host DNA as cells divide.
Activation	**Stress or environmental factors** trigger the virus to become active.
Lytic Cycle Entry	Virus enters the **lytic cycle**, producing new virions and destroying the cell.

Example: Herpes virus remains dormant and can reactivate, causing symptoms like cold sores.

II. How Viruses Differ from Bacteria and Other Living Organisms

1. Are Viruses Alive?

Most scientists **do not consider viruses living organisms** because they **cannot reproduce independently** and **lack metabolism**. They depend entirely on a **host cell for reproduction and survival**.

2. Comparison of Viruses, Bacteria, and Eukaryotic Organisms

Feature	Viruses	Bacteria (Prokaryotes)	Eukaryotic Organisms
Cell Structure	Not cellular; no cytoplasm, no organelles.	Simple **prokaryotic cells**, no nucleus, but with cytoplasm.	Complex **eukaryotic cells** with nucleus and organelles.
Genetic Material	Either **DNA or RNA** (never both).	DNA, circular chromosome in cytoplasm.	DNA in nucleus.
Reproduction	Only by **infecting a host cell** and using its machinery.	Binary fission (asexual reproduction).	**Sexual and asexual reproduction.**
Metabolism	**None** — cannot make energy or proteins on their own.	Have their own metabolism; can **convert nutrients to energy**.	Full metabolism; perform respiration, photosynthesis, etc.
Growth & Development	**Do not grow** or develop — assemble in host cells.	**Grow and divide** independently.	Grow, develop, and respond to environment.
Response to Stimuli	**No independent response** to environment.	Respond to stimuli (e.g., move toward nutrients).	Complex responses to stimuli (e.g., reflexes, behaviors).

3. Importance in Medicine and Biology

Understanding viruses is crucial because:

- **They cause diseases** like the flu, COVID-19, HIV/AIDS.
- Vaccines (like mRNA vaccines for COVID-19) **target viral structures**.
- **Antibiotics do NOT work on viruses**, only on bacteria — this is why understanding the difference is essential for treatment.
- **Viruses can be used in gene therapy** to deliver corrective genes to cells.

III. Recap: Key Differences — Viruses vs. Life Forms

Feature	Viruses	Living Organisms (Bacteria, Eukaryotes)
Cells	**No** (Acellular)	Yes, have cells.
Independent Reproduction	**No**, must infect host cells.	Yes, reproduce on their own (asexual/sexual).
Metabolism	**None** — no energy production.	Yes, perform metabolic processes.
Growth & Development	**No growth or development.**	Yes, grow and develop over life stages.
Response to Stimuli	**No independent response.**	Yes, react to the environment.

Final Thought:

Viruses **blur the line between living and non-living**. Though they cannot live independently, they **evolve** and **affect living organisms profoundly**, making them essential subjects of study in **medicine, genetics, and evolutionary biology**.

Chapter 8: Human Body Systems and Homeostasis

ANATOMY OF THE HUMAN BODY

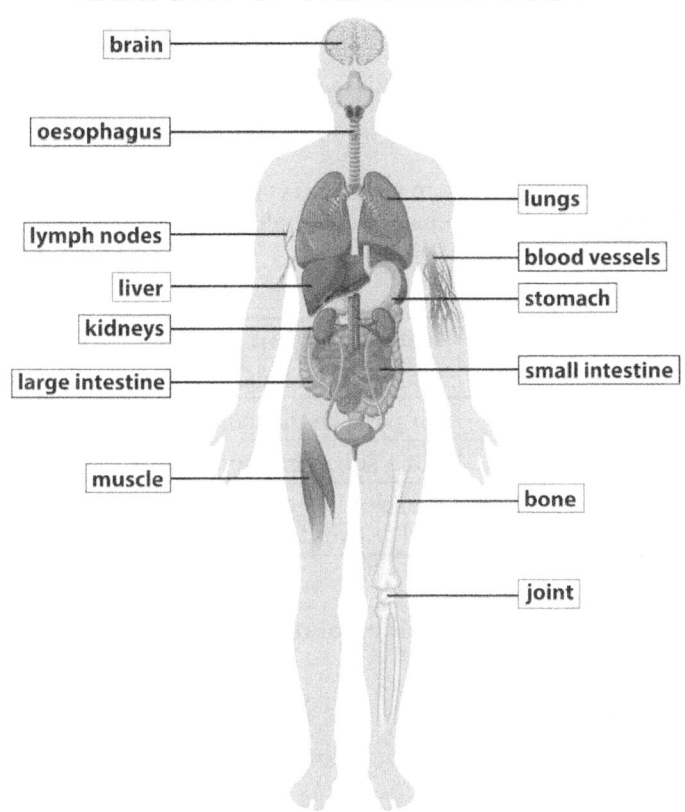

8.1: Major Organ Systems and Their Functions

I. Circulatory System — The Body's Transport Network

Function:

The **circulatory system** is responsible for **transporting blood, nutrients, oxygen, hormones, and waste products** throughout the body. It serves as a **distribution and collection network**, ensuring that every cell receives what it needs to function and that waste products are removed efficiently.

Components:

Organ/Part	Role/Function
Heart	**Pumps blood** throughout the body.
Blood Vessels	**Arteries** carry blood away from the heart, **veins** bring it back, **capillaries** exchange gases, nutrients, and wastes with cells.
Blood	Carries **oxygen, nutrients, hormones,** and **waste products**.

Role in Homeostasis:

- **Regulates body temperature** (e.g., blood flow to skin).
- **Maintains pH balance** by buffering acids and bases in the blood.
- **Balances fluids** between cells and blood vessels (fluid homeostasis).
- **Delivers white blood cells** to fight infections.

II. Respiratory System — The Gas Exchange System

Function:

The **respiratory system** enables the body to **inhale oxygen (O_2)** needed for cellular respiration and **exhale carbon dioxide (CO_2)**, a waste product of metabolism.

Components:

Organ/Part	Role/Function
Nose/Nasal Cavity	Warms, moistens, and filters air.
Trachea	Air passage that connects throat to lungs.
Lungs	Main site of **gas exchange**.
Diaphragm	Muscle that contracts to allow inhalation and relaxes for exhalation.

Role in Homeostasis:

- **Maintains oxygen and carbon dioxide balance** in blood.
- **Regulates pH** of blood via CO_2 levels.
- Supports **cellular respiration** by supplying oxygen for energy production.

III. Digestive System — The Nutrient Processing System

Function:

The **digestive system** is responsible for **breaking down food** into smaller molecules (nutrients), **absorbing nutrients** into the bloodstream, and **eliminating indigestible waste**.

Components:

Organ/Part	Role/Function
Mouth	Starts mechanical and chemical digestion.
Esophagus	Transports food to the stomach.
Stomach	Continues digestion using acids and enzymes.
Small Intestine	Main site of **nutrient absorption**.
Large Intestine	Absorbs water and forms solid waste (feces).
Liver	Produces bile to help digest fats, detoxifies blood.

Organ/Part	Role/Function
Pancreas	Produces digestive enzymes and regulates blood sugar.

Role in Homeostasis:

- **Supplies nutrients** essential for energy, growth, and repair.
- Maintains **glucose levels** in the blood.
- Removes **waste and toxins** through feces and liver detoxification.

IV. Nervous System — The Control and Communication Center

Function:

The **nervous system** coordinates **body responses** to internal and external stimuli, maintaining **communication between body parts** and regulating bodily functions.

Components:

Organ/Part	Role/Function
Brain	Main control center; processes and interprets signals.
Spinal Cord	Connects brain to body; pathway for signals.
Peripheral Nerves	Transmit signals to and from body organs and muscles.

Role in Homeostasis:

- **Monitors internal conditions** (like temperature, blood pressure).
- Initiates **reflexes and voluntary responses** to maintain balance.
- Controls **heartbeat, breathing rate, digestion** through autonomic nervous system.
- Coordinates with **endocrine system** for hormonal balance.

V. Excretory System — The Waste Removal System

Function:

The **excretory system** is responsible for **removing waste products** from the body, especially nitrogenous wastes (like urea), and regulating **water and electrolyte balance**.

Components:

Organ/Part	Role/Function
Kidneys	Filter blood to remove waste, regulate water/salt balance.
Ureters	Carry urine from kidneys to bladder.
Bladder	Stores urine until excretion.
Urethra	Conducts urine out of the body.

Role in Homeostasis:

- **Maintains fluid balance** by controlling water reabsorption.
- Regulates **electrolyte levels** (e.g., sodium, potassium).
- Maintains **acid-base balance** (pH of blood).
- Removes **wastes and toxins** to prevent buildup and poisoning.

VI. Summary Table — Major Human Body Systems and Homeostasis

Organ System	Main Function	Components	Homeostasis Role
Circulatory	Transport nutrients, gases, wastes.	Heart, blood vessels, blood.	Regulates temperature, pH, fluid balance, fights infection.
Respiratory	Gas exchange (O_2 in, CO_2 out).	Lungs, trachea, diaphragm.	Maintains O_2/CO_2 balance and blood pH.
Digestive	Breaks down food, absorbs nutrients, removes waste.	Mouth, stomach, intestines, liver, pancreas.	Provides energy, nutrients, and eliminates waste.
Nervous	Controls body functions and responses.	Brain, spinal cord, nerves.	Detects changes, coordinates responses, maintains balance.
Excretory	Removes waste, regulates water/salt.	Kidneys, bladder, ureters, urethra.	Balances fluids, electrolytes, and removes toxins.

8.2: The Immune System and Disease

I. How the Immune System Fights Infections

The **immune system** is the body's defense system that **detects, attacks, and eliminates pathogens** such as **bacteria, viruses, fungi, and parasites**. It consists of **two main branches — innate immunity** and **adaptive immunity** — which work together to protect the body.

---

1. Innate Immunity — The Body's First Line of Defense (Non-specific Defense)

Innate immunity is the **immediate and general defense** against pathogens. It **does not target specific invaders** but provides a broad defense mechanism.

Components of Innate Immunity:

Defense Type	Description	Example
Physical Barriers	Block pathogen entry.	**Skin, mucous membranes**.
Chemical Barriers	Destroy or inhibit pathogens.	**Stomach acid, enzymes in saliva, lysozyme** in tears.

Defense Type	Description	Example
Inflammatory Response	Increases blood flow, recruits immune cells to infection site.	Redness, swelling, heat, pain.
White Blood Cells (Phagocytes)	Engulf and destroy pathogens.	**Macrophages, neutrophils.**

Key Point: Innate immunity acts **fast** (minutes to hours) and is **always ready to respond**.

---

2. Adaptive Immunity — The Body's Targeted Defense (Specific Defense)

Adaptive immunity develops **after exposure to specific pathogens**. It **recognizes, remembers, and attacks specific invaders** with precision.

Components of Adaptive Immunity:

Defense Mechanism	Description	Example
Antigen Recognition	**B-cells and T-cells** recognize specific antigens (foreign molecules on pathogens).	Recognizing viral protein coat.
Antibody Production (B-cells)	Produce **antibodies** that bind to pathogens, neutralizing them or marking them for destruction.	Antibodies for the flu virus.
T-cells (Helper & Killer)	**Helper T-cells** activate other immune cells; **Cytotoxic (killer) T-cells** destroy infected cells.	Destroying virus-infected cells.
Memory Cells	Long-lived cells that "remember" the pathogen for **faster future response**.	Immunity after chickenpox.

Key Point: Adaptive immunity is **slower to activate (days)** on first exposure but **stronger and faster on subsequent exposures**.

II. Vaccines and Their Role in Disease Prevention

Vaccines are a **powerful tool** that helps **train the immune system to recognize and fight pathogens before** causing disease.

---

1. How Do Vaccines Work? (Mechanism)

Step	Description
Antigen Introduction	Vaccine introduces **harmless antigens** (weakened, dead, or part of pathogen) into the body.

Step	Description
Immune Response Activation	Body **recognizes antigens as foreign** and **produces antibodies and memory cells**.
Long-term Protection	If exposed to the real pathogen later, immune system **responds quickly** to destroy it.

Result: The person gains **immunity** without experiencing the disease.

2. Benefits of Vaccines

Benefit	Explanation
Disease Prevention	Protects individuals from getting sick (e.g., measles, polio).
Herd Immunity	When enough people are vaccinated, the spread of disease is limited, protecting those who **cannot be vaccinated** (e.g., infants, immunocompromised people).
Reduced Disease Outbreaks	Widespread vaccination **eliminates or reduces diseases** in populations (e.g., eradication of smallpox).

3. Safety and Efficacy of Vaccines

Aspect	Explanation
Rigorous Testing	Vaccines undergo **years of testing in clinical trials** to ensure safety and effectiveness.
Approval	Approved by **health agencies** (e.g., FDA, CDC, WHO).
Monitoring	Continuous **monitoring of side effects and effectiveness** after being released to the public.

Key Point: Vaccines are **proven safe and effective** for preventing disease and saving lives.

III. Summary Table — Immune System and Vaccines

System/Process	Key Function	Example
Innate Immunity	First line of defense, non-specific barriers and cells.	Skin, macrophages.
Adaptive Immunity	Specific response, remembers pathogens, makes antibodies.	Memory cells after infection.
Antibody Production (B-cells)	Produces antibodies to neutralize pathogens.	Antibodies for flu virus.

System/Process	Key Function	Example
Memory Cells	Store information for faster future responses.	Immunity to chickenpox.
Vaccines	Introduce antigens to develop immunity.	COVID-19, measles, polio vaccines.
Herd Immunity	Protects whole population by reducing disease spread.	Protecting babies from measles.

IV. Why Understanding the Immune System Matters

1. **Prevents Diseases:** Knowing how the immune system works helps us understand **how to avoid infections**.
2. **Supports Public Health:** Understanding vaccines and herd immunity is crucial for **preventing outbreaks and pandemics**.
3. Guides Treatments: Helps doctors develop **effective treatments and vaccines** for new diseases.
4. Personal Health Choices: Knowing about immunity helps individuals make **informed decisions about vaccines and health**.

Final Thought:

The immune system is our **natural defense** against illness, and vaccines are one of our **greatest tools for preventing disease**. Learning how these systems work helps us protect **ourselves, our families, and our communities**.

Chapter 9: Data Analysis and Scientific Literacy

9.1: Interpreting Graphs and Data Tables

I. Identifying Trends and Patterns in Scientific Data

1. Understanding Data Representation

- **Data tables and graphs** are essential **tools for scientists** to **organize, analyze, and communicate information** clearly.
- They **help visualize large amounts of data**, making it easier to **identify trends, patterns, relationships, and outliers** that might be difficult to see in raw data.

Example: A table showing daily temperatures over a month can be converted into a **line graph** to visualize the trend of warming or cooling.

---

2. Recognizing Patterns in Data

When analyzing scientific data:

- Look for **increases, decreases, fluctuations**, or **stabilization** in data over time.
- Identify **correlations** (when two variables move together) or **inverse relationships** (when one variable increases and the other decreases).

- Spot **anomalies or outliers** — data points that **don't fit the pattern** and may need further investigation.

    Example of pattern recognition:
    If a line graph of plant growth vs. sunlight exposure shows that as sunlight increases, growth increases, this suggests a **positive correlation**.

II. Constructing and Analyzing Different Types of Graphs

Choosing the correct type of graph is critical to **effectively display scientific data**.

1. Types of Graphs and When to Use Them

Type of Graph	When to Use	Example
Bar Charts	To compare **quantities across categories**.	Comparing heights of different plant species.
Line Graphs	To show **changes over time** or continuous data.	Tracking temperature changes over a year.
Pie Charts	To show **proportions or percentages of a whole**.	Proportion of different gases in the atmosphere.
Scatter Plots	To explore **relationships or correlations between two variables**.	Comparing height and weight of individuals.

2. How to Construct Clear and Accurate Graphs

Step	Explanation
Title	Clearly describe what the graph is about.
Labeled Axes	X-axis (independent variable), Y-axis (dependent variable).
Units of Measurement	Include units (e.g., meters, seconds, grams).
Appropriate Scale	Evenly spaced intervals that fit all data points.
Legends (if needed)	Explain symbols, colors, or patterns used.
Avoid Misleading Elements	No distorted scales, unnecessary 3D effects, or confusing visuals.

Important Tip: Always check **which variable is independent and which is dependent** when setting up axes.

---

3. Example of Appropriate Graph Usage

Scenario	Graph Type to Use
Measuring plant height at different fertilizer levels.	**Bar chart** to compare different categories (fertilizer types).
Observing temperature change over several weeks.	**Line graph** to show trend over time.
Showing percentages of nitrogen, oxygen, carbon dioxide in air.	**Pie chart** to show parts of a whole.
Investigating correlation between exercise time and heart rate.	**Scatter plot** to examine relationship between variables.

III. Ensuring Clarity and Accuracy in Graph Design

Why Clarity and Accuracy Matter:

- Poorly designed graphs can **mislead viewers** and **hide true patterns**.
- Clear graphs help **communicate findings effectively** to scientists, teachers, and the public.

Key Guidelines for Clear Graphs:

1. **Titles and labels** must be specific and clear.
2. **Units** must be included to understand measurements.
3. **Scales** should be even and not exaggerated or minimized.
4. Avoid using **unnecessary decorations** (like 3D effects) that distract from the data.
5. **Consistent colors** and **symbols** should be used throughout for comparison.
6. Always **review graphs** for accuracy and completeness before presentation or submission.

Tip: Ask, "If someone else looks at this graph, will they understand what it's showing?"

IV. Interpreting Graphs and Data Tables in Scientific Research

Steps to Analyze a Graph or Data Table:

1. **Read the title and labels** to understand what is being measured.
2. Identify the **independent and dependent variables**.
3. Look for **trends, patterns, and outliers**.
4. Interpret what the patterns mean — **Does one variable affect the other?**
5. Check if the graph **matches the conclusions** presented in a study or report.

Example of Analysis:
A line graph showing "Body Temperature vs. Time" after exercise may show **initial increase** and **gradual return to normal**, indicating how the body maintains **homeostasis**.

V. Summary Table — Graphs and Data Analysis

Skill	Description	Why It's Important
Recognizing Trends	Finding patterns (increases, decreases, steady lines).	Helps understand what the data is showing.
Selecting Graph Type	Choosing bar, line, pie, or scatter plot based on data.	Ensures correct and clear data presentation.
Labeling Graphs Properly	Including titles, axes, units, and legends.	Makes data understandable to others.
Avoiding Misleading Graphs	Using appropriate scales, avoiding unnecessary visuals.	Prevents false interpretation of data.
Interpreting Data	Analyzing what the graph/table means, identifying relationships or anomalies.	Draws valid conclusions from scientific data.

Final Thought:

Being able to **construct and analyze graphs and tables** is a crucial skill in science. It allows us to **communicate results, understand experiments**, and **make informed decisions** based on evidence. Learning how to **read, create, and question data presentations** builds scientific literacy — an essential tool for both students and future scientists.

9.2: Experimental Design and Critical Thinking

I. Identifying Bias in Scientific Research

1. What is Bias?

Bias is a **systematic error** that **distorts research results**, leading to conclusions that may **not reflect the true reality**. Bias can occur **intentionally or unintentionally**, often due to **preconceived beliefs, flawed methods, or external influences**.

> **Key Point:** Detecting bias is essential to ensure scientific research is **fair, accurate, and reliable**.

---

2. Types of Bias in Scientific Research

Type of Bias	Definition	Example
Selection Bias	Sample is **not representative** of the target population.	Studying only young adults to make conclusions about all ages.

Type of Bias	Definition	Example
Measurement Bias	Errors in data collection or tools that affect accuracy.	Using a broken thermometer to measure temperature.
Publication Bias	Only positive or significant results are published, while negative or inconclusive studies are ignored.	Ignoring studies that show a new drug has no effect.

3. How to Detect Bias — Critical Evaluation Checklist

Question to Ask	Why It Matters
Is the sample size large and diverse enough?	Ensures results apply to the general population.
Are the measurement tools accurate and calibrated?	Prevents incorrect data from affecting results.
Who funded the research?	Checks for conflicts of interest (e.g., company funding research on its own product).
Are both positive and negative results reported?	Avoids publication bias, gives a full picture.

Tip: Be skeptical of studies that **only show positive outcomes** or **lack transparent methodology**.

II. Evaluating Scientific Claims Based on Evidence

1. Assessing the Source

- **Credibility** of the **person, institution, or journal** making the claim.
- Consider **reputation, qualifications, and possible bias**.
- **Peer-reviewed sources** (e.g., scientific journals like *Nature*, *Science*) are more reliable than blogs or opinion pieces.

Example: A claim about vaccine safety from the **CDC** or **WHO** is more trustworthy than a claim from a random website.

---

2. Reviewing the Evidence

Criteria	Why It Matters
Study Design	Well-designed experiments with control groups produce valid data.
Sample Size	Large, diverse samples give more reliable results.

Criteria	Why It Matters
Consistency of Results	Findings that are **replicated in multiple studies** are more trustworthy.

Example: If multiple studies by different scientists show similar results, the claim is stronger.

---

3. Understanding Statistical Significance

- **Statistical significance** indicates that results are **unlikely due to chance**.
- Scientists use **p-values** (e.g., **p < 0.05**) to measure significance — meaning there's less than a 5% chance the results happened randomly.
- **Not statistically significant = inconclusive results**.

Important: A statistically significant result still needs **context** and **repetition** to be fully trusted.

---

4. Considering Alternative Explanations

- Ask **whether other factors** could explain the result.
- Consider **confounding variables** — hidden factors that may influence the outcome.

Example: If a study finds people who drink more water are healthier, **could it be because they also exercise more?** Without controlling for exercise, we can't be sure.

III. Why Critical Thinking in Science Matters

1. Making Informed Decisions

- Helps individuals **judge the reliability of scientific information** in news, social media, and healthcare.
- Prevents the spread of **misinformation and pseudoscience**.

2. Evaluating Health and Environmental Claims

- Ensures people choose treatments and actions based on **solid evidence** — not fear or hype.
- Supports public understanding of issues like **climate change, vaccine safety, and nutrition**.

3. Becoming Scientifically Literate Citizens

- A scientifically literate person can **understand complex topics, ask questions**, and **engage in public discussions**.
- Critical thinking promotes **better problem-solving and innovation** in science and society.

IV. Summary Table — Bias and Critical Evaluation in Science

Concept	Definition/Explanation	Importance
Bias	Systematic error that distorts study results.	Affects reliability of scientific conclusions.
Selection Bias	Non-representative sample.	Leads to inaccurate generalizations.
Measurement Bias	Inaccurate data collection tools.	Produces false results.
Publication Bias	Favoring positive results in publication.	Skews understanding of scientific reality.
Assessing Source	Checking credibility of who makes the claim.	Ensures trustworthiness of information.
Reviewing Evidence	Examining quality and amount of supporting data.	Confirms strength of scientific claims.
Statistical Significance	Measures whether results are due to chance.	Helps judge reliability of data.
Alternative Explanations	Considering other reasons for the results.	Ensures correct interpretation of data.
Critical Thinking in Science	Analyzing and questioning evidence logically.	Prevents misinformation and supports informed decisions.

Final Thought:

Critical thinking and understanding experimental design **empower students to question, evaluate, and make sense of scientific claims**. In a world full of information, being able to **spot bias and judge evidence** is key to being an informed and responsible citizen.

Practice Question

Chapter 1: The Nature of Science

1. Scientific Inquiry

A group of students is investigating the effect of different fertilizers on plant growth. They set up three groups of plants, each receiving a different type of fertilizer, while one group receives no fertilizer at all. What is the independent variable in this experiment?

A) The type of plants used
B) The amount of water given to each group
C) The type of fertilizer used
D) The height of the plants measured

Answer: C) The type of fertilizer used

Explanation:

The independent variable is the factor that is deliberately changed or manipulated by the experimenter to observe its effect on the dependent variable. In this case, the students are testing different types of fertilizers to see how they affect plant growth. By varying the type of fertilizer while keeping other conditions constant (like the type of plant and the amount of water), the students can determine which fertilizer, if any, promotes better growth. This setup allows for a clear comparison of the effects of each fertilizer type on the plants.

---

2. Controlled Experiments

In an experiment to test the effect of light on photosynthesis, a scientist uses two identical plants. One plant is kept in sunlight, while the other is kept in the dark. Which of the following is a controlled variable in this experiment?

A) The amount of water given to each plant
B) The type of plant used
C) The duration of the experiment
D) The intensity of light received by the plants

Answer: A) The amount of water given to each plant

Explanation:

A controlled variable, also known as a constant, is a factor that is kept the same throughout the experiment to ensure that the results are due to the independent variable alone. In this case, the amount of water given to each plant must be the same to ensure that any differences in photosynthesis can be attributed solely to the light conditions (sunlight vs. darkness). If the water levels were different, it could confound the results, making it unclear whether changes in photosynthesis were due to light exposure or water availability.

---

3. Data Collection

During an experiment, a researcher measures the growth of bacteria in different temperatures. After collecting data, the researcher finds that bacteria grow best at 37°C. What is the dependent variable in this experiment?

A) The temperature of the environment
B) The type of bacteria used
C) The growth of bacteria
D) The duration of the experiment

Answer: C) The growth of bacteria

Explanation:

The dependent variable is the factor that is measured or observed in response to changes in the independent variable. In this experiment, the researcher is measuring the growth of bacteria at various temperatures to determine how temperature affects bacterial growth. The growth can be quantified in various ways, such as measuring the increase in bacterial colonies or the turbidity of the culture. By focusing on how growth varies with temperature, the researcher can draw conclusions about the optimal conditions for bacterial proliferation.

---

4. Importance of Controls

Why is it important to have a control group in an experiment?

A) To ensure that the experiment can be repeated
B) To provide a standard for comparison
C) To increase the number of variables tested
D) To eliminate the need for data collection

Answer: B) To provide a standard for comparison

Explanation:

A control group is essential in scientific experiments because it serves as a baseline against which the results of the experimental group can be compared. By having a control group that does not receive the experimental treatment (e.g., a group of plants that does not receive fertilizer), researchers can determine the effect of the independent variable (the fertilizer) on the dependent variable (plant growth). This comparison helps to isolate the effects of the treatment and ensures that any observed changes are due to the treatment itself rather than other factors. Without a control group, it would be difficult to attribute changes in the experimental group to the treatment being tested.

---

5. Scientific Theories vs. Laws

Which of the following statements best describes the difference between a scientific theory and a scientific law?

A) A theory describes what happens, while a law explains why it happens.
B) A theory is a well-substantiated explanation, while a law is a statement about observed phenomena.
C) A theory can be proven true, while a law cannot.
D) A theory is based on opinion, while a law is based on facts.

Answer: B) A theory is a well-substantiated explanation, while a law is a statement about observed phenomena.

Explanation:

Scientific theories and laws serve different purposes in the scientific community. A scientific theory is a comprehensive explanation of some aspect of nature that is based on a body of evidence and has withstood rigorous testing and scrutiny. For example, the Theory of Evolution explains how species change over time through mechanisms like natural selection. In contrast, a scientific law describes a consistent and universal observation in nature, such as the Law of Gravity, which states that objects with mass attract each other. While theories provide explanations for why phenomena occur, laws summarize what happens under certain conditions without explaining the underlying reasons.

---

6. Examples of Theories

Which of the following is an example of a widely accepted scientific theory?

A) Law of Gravity
B) Theory of Relativity
C) Law of Conservation of Mass
D) Law of Supply and Demand

Answer: B) Theory of Relativity

Explanation:

The Theory of Relativity, proposed by Albert Einstein, is a well-established scientific theory that explains the relationship between space and time, particularly how they are affected by gravity and velocity. It has been supported by extensive empirical evidence and has fundamentally changed our understanding of physics. The other options listed are laws or principles that describe consistent observations in nature rather than providing comprehensive explanations.

---

7. Empirical Evidence

How does empirical evidence support scientific understanding?

A) By providing opinions and beliefs
B) Through experiments, peer review, and replication
C) By relying on historical data only
D) Through anecdotal evidence

Answer: B) Through experiments, peer review, and replication

Explanation:

Empirical evidence is the foundation of scientific inquiry and is obtained through systematic observation and experimentation. It involves collecting data that can be measured and analyzed to draw conclusions. The process of peer review ensures that research findings are evaluated by other experts in the field, which helps to validate the results. Replication of experiments by different researchers further strengthens the reliability of the findings. This rigorous approach to gathering and validating evidence is what allows scientific knowledge to evolve and improve over time.

---

8. Steps of Scientific Investigation

What is the first step in the scientific method?

A) Forming a hypothesis
B) Conducting an experiment
C) Asking a question
D) Analyzing data

Answer: C) Asking a question

Explanation:

The scientific method begins with asking a question based on observations about the natural world. This question often arises from curiosity or a specific problem that needs to be addressed. Once a question is formulated, researchers can then develop a hypothesis, design experiments, collect data, and analyze the results. This structured approach helps ensure that scientific investigations are systematic and objective.

---

9. Identifying Variables

In an experiment testing the effect of temperature on enzyme activity, the temperature is varied while the pH and substrate concentration are kept constant. What is the independent variable?

A) Enzyme activity
B) pH level
C) Substrate concentration
D) Temperature

Answer: D) Temperature

Explanation:

The independent variable is the factor that is manipulated by the experimenter to observe its effect on the dependent variable. In this case, the temperature is being varied to see how it affects enzyme activity. By controlling other variables such as pH and substrate concentration, the researcher can isolate the effect of temperature on the enzyme's performance.

---

10. Scientific Methodology

A scientist is studying the effect of a new drug on blood pressure. After conducting the experiment, the scientist finds that the drug significantly lowers blood pressure. What should the scientist do next?

A) Publish the results immediately
B) Conduct further experiments to confirm the findings
C) Change the hypothesis
D) Ignore the results

Answer: B) Conduct further experiments to confirm the findings

Explanation:

After obtaining results, it is crucial for scientists to conduct further experiments to validate their findings. This process may involve replicating the experiment under different conditions or with different subjects to ensure that the results are consistent and reliable. Confirmation through additional studies strengthens the credibility of the findings and helps to rule out any potential biases or errors in the initial experiment.

---

11. Case Study: Plant Growth

A researcher is studying how different amounts of sunlight affect the growth of tomato plants. She sets up three groups of plants: one group receives 2 hours of sunlight, another receives 6 hours, and the last receives 10 hours. What is the dependent variable in this study?

A) The amount of sunlight
B) The type of tomato plants
C) The growth of the tomato plants
D) The duration of the experiment

Answer: C) The growth of the tomato plants

Explanation:

The dependent variable is the outcome that is measured in response to changes in the independent variable. In this case, the researcher is measuring the growth of the tomato plants to determine how different amounts of sunlight affect their development. By focusing on plant growth, the researcher can analyze the relationship between sunlight exposure and the health of the plants.

---

12. Case Study: Bacterial Growth

In a study on bacterial growth, a scientist tests the effect of different antibiotics on the growth of bacteria. She measures the diameter of the inhibition zone around each antibiotic disk. What is the independent variable in this experiment?

A) The type of bacteria
B) The diameter of the inhibition zone
C) The type of antibiotic used
D) The temperature of the environment

Answer: C) The type of antibiotic used

Explanation:

The independent variable is the factor that is manipulated in the experiment. In this case, the scientist is testing different antibiotics to see how they affect bacterial growth. By changing the type of antibiotic while keeping other conditions constant, the scientist can determine which antibiotic is most effective at inhibiting bacterial growth.

---

13. Case Study: Water Quality

A group of students is investigating the effect of different pollutants on the growth of aquatic plants. They set up tanks with varying levels of pollutants and measure plant growth over time. What is a controlled variable in this experiment?

A) The type of aquatic plants used
B) The amount of water in each tank
C) The duration of the experiment
D) The type of pollutants used

Answer: A) The type of aquatic plants used

Explanation:

A controlled variable is a factor that is kept constant throughout the experiment to ensure that any changes in the dependent variable can be attributed to the independent variable. In this case, the type of aquatic plants should remain the same across all tanks to ensure that differences in growth can be linked solely to the varying levels of pollutants.

---

14. Case Study: Light Intensity

A researcher is studying the effect of light intensity on the growth of a specific plant species. She sets up her experiment with varying light intensities and measures plant height after four weeks. What is the independent variable?

A) The height of the plants
B) The type of plant
C) The light intensity
D) The duration of the experiment

Answer: C) The light intensity

Explanation:

The independent variable is the factor that is changed by the experimenter. In this case, the researcher is varying the light intensity to observe its effect on plant growth. By manipulating this variable, the researcher can determine how different levels of light exposure influence the height and overall health of the plants.

---

15. Case Study: Soil pH

A scientist is investigating the effect of soil pH on the growth of a particular type of flower. She prepares soil samples with different pH levels and plants the same type of flower in each sample. What is the dependent variable in this study?

A) The type of flower
B) The pH level of the soil
C) The growth of the flowers
D) The amount of water given

Answer: C) The growth of the flowers

Explanation:

The dependent variable is what is being measured in the experiment. In this case, the scientist is measuring the growth of the flowers to see how different soil pH levels affect their development. By focusing on flower growth, the scientist can analyze the relationship between soil acidity and plant health.

---

16. Case Study: Enzyme Activity

A biologist is studying the effect of temperature on enzyme activity. She conducts her experiment at three different temperatures: 25°C, 37°C, and 50°C. What is the independent variable in this experiment?

A) The type of enzyme
B) The temperature
C) The rate of enzyme activity
D) The duration of the experiment

Answer: B) The temperature

Explanation:

The independent variable is the factor that is manipulated by the experimenter. In this case, the biologist is changing the temperature to observe its effect on enzyme activity. By varying the temperature, the biologist can determine how it influences the efficiency and effectiveness of the enzyme being studied.

---

17. Case Study: Fertilizer Types

A farmer tests three different types of fertilizers on his corn crop. He measures the height of the corn plants after six weeks. What is the independent variable in this experiment?

A) The height of the corn plants
B) The type of fertilizer used
C) The amount of water given
D) The duration of the experiment

Answer: B) The type of fertilizer used

Explanation:

The independent variable is the factor that is changed by the experimenter. In this case, the farmer is testing different types of fertilizers to see how they affect the growth of corn plants. By varying the type of fertilizer while keeping other conditions constant, the farmer can determine which fertilizer produces the best results.

---

18. Case Study: Light Exposure

A researcher is studying how different durations of light exposure affect the growth of plants. She sets up four groups of plants, each receiving a different duration of light exposure. What is the independent variable in this study?

A) The growth of the plants
B) The type of plants used
C) The duration of light exposure
D) The amount of water given

Answer: C) The duration of light exposure

Explanation:

The independent variable is the factor that is changed by the experimenter. In this case, the researcher is varying the duration of light exposure to observe its effect on plant growth. By manipulating this variable, the researcher can determine how different lengths of light exposure influence the health and development of the plants.

19. Case Study: Soil Moisture

A researcher is studying the effect of soil moisture on the growth of a specific plant species. She prepares soil samples with different moisture levels and plants the same type of plant in each sample. What is the dependent variable in this study?

A) The type of plant
B) The moisture level of the soil
C) The growth of the plants
D) The amount of sunlight received

Answer: C) The growth of the plants

Explanation:

The dependent variable is what is being measured in the experiment. In this case, the researcher is measuring the growth of the plants to see how different soil moisture levels affect their development. By focusing on plant growth, the researcher can analyze the relationship between soil moisture and plant health.

---

20. Case Study: Antibiotic Resistance

A researcher is studying the effect of different antibiotics on bacterial growth. She measures the size of the inhibition zone around each antibiotic disk. What is the dependent variable in this experiment?

A) The type of bacteria
B) The size of the inhibition zone
C) The type of antibiotic used
D) The temperature of the environment

Answer: B) The size of the inhibition zone

Explanation:

The dependent variable is what is being measured in the experiment. In this case, the researcher is measuring the size of the inhibition zone to determine how effective each antibiotic is at inhibiting bacterial growth. This measurement provides insight into the antibiotic's efficacy and helps to compare the effectiveness of different treatments.

---

21. Case Study: Water Temperature

A researcher is studying how water temperature affects the behavior of fish. She sets up tanks with different water temperatures and observes the fish's activity levels. What is the independent variable in this study?

A) The behavior of the fish
B) The type of fish used
C) The water temperature
D) The duration of the experiment

Answer: C) The water temperature

Explanation:

The independent variable is the factor that is manipulated by the experimenter. In this case, the researcher is changing the water temperature to observe its effect on fish behavior. By varying the temperature, the researcher can determine how it influences the activity and behavior of the fish.

---

22. Case Study: Fertilizer Types on Crop Yield

A farmer tests three different types of fertilizers on his corn crop. He measures the height of the corn plants after six weeks. What is the independent variable in this experiment?

A) The height of the corn plants
B) The type of fertilizer used
C) The amount of water given
D) The duration of the experiment

Answer: B) The type of fertilizer used

Explanation:

The independent variable is the factor that is changed by the experimenter. In this case, the farmer is testing different types of fertilizers to see how they affect the growth of corn plants. By varying the type of fertilizer while keeping other conditions constant, the farmer can determine which fertilizer produces the best results.

---

23. Case Study: Light Intensity on Plant Growth

A researcher is studying how different light intensities affect the growth of a specific plant species. She sets up her experiment with varying light intensities and measures plant height after four weeks. What is the independent variable?

A) The height of the plants
B) The type of plant
C) The light intensity
D) The duration of the experiment

Answer: C) The light intensity

Explanation:

The independent variable is the factor that is changed by the experimenter. In this case, the researcher is varying the light intensity to observe its effect on plant growth. By manipulating this variable, the researcher can determine how different levels of light exposure influence the height and overall health of the plants.

---

24. Case Study: Temperature and Bacterial Growth

A scientist is studying the effect of temperature on bacterial growth. She sets up her experiment at three different temperatures: 20°C, 30°C, and 40°C. What is the dependent variable in this study?

A) The temperature
B) The type of bacteria
C) The growth of the bacteria
D) The duration of the experiment

Answer: C) The growth of the bacteria

Explanation:

The dependent variable is what is being measured in the experiment. In this case, the scientist is measuring the growth of the bacteria to see how different temperatures affect their development. By focusing on bacterial growth, the scientist can analyze the relationship between temperature and bacterial proliferation.

---

25. Case Study: Plant Growth in Different Soils

A researcher is investigating how different soil types affect the growth of tomato plants. She prepares soil samples with varying compositions and measures plant height after six weeks. What is the independent variable in this study?

A) The type of plant
B) The soil composition
C) The height of the plants
D) The amount of water given

Answer: B) The soil composition

Explanation:

The independent variable is the factor that is changed by the experimenter. In this case, the researcher is varying the soil composition to observe its effect on tomato plant growth. By manipulating this variable, the researcher can determine how different soil types influence the height and health of the plants.

---

26. Case Study: Light Exposure on Plant Growth

A researcher is studying how different durations of light exposure affect the growth of plants. She sets up four groups of plants, each receiving a different duration of light exposure. What is the independent variable in this study?

A) The growth of the plants
B) The type of plants used
C) The duration of light exposure
D) The amount of water given

Answer: C) The duration of light exposure

Explanation:

The independent variable is the factor that is changed by the experimenter. In this case, the researcher is varying the duration of light exposure to observe its effect on plant growth. By manipulating this variable, the researcher can determine how different lengths of light exposure influence the health and development of the plants.

---

27. Case Study: Soil Moisture

A researcher is studying the effect of soil moisture on the growth of a specific plant species. She prepares soil samples with different moisture levels and plants the same type of plant in each sample. What is the dependent variable in this study?

A) The type of plant
B) The moisture level of the soil
C) The growth of the plants
D) The amount of sunlight received

Answer: C) The growth of the plants

Explanation:

The dependent variable is what is being measured in the experiment. In this case, the researcher is measuring the growth of the plants to see how different soil moisture levels affect their development. By focusing on plant growth, the researcher can analyze the relationship between soil moisture and plant health.

---

28. Case Study: Antibiotic Resistance

A researcher is studying the effect of different antibiotics on bacterial growth. She measures the size of the inhibition zone around each antibiotic disk. What is the dependent variable in this experiment?

A) The type of bacteria
B) The size of the inhibition zone
C) The type of antibiotic used
D) The temperature of the environment

Answer: B) The size of the inhibition zone

Explanation:

The dependent variable is what is being measured in the experiment. In this case, the researcher is measuring the size of the inhibition zone to determine how effective each antibiotic is at inhibiting bacterial growth. This measurement provides insight into the antibiotic's efficacy and helps to compare the effectiveness of different treatments.

---

29. Case Study: Water Temperature on Fish Behavior

A researcher is studying how water temperature affects the behavior of fish. She sets up tanks with different water temperatures and observes the fish's activity levels. What is the independent variable in this study?

A) The behavior of the fish
B) The type of fish used
C) The water temperature
D) The duration of the experiment

Answer: C) The water temperature

Explanation:

The independent variable is the factor that is manipulated by the experimenter. In this case, the researcher is changing the water temperature to observe its effect on fish behavior. By varying the temperature, the researcher can determine how it influences the activity and behavior of the fish.

---

30. Case Study: Fertilizer Types on Crop Yield

A farmer tests three different types of fertilizers on his corn crop. He measures the height of the corn plants after six weeks. What is the independent variable in this experiment?

A) The height of the corn plants
B) The type of fertilizer used
C) The amount of water given
D) The duration of the experiment

Answer: B) The type of fertilizer used

Explanation:

The independent variable is the factor that is changed by the experimenter. In this case, the farmer is testing different types of fertilizers to see how they affect the growth of corn plants. By varying the type of fertilizer while keeping other conditions constant, the farmer can determine which fertilizer produces the best results.

---

31. Case Study: Light Intensity on Plant Growth

A researcher is studying how different light intensities affect the growth of a specific plant species. She sets up her experiment with varying light intensities and measures plant height after four weeks. What is the independent variable?

A) The height of the plants
B) The type of plant
C) The light intensity
D) The duration of the experiment

Answer: C) The light intensity

Explanation:

The independent variable is the factor that is changed by the experimenter. In this case, the researcher is varying the light intensity to observe its effect on plant growth. By manipulating this variable, the researcher can determine how different levels of light exposure influence the height and overall health of the plants.

32. Case Study: Temperature and Bacterial Growth

A scientist is studying the effect of temperature on bacterial growth. She sets up her experiment at three different temperatures: 20°C, 30°C, and 40°C. What is the dependent variable in this study?

A) The temperature
B) The type of bacteria
C) The growth of the bacteria
D) The duration of the experiment

Answer: C) The growth of the bacteria

Explanation:

The dependent variable is what is being measured in the experiment. In this case, the scientist is measuring the growth of the bacteria to see how different temperatures affect their development. By focusing on bacterial growth, the scientist can analyze the relationship between temperature and bacterial proliferation.

---

33. Case Study: Plant Growth in Different Soils

A researcher is investigating how different soil types affect the growth of tomato plants. She prepares soil samples with varying compositions and measures plant height after six weeks. What is the independent variable in this study?

A) The type of plant
B) The soil composition
C) The height of the plants
D) The amount of water given

Answer: B) The soil composition

Explanation:

The independent variable is the factor that is changed by the experimenter. In this case, the researcher is varying the soil composition to observe its effect on tomato plant growth. By manipulating this variable, the researcher can determine how different soil types influence the height and health of the plants.

---

34. Case Study: Light Exposure on Plant Growth

A researcher is studying how different durations of light exposure affect the growth of plants. She sets up four groups of plants, each receiving a different duration of light exposure. What is the independent variable in this study?

A) The growth of the plants
B) The type of plants used
C) The duration of light exposure
D) The amount of water given

Answer: C) The duration of light exposure

Explanation:

The independent variable is the factor that is changed by the experimenter. In this case, the researcher is varying the duration of light exposure to observe its effect on plant growth. By manipulating this variable, the researcher can determine how different lengths of light exposure influence the health and development of the plants.

---

35. Case Study: Soil pH and Plant Growth

A scientist is investigating the effect of soil pH on the growth of a specific plant species. She prepares soil samples with different pH levels and plants the same type of plant in each sample. What is the dependent variable in this study?

A) The type of plant
B) The pH level of the soil
C) The growth of the plants
D) The amount of sunlight received

Answer: C) The growth of the plants

Explanation:

The dependent variable is what is being measured in the experiment. In this case, the researcher is measuring the growth of the plants to see how different soil pH levels affect their development. By focusing on plant growth, the researcher can analyze the relationship between soil pH and plant health.

---

36. Case Study: Antibiotic Resistance

A researcher is studying the effect of different antibiotics on bacterial growth. She measures the size of the inhibition zone around each antibiotic disk. What is the dependent variable in this experiment?

A) The type of bacteria
B) The size of the inhibition zone
C) The type of antibiotic used
D) The temperature of the environment

Answer: B) The size of the inhibition zone

Explanation:

The dependent variable is what is being measured in the experiment. In this case, the researcher is measuring the size of the inhibition zone to determine how effective each antibiotic is at inhibiting bacterial growth. This measurement provides insight into the antibiotic's efficacy and helps to compare the effectiveness of different treatments.

---

37. Case Study: Water Temperature on Fish Behavior

A researcher is studying how water temperature affects the behavior of fish. She sets up tanks with different water temperatures and observes the fish's activity levels. What is the independent variable in this study?

A) The behavior of the fish
B) The type of fish used
C) The water temperature
D) The duration of the experiment

Answer: C) The water temperature

Explanation:

The independent variable is the factor that is manipulated by the experimenter. In this case, the researcher is changing the water temperature to observe its effect on fish behavior. By varying the temperature, the researcher can determine how it influences the activity and behavior of the fish.

---

38. Case Study: Fertilizer Types on Crop Yield

A farmer tests three different types of fertilizers on his corn crop. He measures the height of the corn plants after six weeks. What is the independent variable in this experiment?

A) The height of the corn plants
B) The type of fertilizer used
C) The amount of water given
D) The duration of the experiment

Answer: B) The type of fertilizer used

Explanation:

The independent variable is the factor that is changed by the experimenter. In this case, the farmer is testing different types of fertilizers to see how they affect the growth of corn plants. By varying the type of fertilizer while keeping other conditions constant, the farmer can determine which fertilizer produces the best results.

---

39. Case Study: Light Intensity on Plant Growth

A researcher is studying how different light intensities affect the growth of a specific plant species. She sets up her experiment with varying light intensities and measures plant height after four weeks. What is the independent variable?

A) The height of the plants
B) The type of plant
C) The light intensity
D) The duration of the experiment

Answer: C) The light intensity

Explanation:

The independent variable is the factor that is changed by the experimenter. In this case, the researcher is varying the light intensity to observe its effect on plant growth. By manipulating this variable, the researcher can determine how different levels of light exposure influence the height and overall health of the plants.

---

40. Case Study: Temperature and Bacterial Growth

A scientist is studying the effect of temperature on bacterial growth. She sets up her experiment at three different temperatures: 20°C, 30°C, and 40°C. What is the dependent variable in this study?

A) The temperature
B) The type of bacteria
C) The growth of the bacteria
D) The duration of the experiment

Answer: C) The growth of the bacteria

Explanation:

The dependent variable is what is being measured in the experiment. In this case, the scientist is measuring the growth of the bacteria to see how different temperatures affect their development. By focusing on bacterial growth, the scientist can analyze the relationship between temperature and bacterial proliferation.

A biology class is using a microscope to observe the structure of plant cells. Which part of the microscope is primarily responsible for adjusting the focus of the specimen?
A) Objective lens
B) Eyepiece
C) Coarse adjustment knob
D) Stage

Answer: C) Coarse adjustment knob
Explanation: The coarse adjustment knob is used to bring the specimen into general focus by moving the stage up

or down. It is particularly useful when starting with low-power objectives. Once the specimen is roughly in focus, the fine adjustment knob can be used for more precise focusing.

---

42. Measuring Mass Accurately

In a laboratory experiment, a student needs to measure the mass of a sample accurately. Which piece of equipment should the student use?
A) Graduated cylinder
B) Thermometer
C) Balance
D) Microscope

Answer: C) Balance
Explanation: A balance is the appropriate tool for measuring mass accurately. It provides precise measurements of the weight of a sample, which is essential for many biological experiments. Graduated cylinders are used for measuring liquid volume, thermometers for temperature, and microscopes for magnifying small specimens.

---

43. Measuring Liquid Volume

During a lab experiment, a student needs to measure 50 mL of a liquid accurately. Which piece of equipment should the student use?
A) Beaker
B) Graduated cylinder
C) Test tube
D) Erlenmeyer flask

Answer: B) Graduated cylinder
Explanation: A graduated cylinder is specifically designed for measuring liquid volumes accurately. It has marked measurements along its side, allowing for precise readings. Beakers and Erlenmeyer flasks are less accurate for measuring specific volumes, while test tubes are not designed for volume measurement.

---

44. Understanding SI Units

Which of the following is the correct SI unit for measuring mass?
A) Liter
B) Meter
C) Gram
D) Second

Answer: C) Gram
Explanation: The SI unit for mass is the gram (g). The liter (L) is used for measuring volume, the meter (m) for length, and the second (s) for time. Understanding these base units is crucial for accurate scientific measurements and communication.

---

45. Prefixes in the Metric System

If a scientist measures a length of 0.005 meters, how can this measurement be expressed using a metric prefix?
A) 5 millimeters
B) 5 centimeters
C) 5 kilometers
D) 5 micrometers

Answer: A) 5 millimeters
Explanation: 0.005 meters is equivalent to 5 millimeters (mm) because 1 meter equals 1,000 millimeters. Understanding metric prefixes is essential for converting and communicating measurements in scientific contexts.

---

46. Importance of Standardization

Why is standardization important in scientific communication?
A) It allows scientists to use different units of measurement.
B) It ensures that experiments can be replicated and results compared.
C) It eliminates the need for data analysis.
D) It simplifies the scientific method.

Answer: B) It ensures that experiments can be replicated and results compared.
Explanation: Standardization in scientific communication allows researchers to share and compare their findings effectively. Using consistent units and methods ensures that experiments can be replicated by others, which is a fundamental aspect of the scientific process.

---

47. Organizing Data in Tables

A researcher collects data on the growth of plants under different light conditions. What is the best way to present this data for analysis?
A) A pie chart
B) A line graph
C) A table
D) A bar graph

Answer: C) A table
Explanation: A table is the best way to organize and present raw data for analysis. It allows for easy comparison of different variables, such as plant growth under various light conditions. Graphs can be used later to visualize trends, but tables are essential for initial data organization.

---

48. Using Bar Graphs

A scientist wants to compare the number of different species of birds observed in a forest over a month. Which type of graph would be most effective for this purpose?
A) Line graph
B) Pie chart
C) Bar graph
D) Scatter plot

Answer: C) Bar graph
Explanation: A bar graph is effective for comparing discrete categories, such as the number of different species of birds. It allows for easy visual comparison of the counts for each species. Line graphs are better for showing trends over time, while pie charts represent parts of a whole, and scatter plots show relationships between two variables.

---

49. Analyzing Trends with Line Graphs

A researcher tracks the temperature changes in a habitat over a year. What type of graph should the researcher use to represent this data?
A) Bar graph
B) Pie chart
C) Line graph
D) Histogram

Answer: C) Line graph
Explanation: A line graph is ideal for displaying data that changes over time, such as temperature fluctuations throughout the year. It allows the researcher to visualize trends and patterns in the data effectively.

---

50. Identifying Patterns in Data

After analyzing data collected from an experiment, a scientist notices a consistent increase in plant height with increased light exposure. What type of relationship does this indicate?
A) No relationship
B) Negative correlation
C) Positive correlation
D) Inverse relationship

Answer: C) Positive correlation
Explanation: A positive correlation indicates that as one variable increases (in this case, light exposure), the other variable (plant height) also increases. This relationship suggests that light exposure positively affects plant growth.

---

51. Sources of Error in Data Analysis

During an experiment, a student accidentally spills water on the balance used to measure mass. What type of error does this represent?
A) Systematic error
B) Random error
C) Human error
D) Instrumental error

Answer: D) Instrumental error
Explanation: Instrumental error occurs when the equipment used in an experiment is affected by external factors, such as water damage. This can lead to inaccurate measurements and affect the reliability of the data collected.

---

52. Measuring Temperature

A scientist is measuring the temperature of a solution during a chemical reaction. Which tool should she use for accurate temperature readings?
A) Graduated cylinder
B) Thermometer
C) Balance
D) Microscope

Answer: B) Thermometer
Explanation: A thermometer is specifically designed to measure temperature accurately. It provides precise readings necessary for monitoring temperature changes during chemical reactions, which can significantly affect the outcome of the experiment.

---

53. Using Graduated Cylinders

When using a graduated cylinder to measure liquid volume, what technique should be employed to ensure accuracy?
A) Measure at eye level to avoid parallax error
B) Fill the cylinder to the top
C) Use the meniscus to read the measurement
D) Both A and C

Answer: D) Both A and C
Explanation: To ensure accurate measurements with a graduated cylinder, it is important to read the meniscus (the curved surface of the liquid) at eye level to avoid parallax error. This technique helps ensure that the measurement is as precise as possible.

---

54. Importance of Measurement Units

Why is it important for scientists to use SI units in their measurements?
A) It allows for more flexibility in data interpretation.
B) It simplifies calculations.

C) It ensures consistency and standardization across scientific disciplines.
D) It eliminates the need for conversions.

Answer: C) It ensures consistency and standardization across scientific disciplines.
Explanation: Using SI units (the International System of Units) provides a standardized framework for measurements, which is crucial for effective communication and comparison of scientific data across different fields and studies. This consistency helps avoid confusion and errors that can arise from using different measurement systems.

---

55. Analyzing Data with Graphs

A researcher collects data on the number of species observed in a specific area over several months. What type of graph would best represent the change in species count over time?
A) Bar graph
B) Pie chart
C) Line graph
D) Histogram

Answer: C) Line graph
Explanation: A line graph is best suited for representing data that changes over time, such as the number of species observed in a specific area. It allows the researcher to visualize trends and fluctuations in species count effectively.

---

56. Using Tables for Data Organization

A scientist records the growth of bacteria in different nutrient solutions over a week. What is the best way to organize this data for analysis?
A) A pie chart
B) A line graph
C) A table
D) A bar graph

Answer: C) A table
Explanation: A table is the most effective way to organize raw data for analysis. It allows for easy comparison of different variables, such as bacterial growth in various nutrient solutions over time. Once the data is organized, graphs can be created to visualize trends.

---

57. Measuring Mass with Balances

When measuring the mass of a solid sample, what is the correct procedure to ensure accurate results using a balance?
A) Place the sample directly on the balance pan.
B) Use a weighing boat or paper to contain the sample.
C) Calibrate the balance before each use.
D) Both B and C

Answer: D) Both B and C
Explanation: Using a weighing boat or paper helps contain the sample and prevents contamination, while calibrating the balance ensures that it provides accurate measurements. Both steps are essential for obtaining reliable mass readings.

---

58. Understanding SI Units

Which of the following is the correct SI unit for measuring volume?
A) Gram
B) Meter
C) Liter
D) Second

Answer: C) Liter
Explanation: The SI unit for measuring volume is the liter (L). Understanding the appropriate units for different measurements is crucial for accurate scientific communication and data interpretation.

---

59. Analyzing Data Patterns

After analyzing the data collected from an experiment, a scientist notices a consistent decrease in plant growth with increased soil salinity. What type of relationship does this indicate?
A) No relationship
B) Negative correlation
C) Positive correlation
D) Inverse relationship

Answer: B) Negative correlation
Explanation: A negative correlation indicates that as one variable increases (in this case, soil salinity), the other variable (plant growth) decreases. This relationship suggests that higher salinity levels negatively affect plant health and growth.

---

60. Importance of Replication

Why is replication important in scientific experiments?
A) It allows scientists to change their hypotheses.
B) It helps to confirm the reliability and validity of results.
C) It reduces the need for controls.
D) It simplifies the experimental design.

Answer: B) It helps to confirm the reliability and validity of results.
Explanation: Replication of experiments is crucial for verifying results and ensuring that they are not due to chance or experimental error. By repeating experiments under the same conditions, scientists can confirm their findings and strengthen the credibility of their conclusions.

Chapter 2: Biochemistry – The Chemistry of Life

1. Elements Essential for Life

A biologist is studying the essential elements for life. Which of the following elements is NOT one of the six key elements that make up most biological molecules?
A) Carbon
B) Hydrogen
C) Calcium
D) Nitrogen

Answer: C) Calcium
Explanation: The six key elements essential for life are carbon (C), hydrogen (H), oxygen (O), nitrogen (N), phosphorus (P), and sulfur (S). Calcium is important for certain biological functions but is not one of the six key elements.

---

2. Role of Carbon in Biological Molecules

Why is carbon considered the backbone of biological molecules?
A) It can form only one bond.
B) It can form four covalent bonds.
C) It is the most abundant element in the universe.
D) It is a trace element in living organisms.

Answer: B) It can form four covalent bonds.
Explanation: Carbon's ability to form four covalent bonds allows it to create a wide variety of complex and diverse organic molecules, making it essential for life.

---

3. Structural Diversity in Macromolecules

Which of the following macromolecules is primarily responsible for energy storage in plants?
A) Proteins
B) Nucleic acids
C) Carbohydrates
D) Lipids

Answer: C) Carbohydrates
Explanation: Carbohydrates, specifically polysaccharides like starch, are the primary energy storage molecules in plants. They can be broken down into glucose when energy is needed.

---

4. Importance of Trace Elements

A patient is diagnosed with an iodine deficiency. Which of the following functions is most likely affected by this deficiency?
A) Oxygen transport in blood
B) Thyroid hormone production
C) Muscle contraction
D) Bone density

Answer: B) Thyroid hormone production
Explanation: Iodine is essential for the synthesis of thyroid hormones, which regulate metabolism. A deficiency can lead to thyroid-related health issues.

5. Lipids and Membrane Structure

Which type of lipid is primarily responsible for forming the cell membrane?
A) Triglycerides
B) Phospholipids
C) Steroids
D) Waxes

Answer: B) Phospholipids
Explanation: Phospholipids are the main components of cell membranes, forming a bilayer that provides structure and regulates the movement of substances in and out of the cell.

---

6. Protein Structure and Function

What type of bond forms between amino acids during protein synthesis?
A) Ionic bond
B) Hydrogen bond
C) Peptide bond
D) Covalent bond

Answer: C) Peptide bond
Explanation: Peptide bonds are covalent bonds that link amino acids together to form proteins. This bond is formed during the process of translation in protein synthesis.

---

7. Nucleic Acids and Genetic Information

Which of the following statements about DNA is true?
A) DNA is single-stranded.
B) DNA contains uracil instead of thymine.
C) DNA stores genetic information.
D) DNA is composed of amino acids.

Answer: C) DNA stores genetic information.
Explanation: DNA (deoxyribonucleic acid) is a double-stranded molecule that contains the genetic instructions for the development and functioning of living organisms.

---

8. Enzymes as Biological Catalysts

What is the primary function of enzymes in biochemical reactions?
A) To increase the temperature of the reaction
B) To lower the activation energy
C) To change the pH of the reaction
D) To provide energy for the reaction

Answer: B) To lower the activation energy
Explanation: Enzymes act as biological catalysts by lowering the activation energy required for biochemical reactions, thereby increasing the reaction rate.

---

9. Lock-and-Key Model of Enzyme Action

In the lock-and-key model of enzyme action, what does the "lock" represent?
A) The enzyme
B) The substrate
C) The active site
D) The product

Answer: C) The active site
Explanation: In the lock-and-key model, the "lock" represents the active site of the enzyme, which is specifically shaped to fit a particular substrate, allowing the reaction to occur.

---

10. Factors Affecting Enzyme Activity

How does an increase in temperature generally affect enzyme activity?
A) It always increases activity.
B) It has no effect.
C) It can increase activity until a certain point, then denature the enzyme.
D) It decreases activity.

Answer: C) It can increase activity until a certain point, then denature the enzyme.
Explanation: Increasing temperature can enhance enzyme activity up to an optimal point. Beyond this point, the enzyme may denature, losing its functional shape and activity.

---

11. pH and Enzyme Activity

Which of the following enzymes works best in a highly acidic environment, such as the stomach?
A) Amylase
B) Pepsin
C) Trypsin
D) DNA polymerase

Answer: B) Pepsin
Explanation: Pepsin is an enzyme that functions optimally in the acidic environment of the stomach, where it helps digest proteins.

---

12. Substrate Concentration and Reaction Speed

What happens to the rate of an enzyme-catalyzed reaction as substrate concentration increases?
A) It decreases.
B) It remains constant.
C) It increases until a saturation point is reached.
D) It becomes negative.

Answer: C) It increases until a saturation point is reached.
Explanation: As substrate concentration increases, the reaction rate increases until all active sites of the enzyme are occupied (saturation point), at which point the rate levels off.

---

13. Competitive Inhibition

In competitive inhibition, how does an inhibitor affect enzyme activity?
A) It binds to the active site, preventing substrate binding.
B) It changes the enzyme's shape.
C) It increases the enzyme's activity.
D) It binds to the substrate.

Answer: A) It binds to the active site, preventing substrate binding.
Explanation: Competitive inhibitors resemble the substrate and compete for binding to the active site of the enzyme, thereby reducing the enzyme's activity.

---

14. Non-Competitive Inhibition

What is the effect of a non-competitive inhibitor on an enzyme?
A) It binds to the active site.
B) It increases the reaction rate.
C) It binds to a site other than the active site, altering enzyme function.
D) It has no effect on the enzyme.

Answer: C) It binds to a site other than the active site, altering enzyme function.
Explanation: Non-competitive inhibitors bind to an allosteric site on the enzyme, changing its shape and reducing its activity regardless of substrate concentration.

---

15. Coenzymes and Cofactors

What role do coenzymes play in enzyme activity?
A) They are substrates for the enzyme.
B) They increase the activation energy.
C) They assist in enzyme function by participating in the reaction.
D) They inhibit enzyme activity.

Answer: C) They assist in enzyme function by participating in the reaction.
Explanation: Coenzymes are organic molecules that assist enzymes by providing additional chemical groups or facilitating the transfer of electrons during biochemical reactions.

---

16. Importance of Iron in Blood

Why is iron considered a trace element essential for life?
A) It is a major component of carbohydrates.
B) It is necessary for the formation of hemoglobin in red blood cells.
C) It helps in the synthesis of DNA.
D) It is a primary energy source for cells.

Answer: B) It is necessary for the formation of hemoglobin in red blood cells.
Explanation: Iron is a crucial component of hemoglobin, the protein in red blood cells that carries oxygen throughout the body.

---

17. Role of Phosphorus in Biological Molecules

What is the primary role of phosphorus in living organisms?
A) Energy storage
B) Structural component of proteins
C) Component of nucleic acids and ATP
D) Oxygen transport

Answer: C) Component of nucleic acids and ATP
Explanation: Phosphorus is a key component of nucleic acids (DNA and RNA) and ATP (adenosine triphosphate), which is essential for energy transfer in cells.

---

18. Hydrocarbons and Functional Groups

Which of the following statements about hydrocarbons is true?
A) They contain only carbon and oxygen.
B) They are always polar molecules.
C) They can form long chains or rings.
D) They are not found in biological molecules.

Answer: C) They can form long chains or rings.
Explanation: Hydrocarbons are organic molecules consisting solely of carbon and hydrogen, and they can form long chains or ring structures, contributing to the diversity of organic compounds.

---

19. Carbohydrates and Energy Storage

Which carbohydrate is primarily used for energy storage in animals?
A) Cellulose
B) Starch
C) Glycogen
D) Chitin

Answer: C) Glycogen
Explanation: Glycogen is the primary energy storage carbohydrate in animals, stored mainly in the liver and muscles, and can be broken down into glucose when energy is needed.

---

20. Role of Lipids in Membrane Structure

What is the primary function of phospholipids in biological membranes?
A) Energy storage
B) Structural support
C) Forming a bilayer that acts as a barrier
D) Catalyzing biochemical reactions

Answer: C) Forming a bilayer that acts as a barrier
Explanation: Phospholipids form a bilayer in cell membranes, providing a barrier that separates the interior of the cell from the external environment while allowing selective permeability.

---

21. Protein Folding and Function

What determines the specific three-dimensional shape of a protein?
A) The type of amino acids present
B) The temperature of the environment
C) The pH of the solution
D) The sequence of amino acids

Answer: D) The sequence of amino acids
Explanation: The specific sequence of amino acids in a protein determines its unique three-dimensional shape, which is crucial for its function.

---

22. Enzyme Specificity

What is meant by enzyme specificity?
A) Enzymes can catalyze any reaction.
B) Enzymes are only active at high temperatures.
C) Enzymes only catalyze specific reactions with particular substrates.
D) Enzymes can work with multiple substrates equally well.

Answer: C) Enzymes only catalyze specific reactions with particular substrates.
Explanation: Enzyme specificity refers to the ability of an enzyme to select and catalyze a specific substrate, ensuring that biochemical reactions occur efficiently and accurately.

---

23. Denaturation of Enzymes

What is the effect of denaturation on an enzyme?
A) It increases the enzyme's activity.
B) It changes the enzyme's shape, rendering it inactive.
C) It has no effect on the enzyme's function.
D) It enhances the enzyme's specificity.

Answer: B) It changes the enzyme's shape, rendering it inactive.
Explanation: Denaturation alters the three-dimensional structure of an enzyme, which can disrupt its active site and prevent it from catalyzing reactions effectively.

---

24. Role of Catalase

What is the primary function of the enzyme catalase in living organisms?
A) To synthesize proteins
B) To break down hydrogen peroxide
C) To facilitate DNA replication
D) To transport oxygen in the blood

Answer: B) To break down hydrogen peroxide
Explanation: Catalase is an enzyme that catalyzes the decomposition of hydrogen peroxide into water and oxygen, protecting cells from oxidative damage.

---

25. Effects of pH on Enzyme Activity

Which of the following statements is true regarding the effect of pH on enzyme activity?
A) All enzymes work best at a neutral pH of 7.
B) Enzymes have an optimal pH range where they function best.
C) Increasing pH always increases enzyme activity.
D) pH has no effect on enzyme activity.

Answer: B) Enzymes have an optimal pH range where they function best.
Explanation: Each enzyme has an optimal pH range that allows it to function most effectively. Deviations from this range can lead to decreased activity or denaturation.

---

26. Substrate Concentration and Enzyme Activity

What happens to the rate of an enzyme-catalyzed reaction when substrate concentration is increased beyond a certain point?
A) The rate continues to increase indefinitely.
B) The rate decreases.
C) The rate levels off and reaches a maximum.
D) The rate becomes negative.

Answer: C) The rate levels off and reaches a maximum.
Explanation: As substrate concentration increases, the reaction rate increases until all active sites of the enzyme are occupied, at which point the rate levels off and reaches a maximum (saturation).

---

27. Role of Functional Groups

Which of the following functional groups is known for making molecules more polar and increasing their solubility in water?
A) Hydroxyl group
B) Methyl group
C) Carbonyl group
D) Phosphate group

Answer: A) Hydroxyl group
Explanation: The hydroxyl group (-OH) is polar and increases the solubility of organic molecules in water, making them more hydrophilic.

---

28. Biological Macromolecules

Which of the following macromolecules is primarily responsible for storing genetic information?
A) Proteins
B) Carbohydrates
C) Nucleic acids
D) Lipids

Answer: C) Nucleic acids
Explanation: Nucleic acids, such as DNA and RNA, are responsible for storing and transmitting genetic information in living organisms.

---

29. Role of Amino Acids

What is the basic building block of proteins?
A) Nucleotides
B) Fatty acids
C) Monosaccharides
D) Amino acids

Answer: D) Amino acids
Explanation: Amino acids are the fundamental building blocks of proteins, linked together by peptide bonds to form polypeptides and ultimately functional proteins.

---

30. Enzyme-Substrate Complex

What is formed when an enzyme binds to its substrate?
A) Enzyme-inhibitor complex
B) Enzyme-product complex
C) Enzyme-substrate complex
D) Enzyme-cofactor complex

Answer: C) Enzyme-substrate complex
Explanation: The enzyme-substrate complex is formed when an enzyme binds to its specific substrate, facilitating the chemical reaction that converts the substrate into products.

---

31. Role of Lipids in Energy Storage

Which type of lipid is primarily used for long-term energy storage in animals?
A) Phospholipids
B) Triglycerides
C) Steroids
D) Waxes

Answer: B) Triglycerides
Explanation: Triglycerides are the main form of stored energy in animals, consisting of three fatty acids linked to a glycerol molecule, providing a dense energy source.

---

32. Enzyme Regulation

What is the role of allosteric sites in enzyme regulation?
A) They are the active sites where substrates bind.
B) They allow for competitive inhibition.
C) They can bind regulatory molecules that change enzyme activity.
D) They are sites for substrate binding only.

Answer: C) They can bind regulatory molecules that change enzyme activity.
Explanation: Allosteric sites are locations on an enzyme where regulatory molecules can bind, leading to changes in enzyme shape and activity, thus regulating the enzyme's function.

---

33. Importance of Carbon in Life

Why is carbon considered the most versatile element in biological molecules?
A) It can form only single bonds.
B) It can form four covalent bonds with various elements.
C) It is the most abundant element in the universe.
D) It is a trace element in living organisms.

Answer: B) It can form four covalent bonds with various elements.
Explanation: Carbon's ability to form four covalent bonds allows it to create a diverse array of organic molecules, making it essential for life.

---

34. Role of Sulfur in Proteins

What role does sulfur play in the structure of proteins?
A) It forms hydrogen bonds between amino acids.
B) It contributes to the formation of disulfide bridges.
C) It acts as a cofactor for enzymes.
D) It is a primary energy source.

Answer: B) It contributes to the formation of disulfide bridges.
Explanation: Sulfur atoms in cysteine residues can form disulfide bridges, which help stabilize the three-dimensional structure of proteins.

---

35. Enzyme Activity and Temperature

What effect does a decrease in temperature generally have on enzyme activity?
A) It increases enzyme activity.
B) It has no effect.
C) It decreases enzyme activity.
D) It denatures the enzyme.

Answer: C) It decreases enzyme activity.
Explanation: Lower temperatures typically reduce the kinetic energy of molecules, leading to fewer collisions between enzymes and substrates, thus decreasing the rate of reaction.

---

36. Role of DNA Polymerase

What is the primary function of the enzyme DNA polymerase?
A) To synthesize RNA from DNA
B) To replicate DNA during cell division
C) To break down DNA
D) To repair damaged DNA

Answer: B) To replicate DNA during cell division.
Explanation: DNA polymerase is essential for synthesizing new DNA strands during replication, ensuring that genetic information is accurately passed on to daughter cells.

---

37. Function of Carbohydrates

Which of the following is a primary function of carbohydrates in living organisms?
A) Energy storage and supply
B) Genetic information storage
C) Catalyzing biochemical reactions
D) Structural support in cell membranes

Answer: A) Energy storage and supply
Explanation: Carbohydrates serve as a primary source of energy for living organisms, with glucose being a key energy molecule.

---

38. Role of Functional Groups in Organic Molecules

Which functional group is associated with alcohols?
A) Carbonyl
B) Hydroxyl
C) Amino
D) Carboxyl

Answer: B) Hydroxyl
Explanation: The hydroxyl group (-OH) is characteristic of alcohols and contributes to their polar nature, making them soluble in water.

---

39. Enzyme Inhibition

What is the effect of a competitive inhibitor on an enzyme-catalyzed reaction?
A) It increases the reaction rate.
B) It decreases the reaction rate by binding to the active site.
C) It has no effect on the reaction rate.
D) It changes the enzyme's shape permanently.

Answer: B) It decreases the reaction rate by binding to the active site.
Explanation: Competitive inhibitors compete with the substrate for binding to the active site of the enzyme, reducing the overall rate of the reaction.

---

40. Importance of Water in Biochemical Reactions

Why is water considered a vital component in biochemical reactions?
A) It is a source of energy.
B) It acts as a solvent and participates in reactions.
C) It is a structural component of proteins.
D) It provides nutrients to cells.

Answer: B) It acts as a solvent and participates in reactions.
Explanation: Water is essential for life because it serves as a solvent for many biochemical reactions and can participate directly in chemical reactions, facilitating metabolic processes.

---

41. Properties of Water: Cohesion

A scientist is studying the surface tension of water. Which property of water is primarily responsible for this phenomenon?
A) Adhesion
B) High specific heat
C) Cohesion
D) Universal solvent

Answer: C) Cohesion
Explanation: Cohesion refers to the attraction between water molecules, which leads to surface tension. This property allows water to form droplets and enables small objects to float on its surface.

---

42. Properties of Water: Adhesion

During an experiment, a student observes that water climbs up a thin glass tube. What property of water is responsible for this behavior?
A) Cohesion
B) High specific heat
C) Adhesion
D) Density

Answer: C) Adhesion
Explanation: Adhesion is the property that allows water molecules to stick to other surfaces, such as the glass of the tube. This results in capillary action, which is essential for the movement of water in plants.

---

43. High Specific Heat of Water

Why is the high specific heat of water important for living organisms?
A) It allows water to evaporate quickly.
B) It helps maintain stable temperatures in the environment.
C) It increases the density of water.
D) It makes water a universal solvent.

Answer: B) It helps maintain stable temperatures in the environment.
Explanation: Water's high specific heat means it can absorb a lot of heat without a significant change in temperature, which helps stabilize temperatures in organisms and their environments.

---

44. Water as a Universal Solvent

Which of the following statements best describes why water is known as the "universal solvent"?
A) It can dissolve all substances.
B) It can dissolve polar and ionic substances.
C) It can only dissolve gases.
D) It does not dissolve any substances.

Answer: B) It can dissolve polar and ionic substances.
Explanation: Water's polarity allows it to interact with and dissolve many polar and ionic compounds, making it an effective solvent for transporting nutrients and waste in biological systems.

---

45. pH Scale

What is the pH range of a solution that is considered acidic?
A) 0-6
B) 7
C) 8-14
D) 6-8

Answer: A) 0-6
Explanation: A pH range of 0-6 indicates an acidic solution, with lower values representing stronger acids. A neutral solution has a pH of 7, while basic solutions have a pH of 8-14.

---

46. Role of Buffers

What is the primary function of buffers in biological systems?
A) To increase the temperature of a solution
B) To maintain stable pH levels
C) To dissolve nutrients
D) To transport waste products

Answer: B) To maintain stable pH levels
Explanation: Buffers help resist changes in pH by neutralizing acids and bases, which is crucial for maintaining homeostasis in biological systems.

---

47. Effects of pH Imbalances

How can extreme pH levels affect enzyme function?
A) They have no effect on enzyme function.
B) They can enhance enzyme activity.
C) They can denature enzymes, disrupting their function.
D) They can increase substrate concentration.

Answer: C) They can denature enzymes, disrupting their function.
Explanation: Extreme pH levels can alter the shape of enzymes, leading to denaturation, which prevents them from binding to substrates and catalyzing reactions effectively.

---

48. Bicarbonate Buffer System

Which of the following best describes the role of the bicarbonate buffer system in the blood?
A) It increases acidity in the blood.
B) It helps maintain a stable pH in the blood.
C) It transports oxygen in the blood.
D) It breaks down glucose.

Answer: B) It helps maintain a stable pH in the blood.
Explanation: The bicarbonate buffer system helps regulate blood pH by neutralizing excess acids or bases, ensuring that the pH remains within a narrow range necessary for proper physiological function.

---

49. Water's Role in Temperature Regulation

How does water's high specific heat contribute to temperature regulation in living organisms?
A) It allows organisms to cool down quickly.
B) It prevents temperature fluctuations.
C) It increases metabolic rates.
D) It decreases the need for energy.

Answer: B) It prevents temperature fluctuations.
Explanation: Water's high specific heat allows it to absorb and release heat without significant temperature changes, helping to stabilize internal temperatures in organisms.

---

50. Capillary Action in Plants

What is the significance of capillary action in plants?
A) It helps in photosynthesis.
B) It allows for the transport of water and nutrients from roots to leaves.
C) It prevents water loss.
D) It increases soil temperature.

Answer: B) It allows for the transport of water and nutrients from roots to leaves.
Explanation: Capillary action, driven by adhesion and cohesion, enables water to move upward through the plant's xylem, facilitating nutrient transport and maintaining hydration.

---

51. pH and Cellular Processes

What can happen to cellular processes if the pH of a cell's environment becomes too acidic?
A) Cellular processes will speed up.
B) Enzyme activity may be inhibited or stopped.
C) The cell will become more efficient.
D) The cell will absorb more nutrients.

Answer: B) Enzyme activity may be inhibited or stopped.
Explanation: An excessively acidic environment can disrupt enzyme function, leading to decreased metabolic activity and potentially harming the cell.

---

52. Water's Role in Chemical Reactions

Why is water often referred to as a reactant in biochemical reactions?
A) It is always produced in reactions.
B) It can participate in hydrolysis and dehydration synthesis reactions.
C) It does not affect reaction rates.
D) It is a waste product.

Answer: B) It can participate in hydrolysis and dehydration synthesis reactions.
Explanation: Water is involved in many biochemical reactions, including hydrolysis (breaking down molecules) and dehydration synthesis (building larger molecules), making it a crucial reactant.

---

53. Water's Density and Ice Formation

What is the significance of water being less dense as a solid (ice) than as a liquid?
A) It allows ice to sink in water.
B) It prevents aquatic ecosystems from freezing solid.
C) It increases the temperature of water.
D) It decreases the solubility of gases in water.

Answer: B) It prevents aquatic ecosystems from freezing solid.
Explanation: Because ice is less dense than liquid water, it floats, insulating the water below and preventing entire bodies of water from freezing solid, which is vital for aquatic life.

---

54. Role of Water in Metabolism

How does water contribute to metabolic processes in living organisms?
A) It provides energy for reactions.
B) It acts as a solvent for biochemical reactions.
C) It increases the temperature of reactions.
D) It decreases the rate of reactions.

Answer: B) It acts as a solvent for biochemical reactions.
Explanation: Water serves as a solvent in which many biochemical reactions occur, facilitating the transport of nutrients and waste products in and out of cells.

---

55. Buffer Systems in the Body

Which buffer system is primarily responsible for maintaining pH balance in the human blood?
A) Phosphate buffer system
B) Bicarbonate buffer system
C) Protein buffer system
D) Sulfate buffer system

Answer: B) Bicarbonate buffer system
Explanation: The bicarbonate buffer system is the main buffer system in human blood, helping to maintain a stable pH by neutralizing excess acids or bases.

---

56. Water's Role in Homeostasis

How does water contribute to homeostasis in living organisms?
A) By providing energy for cellular processes.
B) By regulating temperature and pH levels.
C) By increasing metabolic rates.
D) By transporting oxygen.

Answer: B) By regulating temperature and pH levels.
Explanation: Water helps maintain homeostasis by regulating temperature through its high specific heat and by acting as a solvent and buffer to stabilize pH levels in biological systems.

---

57. Effects of Extreme pH Levels

What effect can extreme pH levels have on cellular enzymes?
A) They can enhance enzyme activity.
B) They can cause enzymes to denature and lose function.
C) They have no effect on enzyme activity.
D) They can increase substrate concentration.

Answer: B) They can cause enzymes to denature and lose function.
Explanation: Extreme pH levels can disrupt the ionic and hydrogen bonds that maintain the enzyme's structure, leading to denaturation and loss of function.

---

58. Water's Role in Nutrient Transport

Why is water considered essential for nutrient transport in living organisms?
A) It is a source of energy.
B) It can dissolve and carry various substances.
C) It increases the temperature of the body.
D) It is a structural component of cells.

Answer: B) It can dissolve and carry various substances.
Explanation: Water's ability to dissolve polar and ionic substances allows it to transport nutrients, gases, and waste products throughout organisms, making it vital for life.

---

59. Capillary Action in the Human Body

What role does capillary action play in the human body?
A) It helps in the digestion of food.
B) It aids in the movement of blood through capillaries.
C) It prevents dehydration.
D) It increases body temperature.

Answer: B) It aids in the movement of blood through capillaries.
Explanation: Capillary action helps facilitate the movement of blood through the small blood vessels (capillaries), allowing for efficient nutrient and gas exchange.

---

60. Water's Role in Hydrolysis

In a hydrolysis reaction, what role does water play?
A) It is a product of the reaction.
B) It provides energy for the reaction.
C) It breaks down larger molecules into smaller ones.
D) It increases the temperature of the reaction.

Answer: C) It breaks down larger molecules into smaller ones.
Explanation: In hydrolysis, water is used to break chemical bonds in larger molecules, resulting in the formation of smaller molecules, such as breaking down polysaccharides into monosaccharides.

Chapter 3: Cell Biology

1. Elements Essential for Life

A biologist is studying the essential elements for life. Which of the following elements is NOT one of the six key elements that make up most biological molecules?
A) Carbon
B) Hydrogen
C) Calcium
D) Nitrogen

Answer: C) Calcium
Explanation: The six key elements essential for life are carbon (C), hydrogen (H), oxygen (O), nitrogen (N), phosphorus (P), and sulfur (S). Calcium is important for certain biological functions but is not one of the six key elements.

---

2. Role of Carbon in Biological Molecules

Why is carbon considered the backbone of biological molecules?
A) It can form only one bond.
B) It can form four covalent bonds.
C) It is the most abundant element in the universe.
D) It is a trace element in living organisms.

Answer: B) It can form four covalent bonds.
Explanation: Carbon's ability to form four covalent bonds allows it to create a wide variety of complex and diverse organic molecules, making it essential for life.

---

3. Structural Diversity in Macromolecules

Which of the following macromolecules is primarily responsible for energy storage in plants?
A) Proteins
B) Nucleic acids
C) Carbohydrates
D) Lipids

Answer: C) Carbohydrates
Explanation: Carbohydrates, specifically polysaccharides like starch, are the primary energy storage molecules in plants. They can be broken down into glucose when energy is needed.

---

4. Importance of Trace Elements

A patient is diagnosed with an iodine deficiency. Which of the following functions is most likely affected by this deficiency?
A) Oxygen transport in blood
B) Thyroid hormone production
C) Muscle contraction
D) Bone density

Answer: B) Thyroid hormone production
Explanation: Iodine is essential for the synthesis of thyroid hormones, which regulate metabolism. A deficiency can lead to thyroid-related health issues.

---

5. Lipids and Membrane Structure

Which type of lipid is primarily responsible for forming the cell membrane?
A) Triglycerides
B) Phospholipids
C) Steroids
D) Waxes

Answer: B) Phospholipids
Explanation: Phospholipids are the main components of cell membranes, forming a bilayer that provides structure and regulates the movement of substances in and out of the cell.

---

6. Protein Structure and Function

What type of bond forms between amino acids during protein synthesis?
A) Ionic bond
B) Hydrogen bond
C) Peptide bond
D) Covalent bond

Answer: C) Peptide bond
Explanation: Peptide bonds are covalent bonds that link amino acids together to form proteins. This bond is formed during the process of translation in protein synthesis.

---

7. Nucleic Acids and Genetic Information

Which of the following statements about DNA is true?
A) DNA is single-stranded.
B) DNA contains uracil instead of thymine.
C) DNA stores genetic information.
D) DNA is composed of amino acids.

Answer: C) DNA stores genetic information.
Explanation: DNA (deoxyribonucleic acid) is a double-stranded molecule that contains the genetic instructions for the development and functioning of living organisms.

---

8. Enzymes as Biological Catalysts

What is the primary function of enzymes in biochemical reactions?
A) To increase the temperature of the reaction
B) To lower the activation energy
C) To change the pH of the reaction
D) To provide energy for the reaction

Answer: B) To lower the activation energy
Explanation: Enzymes act as biological catalysts by lowering the activation energy required for biochemical reactions, thereby increasing the reaction rate.

---

9. Lock-and-Key Model of Enzyme Action

In the lock-and-key model of enzyme action, what does the "lock" represent?
A) The enzyme
B) The substrate
C) The active site
D) The product

Answer: C) The active site
Explanation: In the lock-and-key model, the "lock" represents the active site of the enzyme, which is specifically shaped to fit a particular substrate, allowing the reaction to occur.

---

10. Factors Affecting Enzyme Activity

How does an increase in temperature generally affect enzyme activity?
A) It always increases activity.
B) It has no effect.
C) It can increase activity until a certain point, then denature the enzyme.
D) It decreases activity.

Answer: C) It can increase activity until a certain point, then denature the enzyme.
Explanation: Increasing temperature can enhance enzyme activity up to an optimal point. Beyond this point, the enzyme may denature, losing its functional shape and activity.

---

11. pH and Enzyme Activity

Which of the following enzymes works best in a highly acidic environment, such as the stomach?
A) Amylase
B) Pepsin
C) Trypsin
D) DNA polymerase

Answer: B) Pepsin
Explanation: Pepsin is an enzyme that functions optimally in the acidic environment of the stomach, where it helps digest proteins.

---

12. Substrate Concentration and Reaction Speed

What happens to the rate of an enzyme-catalyzed reaction as substrate concentration increases?
A) It decreases.
B) It remains constant.
C) It increases until a saturation point is reached.
D) It becomes negative.

Answer: C) It increases until a saturation point is reached.
Explanation: As substrate concentration increases, the reaction rate increases until all active sites of the enzyme are occupied (saturation point), at which point the rate levels off.

---

13. Competitive Inhibition

In competitive inhibition, how does an inhibitor affect enzyme activity?
A) It binds to the active site, preventing substrate binding.
B) It changes the enzyme's shape.
C) It increases the enzyme's activity.
D) It binds to the substrate.

Answer: A) It binds to the active site, preventing substrate binding.
Explanation: Competitive inhibitors resemble the substrate and compete for binding to the active site of the enzyme, thereby reducing the enzyme's activity.

---

14. Non-Competitive Inhibition

What is the effect of a non-competitive inhibitor on an enzyme?
A) It binds to the active site.
B) It increases the reaction rate.
C) It binds to a site other than the active site, altering enzyme function.
D) It has no effect on the enzyme.

Answer: C) It binds to a site other than the active site, altering enzyme function.
Explanation: Non-competitive inhibitors bind to an allosteric site on the enzyme, changing its shape and reducing its activity regardless of substrate concentration.

---

15. Coenzymes and Cofactors

What role do coenzymes play in enzyme activity?
A) They are substrates for the enzyme.
B) They increase the activation energy.
C) They assist in enzyme function by participating in the reaction.
D) They inhibit enzyme activity.

Answer: C) They assist in enzyme function by participating in the reaction.
Explanation: Coenzymes are organic molecules that assist enzymes by providing additional chemical groups or facilitating the transfer of electrons during biochemical reactions.

---

16. Importance of Iron in Blood

Why is iron considered a trace element essential for life?
A) It is a major component of carbohydrates.
B) It is necessary for the formation of hemoglobin in red blood cells.
C) It helps in the synthesis of DNA.
D) It is a primary energy source for cells.

Answer: B) It is necessary for the formation of hemoglobin in red blood cells.
Explanation: Iron is a crucial component of hemoglobin, the protein in red blood cells that carries oxygen throughout the body.

---

17. Role of Phosphorus in Biological Molecules

What is the primary role of phosphorus in living organisms?
A) Energy storage
B) Structural component of proteins
C) Component of nucleic acids and ATP
D) Oxygen transport

Answer: C) Component of nucleic acids and ATP
Explanation: Phosphorus is a key component of nucleic acids (DNA and RNA) and ATP (adenosine triphosphate), which is essential for energy transfer in cells.

---

18. Hydrocarbons and Functional Groups

Which of the following statements about hydrocarbons is true?
A) They contain only carbon and oxygen.
B) They are always polar molecules.
C) They can form long chains or rings.
D) They are not found in biological molecules.

Answer: C) They can form long chains or rings.
Explanation: Hydrocarbons are organic molecules consisting solely of carbon and hydrogen, and they can form long chains or ring structures, contributing to the diversity of organic compounds.

---

19. Carbohydrates and Energy Storage

Which carbohydrate is primarily used for energy storage in animals?
A) Cellulose
B) Starch
C) Glycogen
D) Chitin

Answer: C) Glycogen
Explanation: Glycogen is the primary energy storage carbohydrate in animals, stored mainly in the liver and muscles, and can be broken down into glucose when energy is needed.

---

20. Role of Lipids in Membrane Structure

What is the primary function of phospholipids in biological membranes?
A) Energy storage
B) Structural support
C) Forming a bilayer that acts as a barrier
D) Catalyzing biochemical reactions

Answer: C) Forming a bilayer that acts as a barrier
Explanation: Phospholipids form a bilayer in cell membranes, providing a barrier that separates the interior of the cell from the external environment while allowing selective permeability.

---

21. Protein Folding and Function

What determines the specific three-dimensional shape of a protein?
A) The type of amino acids present
B) The temperature of the environment
C) The pH of the solution
D) The sequence of amino acids

Answer: D) The sequence of amino acids
Explanation: The specific sequence of amino acids in a protein determines its unique three-dimensional shape, which is crucial for its function.

---

22. Enzyme Specificity

What is meant by enzyme specificity?
A) Enzymes can catalyze any reaction.
B) Enzymes are only active at high temperatures.
C) Enzymes only catalyze specific reactions with particular substrates.
D) Enzymes can work with multiple substrates equally well.

Answer: C) Enzymes only catalyze specific reactions with particular substrates.
Explanation: Enzyme specificity refers to the ability of an enzyme to select and catalyze a specific substrate, ensuring that biochemical reactions occur efficiently and accurately.

---

23. Denaturation of Enzymes

What is the effect of denaturation on an enzyme?
A) It increases the enzyme's activity.
B) It changes the enzyme's shape, rendering it inactive.
C) It has no effect on the enzyme's function.
D) It enhances the enzyme's specificity.

Answer: B) It changes the enzyme's shape, rendering it inactive.
Explanation: Denaturation alters the three-dimensional structure of an enzyme, which can disrupt its active site and prevent it from catalyzing reactions effectively.

---

24. Role of Catalase

What is the primary function of the enzyme catalase in living organisms?
A) To synthesize proteins
B) To break down hydrogen peroxide
C) To facilitate DNA replication
D) To transport oxygen in the blood

Answer: B) To break down hydrogen peroxide
Explanation: Catalase is an enzyme that catalyzes the decomposition of hydrogen peroxide into water and oxygen, protecting cells from oxidative damage.

---

25. Effects of pH on Enzyme Activity

Which of the following statements is true regarding the effect of pH on enzyme activity?
A) All enzymes work best at a neutral pH of 7.
B) Enzymes have an optimal pH range where they function best.
C) Increasing pH always increases enzyme activity.
D) pH has no effect on enzyme activity.

Answer: B) Enzymes have an optimal pH range where they function best.
Explanation: Each enzyme has an optimal pH range that allows it to function most effectively. Deviations from this range can lead to decreased activity or denaturation.

---

26. Substrate Concentration and Enzyme Activity

What happens to the rate of an enzyme-catalyzed reaction when substrate concentration is increased beyond a certain point?
A) The rate continues to increase indefinitely.
B) The rate decreases.
C) The rate levels off and reaches a maximum.
D) The rate becomes negative.

Answer: C) The rate levels off and reaches a maximum.
Explanation: As substrate concentration increases, the reaction rate increases until all active sites of the enzyme are occupied, at which point the rate levels off and reaches a maximum (saturation).

---

27. Role of Functional Groups

Which of the following functional groups is known for making molecules more polar and increasing their solubility in water?
A) Hydroxyl group
B) Methyl group
C) Carbonyl group
D) Phosphate group

Answer: A) Hydroxyl group
Explanation: The hydroxyl group (-OH) is polar and increases the solubility of organic molecules in water, making them more hydrophilic.

---

28. Biological Macromolecules

Which of the following macromolecules is primarily responsible for storing genetic information?
A) Proteins
B) Carbohydrates
C) Nucleic acids
D) Lipids

Answer: C) Nucleic acids
Explanation: Nucleic acids, such as DNA and RNA, are responsible for storing and transmitting genetic information in living organisms.

---

29. Role of Amino Acids

What is the basic building block of proteins?
A) Nucleotides
B) Fatty acids
C) Monosaccharides
D) Amino acids

Answer: D) Amino acids
Explanation: Amino acids are the fundamental building blocks of proteins, linked together by peptide bonds to form polypeptides and ultimately functional proteins.

---

30. Enzyme-Substrate Complex

What is formed when an enzyme binds to its substrate?
A) Enzyme-inhibitor complex
B) Enzyme-product complex
C) Enzyme-substrate complex
D) Enzyme-cofactor complex

Answer: C) Enzyme-substrate complex
Explanation: The enzyme-substrate complex is formed when an enzyme binds to its specific substrate, facilitating the chemical reaction that converts the substrate into products.

---

31. Role of Lipids in Energy Storage

Which type of lipid is primarily used for long-term energy storage in animals?
A) Phospholipids
B) Triglycerides
C) Steroids
D) Waxes

Answer: B) Triglycerides
Explanation: Triglycerides are the main form of stored energy in animals, consisting of three fatty acids linked to a glycerol molecule, providing a dense energy source.

---

32. Enzyme Regulation

What is the role of allosteric sites in enzyme regulation?
A) They are the active sites where substrates bind.
B) They allow for competitive inhibition.
C) They can bind regulatory molecules that change enzyme activity.
D) They are sites for substrate binding only.

Answer: C) They can bind regulatory molecules that change enzyme activity.
Explanation: Allosteric sites are locations on an enzyme where regulatory molecules can bind, leading to changes in enzyme shape and activity, thus regulating the enzyme's function.

---

33. Importance of Carbon in Life

Why is carbon considered the most versatile element in biological molecules?
A) It can form only single bonds.
B) It can form four covalent bonds with various elements.
C) It is the most abundant element in the universe.
D) It is a trace element in living organisms.

Answer: B) It can form four covalent bonds with various elements.
Explanation: Carbon's ability to form four covalent bonds allows it to create a diverse array of organic molecules, making it essential for life.

---

34. Role of Sulfur in Proteins

What role does sulfur play in the structure of proteins?
A) It forms hydrogen bonds between amino acids.
B) It contributes to the formation of disulfide bridges.
C) It acts as a cofactor for enzymes.
D) It is a primary energy source.

Answer: B) It contributes to the formation of disulfide bridges.
Explanation: Sulfur atoms in cysteine residues can form disulfide bridges, which help stabilize the three-dimensional structure of proteins.

---

35. Enzyme Activity and Temperature

What effect does a decrease in temperature generally have on enzyme activity?
A) It increases enzyme activity.
B) It has no effect.
C) It decreases enzyme activity.
D) It denatures the enzyme.

Answer: C) It decreases enzyme activity.
Explanation: Lower temperatures typically reduce the kinetic energy of molecules, leading to fewer collisions between enzymes and substrates, thus decreasing the rate of reaction.

---

36. Role of DNA Polymerase

What is the primary function of the enzyme DNA polymerase?
A) To synthesize RNA from DNA
B) To replicate DNA during cell division
C) To break down DNA
D) To repair damaged DNA

Answer: B) To replicate DNA during cell division.
Explanation: DNA polymerase is essential for synthesizing new DNA strands during replication, ensuring that genetic information is accurately passed on to daughter cells.

---

37. Function of Carbohydrates

Which of the following is a primary function of carbohydrates in living organisms?
A) Energy storage and supply
B) Genetic information storage
C) Catalyzing biochemical reactions
D) Structural support in cell membranes

Answer: A) Energy storage and supply
Explanation: Carbohydrates serve as a primary source of energy for living organisms, with glucose being a key energy molecule.

---

38. Role of Functional Groups in Organic Molecules

Which functional group is associated with alcohols?
A) Carbonyl
B) Hydroxyl
C) Amino
D) Carboxyl

Answer: B) Hydroxyl
Explanation: The hydroxyl group (-OH) is characteristic of alcohols and contributes to their polar nature, making them soluble in water.

---

39. Enzyme Inhibition

What is the effect of a competitive inhibitor on an enzyme-catalyzed reaction?
A) It increases the reaction rate.
B) It decreases the reaction rate by binding to the active site.
C) It has no effect on the reaction rate.
D) It changes the enzyme's shape permanently.

Answer: B) It decreases the reaction rate by binding to the active site.
Explanation: Competitive inhibitors compete with the substrate for binding to the active site of the enzyme, reducing the overall rate of the reaction.

---

40. Importance of Water in Biochemical Reactions

Why is water considered a vital component in biochemical reactions?
A) It is a source of energy.
B) It acts as a solvent and participates in reactions.
C) It is a structural component of proteins.
D) It provides nutrients to cells.

Answer: B) It acts as a solvent and participates in reactions.
Explanation: Water is essential for life because it serves as a solvent for many biochemical reactions and can participate directly in chemical reactions, facilitating metabolic processes.

---

41. Properties of Water: Cohesion

A scientist is studying the surface tension of water. Which property of water is primarily responsible for this phenomenon?
A) Adhesion
B) High specific heat
C) Cohesion
D) Universal solvent

Answer: C) Cohesion
Explanation: Cohesion refers to the attraction between water molecules, which leads to surface tension. This property allows water to form droplets and enables small objects to float on its surface.

---

42. Properties of Water: Adhesion

During an experiment, a student observes that water climbs up a thin glass tube. What property of water is responsible for this behavior?
A) Cohesion
B) High specific heat
C) Adhesion
D) Density

Answer: C) Adhesion
Explanation: Adhesion is the property that allows water molecules to stick to other surfaces, such as the glass of the tube. This results in capillary action, which is essential for the movement of water in plants.

---

43. High Specific Heat of Water

Why is the high specific heat of water important for living organisms?
A) It allows water to evaporate quickly.
B) It helps maintain stable temperatures in the environment.
C) It increases the density of water.
D) It makes water a universal solvent.

Answer: B) It helps maintain stable temperatures in the environment.
Explanation: Water's high specific heat means it can absorb a lot of heat without a significant change in temperature, which helps stabilize temperatures in organisms and their environments.

---

44. Water as a Universal Solvent

Which of the following statements best describes why water is known as the "universal solvent"?
A) It can dissolve all substances.
B) It can dissolve polar and ionic substances.
C) It can only dissolve gases.
D) It does not dissolve any substances.

Answer: B) It can dissolve polar and ionic substances.
Explanation: Water's polarity allows it to interact with and dissolve many polar and ionic compounds, making it an effective solvent for transporting nutrients and waste in biological systems.

---

45. pH Scale

What is the pH range of a solution that is considered acidic?
A) 0-6
B) 7
C) 8-14
D) 6-8

Answer: A) 0-6
Explanation: A pH range of 0-6 indicates an acidic solution, with lower values representing stronger acids. A neutral solution has a pH of 7, while basic solutions have a pH of 8-14.

---

46. Role of Buffers

What is the primary function of buffers in biological systems?
A) To increase the temperature of a solution
B) To maintain stable pH levels
C) To dissolve nutrients
D) To transport waste products

Answer: B) To maintain stable pH levels
Explanation: Buffers help resist changes in pH by neutralizing acids and bases, which is crucial for maintaining homeostasis in biological systems.

---

47. Effects of pH Imbalances

How can extreme pH levels affect enzyme function?
A) They have no effect on enzyme function.
B) They can enhance enzyme activity.
C) They can denature enzymes, disrupting their function.
D) They can increase substrate concentration.

Answer: C) They can denature enzymes, disrupting their function.
Explanation: Extreme pH levels can alter the shape of enzymes, leading to denaturation, which prevents them from binding to substrates and catalyzing reactions effectively.

---

48. Bicarbonate Buffer System

Which of the following best describes the role of the bicarbonate buffer system in the blood?
A) It increases acidity in the blood.
B) It helps maintain a stable pH in the blood.
C) It transports oxygen in the blood.
D) It breaks down glucose.

Answer: B) It helps maintain a stable pH in the blood.
Explanation: The bicarbonate buffer system helps regulate blood pH by neutralizing excess acids or bases, ensuring that the pH remains within a narrow range necessary for proper physiological function.

---

49. Water's Role in Temperature Regulation

How does water's high specific heat contribute to temperature regulation in living organisms?
A) It allows organisms to cool down quickly.
B) It prevents temperature fluctuations.
C) It increases metabolic rates.
D) It decreases the need for energy.

Answer: B) It prevents temperature fluctuations.
Explanation: Water's high specific heat allows it to absorb and release heat without significant temperature changes, helping to stabilize internal temperatures in organisms.

---

50. Capillary Action in Plants

What is the significance of capillary action in plants?
A) It helps in photosynthesis.
B) It allows for the transport of water and nutrients from roots to leaves.
C) It prevents water loss.
D) It increases soil temperature.

Answer: B) It allows for the transport of water and nutrients from roots to leaves.
Explanation: Capillary action, driven by adhesion and cohesion, enables water to move upward through the plant's xylem, facilitating nutrient transport and maintaining hydration.

---

51. pH and Cellular Processes

What can happen to cellular processes if the pH of a cell's environment becomes too acidic?
A) Cellular processes will speed up.
B) Enzyme activity may be inhibited or stopped.
C) The cell will become more efficient.
D) The cell will absorb more nutrients.

Answer: B) Enzyme activity may be inhibited or stopped.
Explanation: An excessively acidic environment can disrupt enzyme function, leading to decreased metabolic activity and potentially harming the cell.

---

52. Water's Role in Chemical Reactions

Why is water often referred to as a reactant in biochemical reactions?
A) It is always produced in reactions.
B) It can participate in hydrolysis and dehydration synthesis reactions.
C) It does not affect reaction rates.
D) It is a waste product.

Answer: B) It can participate in hydrolysis and dehydration synthesis reactions.
Explanation: Water is involved in many biochemical reactions, including hydrolysis (breaking down molecules) and dehydration synthesis (building larger molecules), making it a crucial reactant.

---

53. Water's Density and Ice Formation

What is the significance of water being less dense as a solid (ice) than as a liquid?
A) It allows ice to sink in water.
B) It prevents aquatic ecosystems from freezing solid.
C) It increases the temperature of water.
D) It decreases the solubility of gases in water.

Answer: B) It prevents aquatic ecosystems from freezing solid.
Explanation: Because ice is less dense than liquid water, it floats, insulating the water below and preventing entire bodies of water from freezing solid, which is vital for aquatic life.

---

54. Role of Water in Metabolism

How does water contribute to metabolic processes in living organisms?
A) It provides energy for reactions.
B) It acts as a solvent for biochemical reactions.
C) It increases the temperature of reactions.
D) It decreases the rate of reactions.

Answer: B) It acts as a solvent for biochemical reactions.
Explanation: Water serves as a solvent in which many biochemical reactions occur, facilitating the transport of nutrients and waste products in and out of cells.

---

55. Buffer Systems in the Body

Which buffer system is primarily responsible for maintaining pH balance in the human blood?
A) Phosphate buffer system
B) Bicarbonate buffer system
C) Protein buffer system
D) Sulfate buffer system

Answer: B) Bicarbonate buffer system
Explanation: The bicarbonate buffer system is the main buffer system in human blood, helping to maintain a stable pH by neutralizing excess acids or bases.

---

56. Water's Role in Homeostasis

How does water contribute to homeostasis in living organisms?
A) By providing energy for cellular processes.
B) By regulating temperature and pH levels.
C) By increasing metabolic rates.
D) By transporting oxygen.

Answer: B) By regulating temperature and pH levels.
Explanation: Water helps maintain homeostasis by regulating temperature through its high specific heat and by acting as a solvent and buffer to stabilize pH levels in biological systems.

---

57. Effects of Extreme pH Levels

What effect can extreme pH levels have on cellular enzymes?
A) They can enhance enzyme activity.
B) They can cause enzymes to denature and lose function.
C) They have no effect on enzyme activity.
D) They can increase substrate concentration.

Answer: B) They can cause enzymes to denature and lose function.
Explanation: Extreme pH levels can disrupt the ionic and hydrogen bonds that maintain the enzyme's structure, leading to denaturation and loss of function.

---

58. Water's Role in Nutrient Transport

Why is water considered essential for nutrient transport in living organisms?
A) It is a source of energy.
B) It can dissolve and carry various substances.
C) It increases the temperature of the body.
D) It is a structural component of cells.

Answer: B) It can dissolve and carry various substances.
Explanation: Water's ability to dissolve polar and ionic substances allows it to transport nutrients, gases, and waste products throughout organisms, making it vital for life.

---

59. Capillary Action in the Human Body

What role does capillary action play in the human body?
A) It helps in the digestion of food.
B) It aids in the movement of blood through capillaries.
C) It prevents dehydration.
D) It increases body temperature.

Answer: B) It aids in the movement of blood through capillaries.
Explanation: Capillary action helps facilitate the movement of blood through the small blood vessels (capillaries), allowing for efficient nutrient and gas exchange.

---

60. Water's Role in Hydrolysis

In a hydrolysis reaction, what role does water play?
A) It is a product of the reaction.
B) It provides energy for the reaction.
C) It breaks down larger molecules into smaller ones.
D) It increases the temperature of the reaction.

Answer: C) It breaks down larger molecules into smaller ones.
Explanation: In hydrolysis, water is used to break chemical bonds in larger molecules, resulting in the formation of smaller molecules, such as breaking down polysaccharides into monosaccharides.

Here are 40 complex scenarios and questions for the Florida Biology EOC Test Prep exam, focusing on cellular energy, photosynthesis, cellular respiration, and cell growth and reproduction. Each question is designed to align with the current format of the Florida Biology EOC exam, and detailed explanations are provided after each question. The numbering starts from 41 and goes to 80.

41. Photosynthesis: Light-Dependent Reactions

A plant is exposed to bright sunlight and has access to water. Which of the following products is generated during the light-dependent reactions of photosynthesis?
A) Glucose
B) Oxygen
C) Carbon dioxide
D) ATP and NADPH

Answer: B) Oxygen
Explanation: During the light-dependent reactions of photosynthesis, water is split, releasing oxygen as a byproduct, while ATP and NADPH are produced for use in the Calvin Cycle.

---

42. Photosynthesis: Calvin Cycle

In the Calvin Cycle, which of the following is used to produce glucose?
A) Oxygen and sunlight
B) ATP, NADPH, and carbon dioxide
C) Water and glucose
D) Light energy and oxygen

Answer: B) ATP, NADPH, and carbon dioxide
Explanation: The Calvin Cycle uses ATP and NADPH produced in the light-dependent reactions, along with carbon dioxide, to synthesize glucose.

---

43. Factors Affecting Photosynthesis

A researcher is studying the effects of light intensity on photosynthesis. What would likely happen to the rate of photosynthesis as light intensity increases, up to a certain point?

A) It decreases.
B) It remains constant.
C) It increases.
D) It stops completely.

Answer: C) It increases.
Explanation: As light intensity increases, the rate of photosynthesis typically increases until it reaches a saturation point, beyond which other factors may limit the process.

---

44. Cellular Respiration: Glycolysis

During glycolysis, which of the following occurs?
A) Glucose is broken down into pyruvate.
B) Oxygen is used to produce ATP.
C) Carbon dioxide is released.
D) Lactic acid is produced.

Answer: A) Glucose is broken down into pyruvate.
Explanation: Glycolysis is the first step of cellular respiration, where glucose is converted into pyruvate, producing a net gain of 2 ATP molecules.

---

45. Krebs Cycle Function

What is the primary purpose of the Krebs Cycle in cellular respiration?
A) To produce glucose
B) To generate electron carriers
C) To break down pyruvate
D) To produce ATP directly

Answer: B) To generate electron carriers
Explanation: The Krebs Cycle produces electron carriers (NADH and $FADH_2$) that are used in the electron transport chain to generate ATP.

---

46. Electron Transport Chain

What is the final electron acceptor in the electron transport chain during aerobic respiration?
A) Carbon dioxide
B) Glucose
C) Oxygen
D) NADH

Answer: C) Oxygen
Explanation: Oxygen serves as the final electron acceptor in the electron transport chain, allowing for the production of water and facilitating the generation of ATP.

---

47. Anaerobic Respiration: Lactic Acid Fermentation

In which type of cells does lactic acid fermentation primarily occur?
A) Plant cells
B) Yeast cells
C) Muscle cells
D) Bacterial cells

Answer: C) Muscle cells
Explanation: Lactic acid fermentation occurs in muscle cells during anaerobic conditions, producing lactic acid and a small amount of ATP.

48. Alcoholic Fermentation

What is produced during alcoholic fermentation?
A) Lactic acid and ATP
B) Ethanol and carbon dioxide
C) Glucose and oxygen
D) Pyruvate and NADH

Answer: B) Ethanol and carbon dioxide
Explanation: Alcoholic fermentation, primarily carried out by yeast, produces ethanol and carbon dioxide as byproducts, along with a small amount of ATP.

---

49. Relationship Between Photosynthesis and Cellular Respiration

How are photosynthesis and cellular respiration related?
A) They are completely independent processes.
B) The products of photosynthesis are the reactants of cellular respiration.
C) They occur in the same organelle.
D) They both produce glucose.

Answer: B) The products of photosynthesis are the reactants of cellular respiration.
Explanation: Photosynthesis produces glucose and oxygen, which are used in cellular respiration to generate ATP, while the byproducts of respiration (carbon dioxide and water) are used in photosynthesis.

---

50. The Cell Cycle: Interphase

During which phase of the cell cycle does DNA replication occur?
A) Mitosis
B) Cytokinesis
C) Interphase
D) Prophase

Answer: C) Interphase
Explanation: Interphase is the phase of the cell cycle where the cell grows, replicates its DNA, and prepares for division.

---

51. Mitosis: Prophase

What occurs during prophase of mitosis?
A) Chromosomes align at the cell's equator.
B) Sister chromatids separate.
C) Chromosomes condense and spindle fibers form.
D) The cytoplasm divides.

Answer: C) Chromosomes condense and spindle fibers form.
Explanation: During prophase, chromatin condenses into visible chromosomes, and the spindle apparatus begins to form, preparing for chromosome alignment.

---

52. Mitosis: Metaphase

What is the key event that occurs during metaphase?
A) Chromosomes are replicated.
B) Chromosomes align at the cell's equator.

C) Nuclear membranes reform.
D) Cytoplasm divides.

Answer: B) Chromosomes align at the cell's equator.
Explanation: In metaphase, chromosomes line up along the metaphase plate (equator) of the cell, preparing for separation.

---

53. Mitosis: Anaphase

What happens during anaphase of mitosis?
A) Chromosomes condense.
B) Sister chromatids separate and move to opposite poles.
C) The nuclear envelope breaks down.
D) The cytoplasm divides.

Answer: B) Sister chromatids separate and move to opposite poles.
Explanation: Anaphase is characterized by the separation of sister chromatids, which are pulled toward opposite ends of the cell by the spindle fibers.

---

54. Mitosis: Telophase

What occurs during telophase of mitosis?
A) Chromosomes condense.
B) Sister chromatids align at the equator.
C) Nuclear membranes reform and chromosomes uncoil.
D) The cytoplasm divides.

Answer: C) Nuclear membranes reform and chromosomes uncoil.
Explanation: During telophase, the nuclear envelope reforms around each set of chromosomes, which begin to uncoil back into chromatin.

---

55. Cytokinesis

What is the process of cytokinesis?
A) Division of the nucleus
B) Division of the cytoplasm
C) DNA replication
D) Chromosome alignment

Answer: B) Division of the cytoplasm
Explanation: Cytokinesis is the process that follows mitosis, resulting in the division of the cytoplasm and the formation of two distinct daughter cells.

---

56. Meiosis: Meiosis I

What is the primary outcome of Meiosis I?
A) Two diploid cells are formed.
B) Four haploid cells are formed.
C) Homologous chromosomes separate.
D) Sister chromatids separate.

Answer: C) Homologous chromosomes separate.
Explanation: Meiosis I results in the separation of homologous chromosomes, leading to two haploid cells, each containing one chromosome from each homologous pair.

57. Meiosis: Crossing Over

What is the significance of crossing over during Prophase I of meiosis?
A) It increases the number of chromosomes.
B) It produces identical daughter cells.
C) It increases genetic diversity.
D) It prevents genetic variation.

Answer: C) It increases genetic diversity.
Explanation: Crossing over allows for the exchange of genetic material between homologous chromosomes, resulting in new combinations of alleles and increased genetic diversity in gametes.

---

58. Meiosis II

What occurs during Meiosis II?
A) Homologous chromosomes separate.
B) Sister chromatids separate.
C) DNA is replicated.
D) Cytokinesis occurs only once.

Answer: B) Sister chromatids separate.
Explanation: Meiosis II is similar to mitosis, where sister chromatids are separated, resulting in four haploid cells from the two haploid cells produced in Meiosis I.

---

59. Differences Between Mitosis and Meiosis

Which of the following statements accurately describes a difference between mitosis and meiosis?
A) Mitosis produces four cells, while meiosis produces two cells.
B) Mitosis is for growth and repair, while meiosis is for reproduction.
C) Mitosis involves two divisions, while meiosis involves one division.
D) Mitosis produces haploid cells, while meiosis produces diploid cells.

Answer: B) Mitosis is for growth and repair, while meiosis is for reproduction.
Explanation: Mitosis is a process of asexual reproduction and cellular repair, producing two identical diploid cells, while meiosis is a sexual reproduction process that produces four genetically diverse haploid gametes.

---

60. Importance of Cellular Respiration

Why is cellular respiration essential for living organisms?
A) It produces glucose.
B) It generates ATP, the energy currency of the cell.
C) It occurs only in plants.
D) It is a form of asexual reproduction.

Answer: B) It generates ATP, the energy currency of the cell.
Explanation: Cellular respiration is crucial because it converts biochemical energy from nutrients into ATP, which powers various cellular processes necessary for life.

Chapter 4: Genetics and Heredity

1. Mendel's Pea Plant Experiments

Gregor Mendel conducted experiments with pea plants to study inheritance. What trait did he observe in the F1 generation when he crossed purebred tall plants with purebred short plants?
A) All offspring were short.
B) All offspring were tall.
C) Offspring showed a blend of tall and short.
D) Offspring were of varying heights.

Answer: B) All offspring were tall.
Explanation: Mendel found that when he crossed purebred tall plants (TT) with purebred short plants (tt), all the F1 offspring were tall (Tt), demonstrating the dominance of the tall trait.

---

2. Law of Segregation

According to Mendel's Law of Segregation, what happens to alleles during gamete formation?
A) They blend together.
B) They remain paired.
C) They separate into different gametes.
D) They are lost.

Answer: C) They separate into different gametes.
Explanation: The Law of Segregation states that during gamete formation, the two alleles for a trait separate so that each gamete carries only one allele for each trait.

---

3. Law of Independent Assortment

What does Mendel's Law of Independent Assortment state?
A) Alleles for different traits are inherited together.
B) Alleles for different traits are inherited independently.
C) Dominant alleles mask recessive alleles.
D) Traits are blended in the offspring.

Answer: B) Alleles for different traits are inherited independently.
Explanation: The Law of Independent Assortment states that the inheritance of one trait does not affect the inheritance of another trait, allowing for independent combinations of traits.

---

4. Dominant vs. Recessive Alleles

In a genetic cross between a homozygous dominant (AA) and a homozygous recessive (aa) individual, what will be the genotype of the offspring?
A) AA
B) Aa
C) aa
D) Aaa

Answer: B) Aa
Explanation: The offspring from a cross between a homozygous dominant (AA) and a homozygous recessive (aa) will all be heterozygous (Aa).

---

5. Complete Dominance

In a complete dominance scenario, if a plant with a dominant allele for flower color (R) is crossed with a plant with a recessive allele (r), what will be the phenotype of the offspring?
A) All offspring will have the recessive phenotype.
B) All offspring will have the dominant phenotype.
C) Offspring will show a blend of phenotypes.
D) Offspring will have varying phenotypes.

Answer: B) All offspring will have the dominant phenotype.
Explanation: In complete dominance, the presence of at least one dominant allele (R) will result in the dominant phenotype being expressed in the offspring.

---

6. Incomplete Dominance

In a case of incomplete dominance, a red flower (RR) is crossed with a white flower (WW). What will be the phenotype of the offspring?
A) Red flowers
B) White flowers
C) Pink flowers
D) Red and white flowers

Answer: C) Pink flowers
Explanation: In incomplete dominance, the offspring exhibit a blending of traits, resulting in pink flowers (RW) when red and white flowers are crossed.

---

7. Codominance

Which of the following is an example of codominance?
A) A red flower crossed with a white flower producing pink flowers.
B) A black chicken crossed with a white chicken producing black and white speckled offspring.
C) A tall plant crossed with a short plant producing all tall offspring.
D) A yellow pea crossed with a green pea producing yellow peas.

Answer: B) A black chicken crossed with a white chicken producing black and white speckled offspring.
Explanation: In codominance, both alleles are expressed equally in the phenotype, as seen in the black and white speckled offspring.

---

8. Multiple Alleles

Which of the following traits is an example of multiple alleles?
A) Flower color in snapdragons
B) Blood type in humans
C) Height in pea plants
D) Seed shape in peas

Answer: B) Blood type in humans
Explanation: Human blood type is determined by multiple alleles (A, B, O), allowing for various combinations and phenotypes.

---

9. Sex-Linked Traits

Which of the following traits is an example of a sex-linked trait?
A) Eye color
B) Hemophilia
C) Height
D) Flower color

Answer: B) Hemophilia
Explanation: Hemophilia is a sex-linked trait located on the X chromosome, affecting primarily males who inherit the recessive allele.

---

10. Punnett Squares: Monohybrid Cross

In a monohybrid cross between two heterozygous individuals (Aa x Aa), what is the expected genotype ratio of the offspring?
A) 1 AA : 2 Aa : 1 aa
B) 3 AA : 1 aa
C) 1 Aa : 1 aa
D) 2 AA : 1 Aa : 1 aa

Answer: A) 1 AA : 2 Aa : 1 aa
Explanation: The Punnett square for a monohybrid cross between two heterozygous individuals (Aa x Aa) results in a genotype ratio of 1 AA : 2 Aa : 1 aa.

---

11. Punnett Squares: Dihybrid Cross

In a dihybrid cross between two heterozygous individuals (AaBb x AaBb), what is the expected phenotype ratio of the offspring?
A) 9:3:3:1
B) 1:1:1:1
C) 3:1
D) 1:2:1

Answer: A) 9:3:3:1
Explanation: The expected phenotype ratio from a dihybrid cross (AaBb x AaBb) is 9:3:3:1, representing the combinations of two traits.

---

12. DNA Structure

Which of the following correctly describes the structure of DNA?
A) Single-stranded helix
B) Double-stranded helix
C) Triple-stranded helix
D) Circular structure

Answer: B) Double-stranded helix
Explanation: DNA is structured as a double helix, consisting of two strands of nucleotides twisted around each other.

---

13. Nucleotide Components

Which of the following components is NOT part of a DNA nucleotide?
A) Ribose sugar
B) Phosphate group
C) Nitrogenous base
D) Deoxyribose sugar

Answer: A) Ribose sugar
Explanation: DNA nucleotides contain deoxyribose sugar, not ribose sugar, which is found in RNA nucleotides.

---

14. Base-Pairing Rules

According to the base-pairing rules in DNA, which of the following pairs is correct?
A) Adenine - Cytosine
B) Guanine - Thymine
C) Adenine - Thymine
D) Cytosine - Uracil

Answer: C) Adenine - Thymine
Explanation: In DNA, adenine pairs with thymine (A-T) and cytosine pairs with guanine (C-G).

---

15. RNA Differences from DNA

Which of the following is a key difference between RNA and DNA?
A) RNA is double-stranded, while DNA is single-stranded.
B) RNA contains uracil, while DNA contains thymine.
C) RNA is found only in the nucleus, while DNA is found in the cytoplasm.
D) RNA is larger than DNA.

Answer: B) RNA contains uracil, while DNA contains thymine.
Explanation: RNA contains uracil (U) instead of thymine (T), which is a distinguishing feature between RNA and DNA.

---

16. Types of RNA

What is the primary function of messenger RNA (mRNA)?
A) To bring amino acids to the ribosome
B) To form the ribosome
C) To carry genetic information from DNA to the ribosome
D) To catalyze biochemical reactions

Answer: C) To carry genetic information from DNA to the ribosome
Explanation: mRNA serves as the template that carries genetic information from the DNA in the nucleus to the ribosome for protein synthesis.

---

17. DNA Replication Process

During DNA replication, which enzyme is responsible for unzipping the DNA double helix?
A) DNA polymerase
B) Ligase
C) Helicase
D) RNA polymerase

Answer: C) Helicase
Explanation: Helicase is the enzyme that unwinds and unzips the DNA double helix, allowing for replication to occur.

---

18. Role of DNA Polymerase

What is the primary role of DNA polymerase during DNA replication?
A) To unzip the DNA strands
B) To add nucleotides to the growing DNA strand
C) To seal the gaps between Okazaki fragments
D) To synthesize RNA

Answer: B) To add nucleotides to the growing DNA strand
Explanation: DNA polymerase adds complementary nucleotides to the growing DNA strand during replication, ensuring accurate copying of the genetic material.

19. Semi-Conservative Model

What does the semi-conservative model of DNA replication imply?
A) Both strands of DNA are completely new.
B) Each new DNA molecule consists of one old strand and one new strand.
C) DNA replication occurs in a circular manner.
D) DNA replication is a random process.

Answer: B) Each new DNA molecule consists of one old strand and one new strand.
Explanation: The semi-conservative model indicates that during replication, each new DNA molecule retains one original strand and incorporates one new strand.

---

20. Transcription Process

During transcription, what is the role of RNA polymerase?
A) To replicate DNA
B) To synthesize mRNA from the DNA template
C) To translate mRNA into protein
D) To splice introns from mRNA

Answer: B) To synthesize mRNA from the DNA template
Explanation: RNA polymerase is responsible for synthesizing mRNA by copying the DNA template during the transcription process.

---

21. Translation Process

What occurs during the translation phase of protein synthesis?
A) DNA is replicated.
B) mRNA is synthesized from DNA.
C) Amino acids are linked together to form proteins.
D) RNA is spliced.

Answer: C) Amino acids are linked together to form proteins.
Explanation: During translation, the ribosome reads the mRNA sequence and tRNA brings the appropriate amino acids to form a polypeptide chain, resulting in protein synthesis.

---

22. Role of tRNA

What is the primary function of transfer RNA (tRNA) in protein synthesis?
A) To carry genetic information
B) To bring amino acids to the ribosome
C) To form the ribosome
D) To catalyze the formation of peptide bonds

Answer: B) To bring amino acids to the ribosome
Explanation: tRNA transports specific amino acids to the ribosome, where they are added to the growing polypeptide chain during translation.

---

23. Codons in mRNA

What is a codon?
A) A sequence of amino acids
B) A three-base sequence on mRNA that codes for an amino acid

C) A type of RNA
D) A sequence of nucleotides in DNA

Answer: B) A three-base sequence on mRNA that codes for an amino acid
Explanation: A codon is a sequence of three nucleotides in mRNA that specifies a particular amino acid during protein synthesis.

---

24. Start and Stop Codons

What is the role of start and stop codons in protein synthesis?
A) They determine the sequence of amino acids.
B) They signal the beginning and end of translation.
C) They are involved in DNA replication.
D) They are responsible for splicing RNA.

Answer: B) They signal the beginning and end of translation.
Explanation: Start codons (AUG) signal the beginning of translation, while stop codons (UAA, UAG, UGA) signal the termination of the polypeptide chain.

---

25. Genetic Variation

How does crossing over during meiosis contribute to genetic variation?
A) It produces identical gametes.
B) It allows for the exchange of genetic material between homologous chromosomes.
C) It ensures that all offspring are genetically identical.
D) It prevents mutations.

Answer: B) It allows for the exchange of genetic material between homologous chromosomes.
Explanation: Crossing over during Prophase I of meiosis results in the exchange of genetic material, increasing genetic diversity in the resulting gametes.

---

26. Mendelian Genetics: Dihybrid Cross

In a dihybrid cross between two heterozygous individuals (AaBb x AaBb), what is the expected genotype ratio of the offspring?
A) 1:2:1
B) 9:3:3:1
C) 3:1
D) 1:1:1:1

Answer: B) 9:3:3:1
Explanation: The expected genotype ratio from a dihybrid cross (AaBb x AaBb) is 9:3:3:1, representing the combinations of two traits.

---

27. Genetic Disorders: Sex-Linked Traits

A mother is a carrier for color blindness ($X^C X^c$) and the father has normal vision ($X^C Y$). What is the probability that their son will be color blind?
A) 0%
B) 25%
C) 50%
D) 100%

Answer: C) 50%
Explanation: Sons inherit their X chromosome from their mother. There is a 50% chance that the son will inherit the X^c chromosome, making him color blind.

28. Incomplete Dominance in Flowers

In a plant species, red flowers (RR) and white flowers (WW) exhibit incomplete dominance, producing pink flowers (RW) in the F1 generation. What will be the phenotypic ratio of the F2 generation when two pink flowers are crossed?
A) 1 red : 2 pink : 1 white
B) 3 red : 1 white
C) 1 red : 1 white
D) 1 pink : 1 white

Answer: A) 1 red : 2 pink : 1 white
Explanation: When two pink flowers (RW) are crossed, the F2 generation will have a phenotypic ratio of 1 red (RR) : 2 pink (RW) : 1 white (WW).

29. Genetic Mutations

What is a mutation?
A) A change in the DNA sequence
B) A normal variation in traits
C) A type of genetic recombination
D) A process of DNA replication

Answer: A) A change in the DNA sequence
Explanation: A mutation is a permanent alteration in the DNA sequence that can lead to changes in phenotype or function.

30. DNA Replication Enzymes

Which enzyme is responsible for sealing the gaps between Okazaki fragments during DNA replication?
A) Helicase
B) DNA polymerase
C) Ligase
D) RNA polymerase

Answer: C) Ligase
Explanation: DNA ligase is the enzyme that seals the gaps between Okazaki fragments on the lagging strand during DNA replication.

31. RNA Processing

What happens to mRNA before it leaves the nucleus?
A) It is translated into protein.
B) It is spliced to remove introns.
C) It is replicated.
D) It is degraded.

Answer: B) It is spliced to remove introns.
Explanation: Before mRNA exits the nucleus, it undergoes processing, which includes splicing to remove non-coding regions (introns) and joining coding regions (exons).

32. Genetic Engineering

What is the purpose of using restriction enzymes in genetic engineering?
A) To replicate DNA
B) To cut DNA at specific sequences

C) To synthesize RNA
D) To repair DNA

Answer: B) To cut DNA at specific sequences
Explanation: Restriction enzymes are used in genetic engineering to cut DNA at specific sequences, allowing for the manipulation and recombination of genetic material.

---

33. Chromosomal Abnormalities

What is a common result of nondisjunction during meiosis?
A) Normal chromosome number
B) Genetic variation
C) Chromosomal abnormalities such as Down syndrome
D) Increased fertility

Answer: C) Chromosomal abnormalities such as Down syndrome
Explanation: Nondisjunction, the failure of chromosomes to separate properly during meiosis, can lead to an abnormal number of chromosomes in gametes, resulting in conditions like Down syndrome.

---

34. Genetic Drift

What is genetic drift?
A) The movement of alleles between populations
B) A change in allele frequencies due to random sampling
C) The introduction of new alleles into a population
D) The selection of traits based on environmental pressures

Answer: B) A change in allele frequencies due to random sampling
Explanation: Genetic drift refers to random changes in allele frequencies in a population, often having a more significant effect in small populations.

---

35. Natural Selection

Which of the following best describes natural selection?
A) The process by which organisms with favorable traits survive and reproduce
B) The random change in allele frequencies
C) The introduction of new species into an ecosystem
D) The extinction of all individuals in a population

Answer: A) The process by which organisms with favorable traits survive and reproduce
Explanation: Natural selection is the mechanism by which individuals with advantageous traits are more likely to survive and reproduce, leading to the adaptation of populations over time.

---

36. Phenotype vs. Genotype

What is the difference between genotype and phenotype?
A) Genotype refers to the physical appearance, while phenotype refers to the genetic makeup.
B) Genotype refers to the genetic makeup, while phenotype refers to the physical appearance.
C) Genotype is always dominant, while phenotype is always recessive.
D) There is no difference; they are the same.

Answer: B) Genotype refers to the genetic makeup, while phenotype refers to the physical appearance.
Explanation: The genotype is the genetic constitution of an organism, while the phenotype is the observable characteristics resulting from the genotype.

---

37. Genetic Recombination

What is the significance of genetic recombination during meiosis?
A) It produces identical gametes.
B) It increases genetic diversity in offspring.
C) It ensures that all offspring are genetically identical.
D) It prevents mutations.

Answer: B) It increases genetic diversity in offspring.
Explanation: Genetic recombination during meiosis, particularly through crossing over, increases genetic diversity by producing new combinations of alleles in gametes.

---

38. Role of Codons in Translation

What is the role of codons during translation?
A) They signal the start and stop of transcription.
B) They determine the sequence of amino acids in a protein.
C) They are involved in DNA replication.
D) They are responsible for splicing RNA.

Answer: B) They determine the sequence of amino acids in a protein.
Explanation: Codons are three-nucleotide sequences in mRNA that specify which amino acids will be added to the growing polypeptide chain during translation.

---

39. Genetic Testing

What is the purpose of genetic testing?
A) To determine an individual's blood type
B) To identify genetic disorders or predispositions
C) To measure physical fitness
D) To assess environmental impacts on health

Answer: B) To identify genetic disorders or predispositions
Explanation: Genetic testing is used to identify genetic disorders, carrier status, and predispositions to certain diseases, providing valuable information for health management.

---

40. Epigenetics

What does the field of epigenetics study?
A) The structure of DNA
B) The influence of environmental factors on gene expression
C) The inheritance of traits
D) The process of natural selection

Answer: B) The influence of environmental factors on gene expression
Explanation: Epigenetics examines how environmental factors can affect gene expression without altering the underlying DNA sequence, influencing traits and disease susceptibility.

Here are 20 complex scenarios and questions for the Florida Biology EOC Test Prep exam, focusing on genetic disorders and biotechnology. Each question is designed to align with the current format of the Florida Biology EOC exam, and detailed explanations are provided after each question. The numbering starts from 41 and goes to 60.

41. Causes of Genetic Mutations

A scientist is studying a new genetic disorder caused by a mutation in a single nucleotide. What type of mutation is most likely responsible for this disorder?

A) Frameshift mutation
B) Point mutation
C) Deletion mutation
D) Inversion mutation

Answer: B) Point mutation
Explanation: A point mutation involves a change in a single nucleotide, which can lead to genetic disorders if it occurs in a critical region of a gene.

---

42. Effects of Mutations

A mutation in a gene results in a premature stop codon during protein synthesis. What type of mutation is this most likely to be?
A) Silent mutation
B) Missense mutation
C) Nonsense mutation
D) Frameshift mutation

Answer: C) Nonsense mutation
Explanation: A nonsense mutation introduces a premature stop codon, leading to a truncated protein that is often nonfunctional.

---

43. Mutagens

A group of researchers is investigating the effects of UV radiation on DNA. What type of genetic change can UV radiation cause?
A) Point mutation
B) Frameshift mutation
C) Chromosomal translocation
D) All of the above

Answer: D) All of the above
Explanation: UV radiation can cause various types of mutations, including point mutations, frameshift mutations, and chromosomal changes.

---

44. Genetic Engineering: GMOs

A farmer is using genetically modified organisms (GMOs) to increase crop yield. What is one potential benefit of using GMOs in agriculture?
A) Increased pesticide use
B) Reduced nutritional value
C) Enhanced resistance to pests and diseases
D) Decreased crop diversity

Answer: C) Enhanced resistance to pests and diseases
Explanation: GMOs can be engineered to be resistant to pests and diseases, potentially leading to higher crop yields and reduced reliance on chemical pesticides.

---

45. CRISPR Technology

What is the primary function of CRISPR-Cas9 technology in genetic engineering?
A) To replicate DNA
B) To edit specific DNA sequences
C) To synthesize RNA
D) To clone organisms

Answer: B) To edit specific DNA sequences
Explanation: CRISPR-Cas9 is a powerful gene-editing tool that allows scientists to make precise modifications to specific DNA sequences in the genome.

---

46. Cloning: Dolly the Sheep

Dolly the sheep was the first mammal to be cloned from an adult somatic cell. What process was used to create Dolly?
A) Natural reproduction
B) In vitro fertilization
C) Somatic cell nuclear transfer
D) Gene editing

Answer: C) Somatic cell nuclear transfer
Explanation: Dolly was created using somatic cell nuclear transfer, where the nucleus of an adult somatic cell was transferred into an enucleated egg cell.

---

47. Applications in Medicine

Gene therapy is being researched as a treatment for genetic disorders. What is the goal of gene therapy?
A) To replace damaged or missing genes
B) To clone healthy cells
C) To create genetically modified organisms
D) To enhance physical traits

Answer: A) To replace damaged or missing genes
Explanation: Gene therapy aims to treat or prevent disease by introducing, removing, or altering genetic material within a patient's cells.

---

48. Ethical Considerations: Designer Babies

The concept of "designer babies" raises ethical concerns. What is one potential ethical issue associated with this practice?
A) Increased genetic diversity
B) Unintended health consequences
C) Improved public health
D) Enhanced genetic variation

Answer: B) Unintended health consequences
Explanation: The manipulation of genes in embryos could lead to unintended health consequences, raising ethical concerns about the long-term effects on individuals and future generations.

---

49. Laws and Regulations

Which of the following is a key consideration in the regulation of biotechnology research?
A) Ensuring all research is conducted in secret
B) Protecting intellectual property rights
C) Eliminating all forms of genetic research
D) Promoting unrestricted access to genetic modifications

Answer: B) Protecting intellectual property rights
Explanation: Regulations in biotechnology often focus on protecting intellectual property rights while ensuring safety and ethical standards in research and applications.

---

50. Genetic Disorders: Inherited Conditions

A child is diagnosed with cystic fibrosis, a genetic disorder caused by a mutation in the CFTR gene. What type of inheritance pattern does cystic fibrosis follow?
A) Autosomal dominant
B) Autosomal recessive
C) X-linked dominant
D) Mitochondrial inheritance

Answer: B) Autosomal recessive
Explanation: Cystic fibrosis is inherited in an autosomal recessive pattern, meaning that an individual must inherit two copies of the mutated gene to express the disorder.

---

51. Point Mutations

A point mutation changes a single nucleotide in a gene from adenine (A) to guanine (G). What type of mutation is this?
A) Silent mutation
B) Missense mutation
C) Nonsense mutation
D) Frameshift mutation

Answer: B) Missense mutation
Explanation: A point mutation that results in a change in the amino acid sequence of a protein is called a missense mutation, which can alter protein function.

---

52. Frameshift Mutations

What is the effect of a frameshift mutation on a gene?
A) It does not affect the protein produced.
B) It shifts the reading frame, altering all downstream amino acids.
C) It creates a stop codon.
D) It only affects the first amino acid.

Answer: B) It shifts the reading frame, altering all downstream amino acids.
Explanation: A frameshift mutation, caused by insertion or deletion of nucleotides, changes the reading frame of the gene, potentially resulting in a completely different protein.

---

53. Genetic Engineering: Ethical Debates

What is one ethical concern regarding the use of genetic engineering in agriculture?
A) Increased crop yields
B) Potential harm to non-target species
C) Enhanced nutritional content
D) Reduced pesticide use

Answer: B) Potential harm to non-target species
Explanation: One ethical concern is that genetically engineered crops may unintentionally harm non-target species or disrupt local ecosystems.

---

54. Biotechnology in Medicine

How is synthetic insulin produced using biotechnology?
A) By extracting insulin from animal pancreas
B) By genetically modifying bacteria to produce human insulin
C) By synthesizing insulin in a laboratory
D) By using plant cells to produce insulin

Answer: B) By genetically modifying bacteria to produce human insulin
Explanation: Synthetic insulin is produced by inserting the human insulin gene into bacteria, allowing them to produce insulin that is identical to human insulin.

---

55. Genetic Testing

What is the primary purpose of genetic testing in individuals?
A) To determine physical appearance
B) To identify genetic disorders or predispositions
C) To assess environmental impacts on health
D) To measure fitness levels

Answer: B) To identify genetic disorders or predispositions
Explanation: Genetic testing is used to identify genetic disorders, carrier status, and predispositions to certain diseases, providing valuable information for health management.

---

56. Gene Therapy Techniques

Which of the following is a common method used in gene therapy?
A) Cloning
B) CRISPR-Cas9
C) In vitro fertilization
D) Natural selection

Answer: B) CRISPR-Cas9
Explanation: CRISPR-Cas9 is a widely used gene-editing technology in gene therapy to modify genes and potentially correct genetic disorders.

---

57. Genetic Engineering: Risks

What is one potential risk associated with genetic engineering in humans?
A) Increased genetic diversity
B) Unintended genetic consequences
C) Improved health outcomes
D) Enhanced physical traits

Answer: B) Unintended genetic consequences
Explanation: Genetic engineering in humans carries the risk of unintended genetic consequences, which could lead to unforeseen health issues or genetic disorders.

---

58. Ethical Considerations in Cloning

What is a major ethical concern regarding cloning animals?
A) Increased biodiversity
B) Potential suffering of cloned animals
C) Improved agricultural efficiency
D) Enhanced genetic variation

Answer: B) Potential suffering of cloned animals
Explanation: Ethical concerns about cloning include the potential suffering and health issues that cloned animals may experience, as well as the implications for animal welfare.

---

59. Genetic Modification in Plants

What is one benefit of genetically modifying plants?
A) Increased susceptibility to pests
B) Enhanced nutritional content
C) Reduced crop yields
D) Increased use of chemical fertilizers

Answer: B) Enhanced nutritional content
Explanation: Genetically modifying plants can enhance their nutritional content, making them more beneficial for human consumption and addressing nutritional deficiencies.

---

60. Genetic Disorders: Screening

What is the purpose of newborn screening for genetic disorders?
A) To determine the child's height and weight
B) To identify genetic disorders early for treatment
C) To assess the child's intelligence
D) To evaluate the child's physical fitness

Answer: B) To identify genetic disorders early for treatment
Explanation: Newborn screening is conducted to identify genetic disorders early, allowing for timely intervention and treatment to improve health outcomes.

Chapter 5: Evolution and Natural Selection

1. Darwin's Observations

During his voyage on the HMS Beagle, Charles Darwin observed various species of finches on the Galápagos Islands. What was one of his key observations regarding these finches?
A) They all had identical beak shapes.
B) They exhibited variations in beak size and shape based on their food sources.
C) They were all the same species.
D) They migrated to the mainland every year.

Answer: B) They exhibited variations in beak size and shape based on their food sources.
Explanation: Darwin noted that the finches had different beak shapes adapted to their specific diets, which contributed to his theory of natural selection.

---

2. Principles of Natural Selection

Which of the following is NOT one of the four main principles of natural selection?
A) Variation
B) Overproduction
C) Genetic drift
D) Adaptation

Answer: C) Genetic drift
Explanation: The four main principles of natural selection are variation, overproduction, adaptation, and descent with modification. Genetic drift is a separate mechanism of evolution.

---

3. Overproduction

A species of sea turtles lays hundreds of eggs each breeding season. What is the significance of overproduction in the context of natural selection?
A) It ensures that all offspring survive.
B) It increases competition for resources among offspring.
C) It leads to genetic drift.
D) It eliminates the need for adaptation.

Answer: B) It increases competition for resources among offspring.
Explanation: Overproduction leads to competition for limited resources, which can result in natural selection favoring those individuals best adapted to survive.

---

4. Adaptation

Which of the following best describes an adaptation?
A) A trait that is always beneficial.
B) A trait that provides a survival advantage in a specific environment.
C) A trait that is inherited from ancestors.
D) A trait that is acquired during an organism's lifetime.

Answer: B) A trait that provides a survival advantage in a specific environment.
Explanation: Adaptations are characteristics that enhance an organism's ability to survive and reproduce in its environment.

---

5. Descent with Modification

What does the principle of descent with modification imply?
A) All species are identical to their ancestors.
B) Species change over time, and new species arise from common ancestors.
C) Evolution occurs only in response to environmental changes.
D) Traits are inherited only from the mother.

Answer: B) Species change over time, and new species arise from common ancestors.
Explanation: Descent with modification suggests that species evolve and diverge from common ancestors, leading to the diversity of life.

---

6. Evidence of Evolution: Fossil Record

What do transitional fossils, such as Tiktaalik, provide evidence for?
A) The extinction of species
B) The chronological history of life on Earth
C) The existence of dinosaurs
D) The process of natural selection

Answer: B) The chronological history of life on Earth
Explanation: Transitional fossils illustrate the evolutionary changes that have occurred over time, linking major evolutionary groups.

---

7. Comparative Anatomy: Homologous Structures

Which of the following is an example of homologous structures?
A) The wings of a butterfly and a bird
B) The forelimb of a human and the flipper of a whale
C) The eyes of a squid and a human
D) The fins of a fish and the legs of a frog

Answer: B) The forelimb of a human and the flipper of a whale
Explanation: Homologous structures are similar in structure due to common ancestry, even if they serve different functions.

---

8. Analogous Structures

Which of the following is an example of analogous structures?
A) The forelimbs of mammals
B) The wings of birds and the wings of insects
C) The pelvis of a whale and the pelvis of a human
D) The roots of plants

Answer: B) The wings of birds and the wings of insects
Explanation: Analogous structures have similar functions but different evolutionary origins, resulting from convergent evolution.

---

9. Vestigial Structures

What is a vestigial structure?
A) A structure that has a current function
B) A structure that is fully developed and functional
C) A remnant of a structure that had a function in an ancestor
D) A structure that is essential for survival

Answer: C) A remnant of a structure that had a function in an ancestor
Explanation: Vestigial structures are remnants of features that served a purpose in ancestral species but are reduced or nonfunctional in modern descendants.

---

10. DNA and Molecular Evidence

How do similarities in DNA sequences among different species provide evidence for evolution?
A) They show that all species are identical.
B) They indicate that species share a common ancestor.
C) They prove that evolution does not occur.
D) They demonstrate that mutations are harmful.

Answer: B) They indicate that species share a common ancestor.
Explanation: Similarities in DNA sequences suggest that species have diverged from a common ancestor, supporting the theory of evolution.

---

11. Genetic Drift: Bottleneck Effect

A natural disaster drastically reduces the population of a species, leading to a loss of genetic diversity. What is this phenomenon called?
A) Founder effect
B) Gene flow
C) Bottleneck effect
D) Natural selection

Answer: C) Bottleneck effect
Explanation: The bottleneck effect occurs when a significant reduction in population size leads to a loss of genetic diversity.

---

12. Genetic Drift: Founder Effect

A small group of individuals from a population migrates to a new area and establishes a new population. What is this an example of?
A) Bottleneck effect
B) Gene flow
C) Founder effect
D) Natural selection

Answer: C) Founder effect
Explanation: The founder effect occurs when a small group establishes a new population, leading to limited genetic variation compared to the original population.

---

13. Gene Flow

What is gene flow?
A) The movement of alleles between populations
B) The random change in allele frequencies
C) The process of natural selection
D) The formation of new species

Answer: A) The movement of alleles between populations
Explanation: Gene flow involves the transfer of genetic material between populations, which can increase genetic diversity and reduce differences between populations.

---

14. Mutations and Evolution

How do mutations contribute to evolution?
A) They always have harmful effects.
B) They introduce new genetic variations into a population.
C) They prevent adaptation.
D) They eliminate genetic diversity.

Answer: B) They introduce new genetic variations into a population.
Explanation: Mutations are random changes in DNA that can create new alleles, providing the raw material for evolution and adaptation.

---

15. Speciation

What is speciation?
A) The extinction of a species
B) The formation of new species
C) The adaptation of a species to its environment
D) The migration of species

Answer: B) The formation of new species
Explanation: Speciation is the evolutionary process by which new biological species arise, often through mechanisms like reproductive isolation.

---

16. Geographic Isolation

How does geographic isolation contribute to speciation?
A) It prevents genetic drift.
B) It allows for gene flow between populations.
C) It leads to different evolutionary paths due to physical separation.
D) It eliminates competition for resources.

Answer: C) It leads to different evolutionary paths due to physical separation.
Explanation: Geographic isolation can result in populations evolving independently, leading to the formation of new species.

---

17. Behavioral Isolation

What is behavioral isolation?
A) When two species occupy different habitats
B) When two species reproduce at different times
C) When differences in mating behaviors prevent interbreeding
D) When physical barriers prevent mating

Answer: C) When differences in mating behaviors prevent interbreeding
Explanation: Behavioral isolation occurs when two populations develop different mating rituals or behaviors, preventing them from interbreeding.

---

18. Temporal Isolation

Which of the following is an example of temporal isolation?
A) Two species of frogs that mate in different seasons
B) Two species of birds that have different mating calls
C) Two species of plants that grow in different habitats
D) Two species of fish that cannot mate due to physical differences

Answer: A) Two species of frogs that mate in different seasons
Explanation: Temporal isolation occurs when species reproduce at different times, preventing them from interbreeding.

---

19. Adaptive Radiation

What is adaptive radiation?
A) The extinction of a species
B) The rapid evolution of multiple species from a common ancestor
C) The migration of species to new environments
D) The gradual change of a species over time

Answer: B) The rapid evolution of multiple species from a common ancestor
Explanation: Adaptive radiation occurs when a single ancestral species evolves into a variety of forms to adapt to different environments.

---

20. Evidence of Evolution: Antibiotic Resistance

A population of bacteria develops resistance to an antibiotic after repeated exposure. What evolutionary principle does this scenario illustrate?
A) Genetic drift
B) Natural selection
C) Gene flow
D) Speciation

Answer: B) Natural selection
Explanation: The development of antibiotic resistance in bacteria is an example of natural selection, where individuals with advantageous traits survive and reproduce, leading to a population that is resistant to the antibiotic.

Here are 20 complex scenarios and questions for the Florida Biology EOC Test Prep exam, focusing on human evolution. Each question is designed to align with the current format of the Florida Biology EOC exam, and detailed explanations are provided after each question. The numbering starts from 41 and goes to 60.

41. Fossil Evidence: Australopithecus afarensis

A team of paleontologists discovers a fossilized skeleton of a hominid that walked upright and had a small brain size. This species is believed to be one of the earliest ancestors of modern humans. Which hominid does this fossil most likely represent?
A) Homo habilis
B) Homo erectus
C) Australopithecus afarensis
D) Neanderthal

Answer: C) Australopithecus afarensis
Explanation: Australopithecus afarensis, exemplified by the famous fossil "Lucy," is known for being an early bipedal ancestor with a small brain size.

---

42. Tool Use in Early Hominids

A recent archaeological dig uncovers stone tools associated with a hominid species that lived approximately 2.4 million years ago. Which species is most likely responsible for the creation of these tools?
A) Australopithecus afarensis
B) Homo habilis
C) Homo erectus
D) Neanderthal

Answer: B) Homo habilis
Explanation: Homo habilis is recognized as the first tool user, and the tools found at archaeological sites date back to their time.

---

43. Migration of Homo erectus

Homo erectus is known for being the first hominid to migrate out of Africa. What significant adaptation did they develop that aided in their survival during this migration?
A) Increased brain size
B) Ability to use fire
C) Development of language
D) Bipedal locomotion

Answer: B) Ability to use fire
Explanation: The ability to use fire was a crucial adaptation for Homo erectus, providing warmth, protection, and a means to cook food, which facilitated their migration and survival in diverse environments.

---

44. Neanderthals and Homo sapiens

Recent studies suggest that Neanderthals and modern humans coexisted and interacted in certain regions. What evidence supports the idea of interbreeding between these two species?
A) Fossilized tools found in the same layers
B) Genetic material from Neanderthals found in modern human DNA
C) Similarities in skeletal structure
D) Shared cultural practices

Answer: B) Genetic material from Neanderthals found in modern human DNA
Explanation: Genetic studies have shown that non-African modern humans carry a small percentage of Neanderthal DNA, indicating that interbreeding occurred between the two species.

---

45. Out-of-Africa Theory

The Out-of-Africa theory posits that modern humans evolved in Africa and migrated to other parts of the world. What evidence supports this theory?
A) Fossils of early humans found only in Europe
B) Genetic similarities among modern human populations
C) The absence of human fossils in Africa
D) The presence of identical species in different continents

Answer: B) Genetic similarities among modern human populations
Explanation: Genetic studies indicate that all modern humans share a common ancestry that traces back to Africa, supporting the Out-of-Africa theory.

---

46. Lactose Tolerance

In certain populations, individuals have developed the ability to digest lactose into adulthood. What is the evolutionary advantage of lactose tolerance in these populations?
A) Increased risk of disease
B) Enhanced ability to utilize dairy as a food source
C) Decreased reproductive success
D) Reduced genetic diversity

Answer: B) Enhanced ability to utilize dairy as a food source
Explanation: Lactose tolerance provides a nutritional advantage in populations that consume dairy products, allowing individuals to access a reliable source of calories and nutrients.

47. Sickle Cell Trait

In regions where malaria is prevalent, individuals with the sickle cell trait have a survival advantage. What is the mechanism behind this advantage?
A) Increased oxygen transport
B) Resistance to malaria parasites
C) Enhanced physical strength
D) Improved reproductive success

Answer: B) Resistance to malaria parasites
Explanation: The sickle cell trait provides some resistance to malaria, as the malaria parasite has difficulty surviving in sickle-shaped red blood cells.

48. Skin Color Variation

Skin color variations in human populations are primarily influenced by which environmental factor?
A) Altitude
B) Temperature
C) UV radiation
D) Humidity

Answer: C) UV radiation
Explanation: Skin color variations are adaptations to different levels of UV radiation, with darker skin providing protection against UV damage and lighter skin facilitating vitamin D production in low UV environments.

49. Impact of Agriculture

The development of agriculture had a profound impact on human evolution. What was one significant effect of this transition from hunter-gatherer societies to agricultural societies?
A) Decreased population density
B) Increased reliance on wild food sources
C) Changes in social structures and population growth
D) Reduced brain size

Answer: C) Changes in social structures and population growth
Explanation: The shift to agriculture allowed for larger, more stable populations and the development of complex social structures, leading to significant changes in human society.

50. Evolution of Brain Size

Research indicates that the evolution of brain size in hominids is linked to which of the following factors?
A) Increased physical strength
B) Development of language and social structures
C) Ability to run long distances
D) Changes in diet

Answer: B) Development of language and social structures
Explanation: The increase in brain size is associated with the development of complex language and social interactions, which are crucial for survival and cooperation in larger groups.

51. Modern Medicine and Natural Selection

How has modern medicine influenced natural selection in human populations?
A) It has eliminated all genetic disorders.

B) It has increased the survival of individuals with genetic disorders.
C) It has no impact on natural selection.
D) It has decreased the average lifespan of humans.

Answer: B) It has increased the survival of individuals with genetic disorders.
Explanation: Modern medicine allows individuals with genetic disorders to survive and reproduce, which can affect the dynamics of natural selection in human populations.

---

52. Fossil Evidence: Major Hominids

A paleontologist discovers a fossil that exhibits both ape-like and human-like features. Which of the following hominids is this fossil most likely to represent?
A) Homo sapiens
B) Homo erectus
C) Australopithecus afarensis
D) Neanderthal

Answer: C) Australopithecus afarensis
Explanation: Australopithecus afarensis, such as "Lucy," displays a mix of ape-like and human-like characteristics, making it a key species in understanding human evolution.

---

53. Genetic Adaptations: Skin Color

A population living in a region with high UV radiation has predominantly dark skin. What is the evolutionary advantage of this adaptation?
A) Increased vitamin D production
B) Protection against skin cancer
C) Enhanced ability to absorb UV radiation
D) Improved camouflage

Answer: B) Protection against skin cancer
Explanation: Dark skin provides protection against the harmful effects of UV radiation, reducing the risk of skin cancer and other UV-related health issues.

---

54. Cultural Evolution

The transition from nomadic lifestyles to settled agricultural communities led to significant changes in human culture. What is one major cultural development that arose from this transition?
A) Decreased population size
B) Development of written language
C) Increased reliance on hunting
D) Reduced social complexity

Answer: B) Development of written language
Explanation: The establishment of agricultural societies facilitated the development of written language, which was essential for record-keeping and communication in larger communities.

---

55. Evolutionary Pressure: Disease Resistance

In a population where malaria is endemic, individuals with the sickle cell trait have a survival advantage. What type of evolutionary pressure does this scenario illustrate?
A) Stabilizing selection
B) Directional selection
C) Disruptive selection
D) Sexual selection

Answer: B) Directional selection
Explanation: Directional selection occurs when individuals with a particular trait (sickle cell trait) have a higher fitness in a specific environment (malaria prevalence), leading to an increase in that trait in the population.

---

56. Human Evolution: Neanderthals

Neanderthals are often depicted as primitive, but recent research suggests they had complex behaviors. Which of the following behaviors is evidence of their cognitive abilities?
A) Use of simple tools
B) Burial of their dead
C) Migration patterns
D) Hunting large animals

Answer: B) Burial of their dead
Explanation: The practice of burying their dead indicates that Neanderthals had complex social structures and possibly a sense of ritual, reflecting advanced cognitive abilities.

---

57. Genetic Variation in Humans

What is one reason for the high level of genetic variation observed in human populations?
A) Limited migration
B) High mutation rates
C) Cultural practices
D) Gene flow through migration

Answer: D) Gene flow through migration
Explanation: Gene flow, resulting from migration and interbreeding among populations, contributes to the high level of genetic variation observed in humans.

---

58. Evolutionary Adaptations: Lactose Tolerance

In populations with a long history of dairy farming, what genetic adaptation has evolved in response to the consumption of milk?
A) Increased lactose intolerance
B) Lactose tolerance into adulthood
C) Decreased bone density
D) Enhanced digestive enzymes for starch

Answer: B) Lactose tolerance into adulthood
Explanation: In populations that consume dairy products, individuals have developed lactose tolerance, allowing them to digest lactose beyond infancy.

---

59. Fossil Record: Transitional Forms

The discovery of a transitional fossil that exhibits both fish and amphibian characteristics provides evidence for which evolutionary concept?
A) Convergent evolution
B) Divergent evolution
C) Common ancestry
D) Genetic drift

Answer: C) Common ancestry
Explanation: Transitional fossils demonstrate the evolutionary link between different groups, supporting the idea of common ancestry among species.

60. Impact of Environment on Evolution

How does environmental change influence the process of natural selection?
A) It has no effect on species survival.
B) It creates new species instantly.
C) It can favor certain traits that enhance survival in the new conditions.
D) It eliminates all genetic variation.

Answer: C) It can favor certain traits that enhance survival in the new conditions.
Explanation: Environmental changes can shift the selective pressures on a population, favoring traits that improve survival and reproduction in the altered environment.

Chapter 6: Ecology and Environmental Science

1. Food Chains and Energy Transfer

A food chain in a grassland ecosystem is represented as follows: Grass → Grasshopper → Frog → Snake. If the grass produces 1,000 kcal of energy, how much energy is available to the snake?
A) 100 kcal
B) 10 kcal
C) 1,000 kcal
D) 1 kcal

Answer: A) 100 kcal
Explanation: According to the 10% rule of energy transfer, only 10% of the energy from one trophic level is available to the next. Therefore, the energy available to the snake (tertiary consumer) is 10% of the energy available to the frog (secondary consumer), which is 10% of the energy available to the grasshopper (primary consumer).

---

2. Food Web Complexity

In a forest ecosystem, a food web includes the following organisms: oak tree, caterpillar, blue jay, and fox. If the caterpillar population decreases significantly, what is the most likely immediate effect on the blue jay population?
A) Increase in blue jay population
B) Decrease in blue jay population
C) No effect on blue jay population
D) Blue jays will migrate to another area

Answer: B) Decrease in blue jay population
Explanation: The blue jay, as a primary consumer, relies on the caterpillar for food. A significant decrease in the caterpillar population would likely lead to a decrease in the blue jay population due to reduced food availability.

---

3. Trophic Levels

Which of the following correctly identifies the trophic levels in a typical food chain?
A) Producers → Primary consumers → Secondary consumers → Tertiary consumers
B) Primary consumers → Producers → Tertiary consumers → Secondary consumers
C) Tertiary consumers → Secondary consumers → Primary consumers → Producers
D) Secondary consumers → Tertiary consumers → Producers → Primary consumers

Answer: A) Producers → Primary consumers → Secondary consumers → Tertiary consumers
Explanation: The correct order of trophic levels starts with producers (autotrophs), followed by primary consumers (herbivores), then secondary consumers (carnivores that eat herbivores), and finally tertiary consumers (higher-level carnivores).

---

4. Biotic vs. Abiotic Factors

In a freshwater lake ecosystem, which of the following is an example of an abiotic factor?
A) Fish
B) Algae
C) Water temperature
D) Bacteria

Answer: C) Water temperature
Explanation: Abiotic factors are non-living components of an ecosystem, such as temperature, water, soil, and sunlight. Fish, algae, and bacteria are all biotic factors.

5. Symbiotic Relationships

In a mutualistic relationship, both species involved benefit. Which of the following is an example of mutualism?
A) A clownfish living among the tentacles of a sea anemone
B) A tick feeding on a deer
C) Bees pollinating flowers while collecting nectar
D) A barnacle attaching to a whale

Answer: C) Bees pollinating flowers while collecting nectar
Explanation: In mutualism, both species benefit; bees receive food (nectar) while helping flowers reproduce through pollination.

6. Predation and Competition

In a savanna ecosystem, lions and hyenas compete for the same prey. What type of interaction does this represent?
A) Mutualism
B) Commensalism
C) Predation
D) Competition

Answer: D) Competition
Explanation: Competition occurs when two or more species vie for the same resources, such as food, in this case, the prey.

7. Water Cycle Processes

Which of the following processes is NOT part of the water cycle?
A) Evaporation
B) Transpiration
C) Photosynthesis
D) Precipitation

Answer: C) Photosynthesis
Explanation: Photosynthesis is not a part of the water cycle; it is a process by which plants convert sunlight into energy. The water cycle includes evaporation, transpiration, and precipitation.

8. Importance of the Water Cycle

Why is the water cycle essential for maintaining ecosystems?
A) It increases soil salinity.
B) It regulates climate and supports life.
C) It decreases biodiversity.
D) It eliminates pollutants from the environment.

Answer: B) It regulates climate and supports life.
Explanation: The water cycle is crucial for maintaining freshwater supplies, regulating climate, and supporting all forms of life by providing necessary water resources.

9. Carbon Cycle Processes

Which of the following processes in the carbon cycle involves the conversion of carbon dioxide into organic compounds?
A) Respiration
B) Decomposition

C) Photosynthesis
D) Combustion

Answer: C) Photosynthesis
Explanation: Photosynthesis is the process by which plants convert carbon dioxide and sunlight into organic compounds, such as glucose, while releasing oxygen.

---

10. Human Impact on the Carbon Cycle

How do human activities, such as burning fossil fuels, affect the carbon cycle?
A) They decrease atmospheric CO_2 levels.
B) They increase atmospheric CO_2 levels.
C) They have no impact on the carbon cycle.
D) They enhance photosynthesis in plants.

Answer: B) They increase atmospheric CO_2 levels.
Explanation: Burning fossil fuels releases large amounts of carbon dioxide into the atmosphere, contributing to climate change and disrupting the natural carbon cycle.

---

11. Nitrogen Cycle: Nitrogen Fixation

Which of the following organisms is primarily responsible for nitrogen fixation in the nitrogen cycle?
A) Fungi
B) Bacteria
C) Plants
D) Animals

Answer: B) Bacteria
Explanation: Nitrogen-fixing bacteria convert atmospheric nitrogen (N_2) into usable forms (ammonia) for plants, playing a crucial role in the nitrogen cycle.

---

12. Human Impact on the Nitrogen Cycle

How do fertilizers impact the nitrogen cycle?
A) They decrease nitrogen levels in the soil.
B) They increase nitrogen levels, leading to runoff and pollution.
C) They have no effect on the nitrogen cycle.
D) They promote nitrogen fixation.

Answer: B) They increase nitrogen levels, leading to runoff and pollution.
Explanation: The use of nitrogen-rich fertilizers can lead to excess nitrogen in the soil, which may runoff into water bodies, causing pollution and eutrophication.

---

13. Phosphorus Cycle

What is the primary source of phosphorus in ecosystems?
A) Atmospheric gases
B) Rocks and soil
C) Water vapor
D) Animal waste

Answer: B) Rocks and soil
Explanation: Phosphorus is primarily found in rocks and soil, and it is released through weathering processes, making it available for biological uptake.

---

14. Oxygen Cycle

How is the oxygen cycle linked to the carbon cycle?
A) Oxygen is produced during photosynthesis and consumed during respiration.
B) Oxygen is released during decomposition.
C) Oxygen levels are unaffected by carbon levels.
D) Oxygen is only produced by animals.

Answer: A) Oxygen is produced during photosynthesis and consumed during respiration.
Explanation: The oxygen cycle is closely linked to the carbon cycle, as plants produce oxygen during photosynthesis while consuming carbon dioxide, and animals consume oxygen during respiration while releasing carbon dioxide.

---

15. Energy Flow in Ecosystems

In an energy pyramid, if the primary producers have 1,000 kcal of energy, how much energy is available to the secondary consumers?
A) 100 kcal
B) 1,000 kcal
C) 10 kcal
D) 1 kcal

Answer: A) 100 kcal
Explanation: According to the 10% rule, only about 10% of the energy is transferred from one trophic level to the next. Therefore, secondary consumers would receive approximately 100 kcal from primary producers.

---

16. Ecosystem Interactions: Mutualism

In a mutualistic relationship between oxpeckers and large mammals, what do the oxpeckers gain from the relationship?
A) Protection from predators
B) Food by eating parasites on the mammals
C) Shelter from the elements
D) Mating opportunities

Answer: B) Food by eating parasites on the mammals
Explanation: Oxpeckers benefit from this mutualistic relationship by feeding on parasites and dead skin found on large mammals, while the mammals benefit from reduced parasite loads.

---

17. Biogeochemical Cycles: Importance

Why are biogeochemical cycles important for ecosystems?
A) They prevent the extinction of species.
B) They recycle essential nutrients and elements.
C) They eliminate waste products from ecosystems.
D) They increase biodiversity.

Answer: B) They recycle essential nutrients and elements.
Explanation: Biogeochemical cycles are crucial for recycling nutrients and elements, ensuring that they are available for use by living organisms in ecosystems.

---

18. Energy Transfer Efficiency

What percentage of energy is typically transferred from one trophic level to the next in an energy pyramid?
A) 1%
B) 10%

C) 50%
D) 100%

Answer: B) 10%
Explanation: The 10% rule states that only about 10% of the energy is transferred from one trophic level to the next, with the rest lost as heat.

---

19. Ecosystem Resilience

What is ecosystem resilience?
A) The ability of an ecosystem to remain unchanged over time.
B) The ability of an ecosystem to recover from disturbances.
C) The diversity of species within an ecosystem.
D) The total biomass of an ecosystem.

Answer: B) The ability of an ecosystem to recover from disturbances.
Explanation: Ecosystem resilience refers to the capacity of an ecosystem to recover from disturbances, such as natural disasters or human impacts, and return to its original state.

---

20. Human Impact on Ecosystems

Which of the following human activities is most likely to disrupt the balance of an ecosystem?
A) Planting native species
B) Deforestation
C) Recycling materials
D) Creating wildlife reserves

Answer: B) Deforestation
Explanation: Deforestation significantly disrupts ecosystems by removing habitats, altering water cycles, and affecting biodiversity, leading to imbalances in the ecosystem.

---

21. Food Web Dynamics

In a marine ecosystem, if the population of phytoplankton decreases due to pollution, what is the most likely consequence for the entire food web?
A) Increased fish populations
B) Decreased populations of primary consumers like zooplankton
C) No effect on the food web
D) Increased biodiversity

Answer: B) Decreased populations of primary consumers like zooplankton
Explanation: Phytoplankton are primary producers; a decrease in their population would lead to a decline in primary consumers, disrupting the entire food web.

---

22. Biotic Factors in Ecosystems

Which of the following is an example of a biotic factor affecting an ecosystem?
A) Soil pH
B) Temperature
C) Competition between species
D) Sunlight

Answer: C) Competition between species
Explanation: Biotic factors are living components of an ecosystem, such as competition, predation, and symbiotic relationships.

23. Energy Pyramid Representation

If an energy pyramid shows that primary producers have 500 kcal, how much energy would be available to tertiary consumers?
A) 50 kcal
B) 5 kcal
C) 500 kcal
D) 5000 kcal

Answer: B) 5 kcal
Explanation: Following the 10% rule, the energy available to tertiary consumers would be 0.1% of the energy from primary producers, which is 5 kcal.

---

24. Nitrogen Cycle: Nitrification

What is the process of nitrification in the nitrogen cycle?
A) Conversion of nitrogen gas into ammonia
B) Conversion of ammonia into nitrites and nitrates
C) Conversion of nitrates back into nitrogen gas
D) Uptake of nitrogen by plants

Answer: B) Conversion of ammonia into nitrites and nitrates
Explanation: Nitrification is the process by which ammonia is converted into nitrites and then nitrates by nitrifying bacteria, making nitrogen available for plant uptake.

---

25. Carbon Cycle: Human Impact

Which human activity is most directly responsible for increasing carbon dioxide levels in the atmosphere?
A) Deforestation
B) Planting trees
C) Recycling
D) Sustainable agriculture

Answer: A) Deforestation
Explanation: Deforestation reduces the number of trees that can absorb carbon dioxide, while also releasing stored carbon when trees are cut down or burned.

---

26. Ecosystem Succession

What type of succession occurs in an area where a volcanic eruption has destroyed the existing ecosystem?
A) Primary succession
B) Secondary succession
C) Tertiary succession
D) Climax succession

Answer: A) Primary succession
Explanation: Primary succession occurs in lifeless areas where soil has not yet formed, such as after a volcanic eruption, leading to the gradual establishment of a new ecosystem.

---

27. Biogeochemical Cycles: Phosphorus

Why is phosphorus considered a limiting nutrient in many ecosystems?
A) It is abundant in the atmosphere.
B) It is often found in low concentrations in soil and water.

C) It is not essential for plant growth.
D) It is easily recycled in the ecosystem.

Answer: B) It is often found in low concentrations in soil and water.
Explanation: Phosphorus is often a limiting nutrient because it is less abundant in the environment compared to other nutrients like nitrogen and potassium, affecting plant growth.

---

28. Ecosystem Interactions: Commensalism

Which of the following is an example of commensalism?
A) A bee pollinating a flower
B) A barnacle attaching to a whale
C) A lion hunting a zebra
D) A parasite living in a host

Answer: B) A barnacle attaching to a whale
Explanation: In commensalism, one species benefits while the other is neither helped nor harmed. Barnacles benefit from being transported by the whale, while the whale is unaffected.

---

29. Energy Flow: Trophic Levels

If a food web shows that a secondary consumer has 200 kcal of energy, how much energy would be available to the primary consumer?
A) 20 kcal
B) 200 kcal
C) 2000 kcal
D) 2 kcal

Answer: C) 2000 kcal
Explanation: If the secondary consumer has 200 kcal, the primary consumer would have approximately 2000 kcal, following the 10% rule of energy transfer.

---

30. Water Cycle: Transpiration

What role does transpiration play in the water cycle?
A) It decreases humidity in the atmosphere.
B) It contributes to the formation of clouds.
C) It prevents water loss in plants.
D) It increases soil erosion.

Answer: B) It contributes to the formation of clouds.
Explanation: Transpiration is the process by which water vapor is released from plant leaves into the atmosphere, contributing to humidity and cloud formation.

---

31. Ecosystem Services

Which of the following is an example of an ecosystem service provided by wetlands?
A) Increased urban development
B) Water filtration and flood control
C) Deforestation
D) Soil degradation

Answer: B) Water filtration and flood control
Explanation: Wetlands provide essential ecosystem services, including filtering pollutants from water and controlling flooding by absorbing excess water.

32. Human Impact: Urbanization

How does urbanization typically affect local ecosystems?
A) It increases biodiversity.
B) It creates more natural habitats.
C) It leads to habitat fragmentation and loss.
D) It has no impact on ecosystems.

Answer: C) It leads to habitat fragmentation and loss.
Explanation: Urbanization often results in the destruction of natural habitats, leading to fragmentation and loss of biodiversity.

33. Biogeochemical Cycles: Oxygen

What is the primary process that drives the oxygen cycle?
A) Respiration
B) Photosynthesis
C) Decomposition
D) Combustion

Answer: B) Photosynthesis
Explanation: Photosynthesis is the primary process that produces oxygen in the atmosphere, while respiration consumes oxygen.

34. Ecosystem Dynamics: Invasive Species

What is the impact of invasive species on native ecosystems?
A) They enhance biodiversity.
B) They have no effect on native species.
C) They can outcompete native species for resources.
D) They promote ecosystem stability.

Answer: C) They can outcompete native species for resources.
Explanation: Invasive species often outcompete native species for resources, leading to declines in native populations and disruptions in ecosystem balance.

35. Energy Flow: Biomass

In an energy pyramid, if the biomass of primary producers is 1,000 kg, what is the expected biomass of secondary consumers?
A) 100 kg
B) 1,000 kg
C) 10 kg
D) 1 kg

Answer: A) 100 kg
Explanation: Following the 10% rule, the biomass of secondary consumers would be approximately 10% of the biomass of primary producers, which is 100 kg.

36. Nitrogen Cycle: Denitrification

What is the role of denitrifying bacteria in the nitrogen cycle?
A) They convert nitrogen gas into ammonia.
B) They convert nitrates back into nitrogen gas.

C) They fix atmospheric nitrogen into usable forms.
D) They promote plant growth.

Answer: B) They convert nitrates back into nitrogen gas.
Explanation: Denitrifying bacteria play a crucial role in the nitrogen cycle by converting nitrates into nitrogen gas, returning it to the atmosphere.

---

37. Ecosystem Interactions: Parasitism

Which of the following is an example of parasitism?
A) A bird building a nest in a tree
B) A dog and its owner
C) A tapeworm living in the intestines of a mammal
D) A flower and its pollinator

Answer: C) A tapeworm living in the intestines of a mammal
Explanation: In parasitism, one organism benefits at the expense of another. The tapeworm benefits by feeding on the host, while the host suffers from the relationship.

---

38. Carbon Cycle: Decomposition

What role do decomposers play in the carbon cycle?
A) They produce carbon dioxide through photosynthesis.
B) They release carbon dioxide back into the atmosphere during decomposition.
C) They store carbon in plant biomass.
D) They prevent carbon from entering the soil.

Answer: B) They release carbon dioxide back into the atmosphere during decomposition.
Explanation: Decomposers break down dead organic matter, releasing carbon dioxide back into the atmosphere, thus playing a vital role in the carbon cycle.

---

39. Ecosystem Stability

What is a characteristic of a stable ecosystem?
A) High biodiversity
B) Low productivity
C) Limited species interactions
D) Constant environmental conditions

Answer: A) High biodiversity
Explanation: A stable ecosystem typically has high biodiversity, which contributes to resilience and the ability to withstand environmental changes.

---

40. Human Impact: Climate Change

How does climate change affect ecosystems?
A) It has no impact on ecosystems.
B) It stabilizes ecosystems by reducing variability.
C) It alters species distributions and disrupts food webs.
D) It increases biodiversity in all ecosystems.

Answer: C) It alters species distributions and disrupts food webs.
Explanation: Climate change can lead to shifts in species distributions, affecting interactions within food webs and potentially leading to declines in biodiversity.

41. Carrying Capacity

A wildlife biologist studies a population of deer in a forest. The forest can sustainably support 150 deer. If the population exceeds this number, what is likely to happen?
A) The population will continue to grow indefinitely.
B) The population will stabilize at 150 deer.
C) The population will decline due to limited resources.
D) The population will migrate to another area.

Answer: C) The population will decline due to limited resources.
Explanation: When a population exceeds its carrying capacity, resources become limited, leading to competition, starvation, and a decline in population size.

---

42. Density-Dependent Factors

In a pond ecosystem, as the fish population increases, competition for food and space also rises. What type of limiting factor does this scenario represent?
A) Density-independent
B) Density-dependent
C) Environmental
D) Biotic

Answer: B) Density-dependent
Explanation: Density-dependent factors, such as competition, become more significant as the population density increases, affecting population growth and survival.

---

43. Exponential Growth Model

A population of bacteria doubles every hour under ideal conditions. If the initial population is 10 bacteria, how many will there be after 3 hours?
A) 20
B) 40
C) 80
D) 160

Answer: D) 160
Explanation: The population doubles every hour:

- After 1 hour: 10 × 2 = 20
- After 2 hours: 20 × 2 = 40
- After 3 hours: 40 × 2 = 80
- After 3 hours: 80 × 2 = 160

---

44. Logistic Growth Model

A population of rabbits in a controlled environment grows rapidly at first but then levels off as it reaches the carrying capacity of the habitat. What type of growth model does this represent?
A) Exponential growth
B) Logistic growth
C) Linear growth
D) Cyclical growth

Answer: B) Logistic growth
Explanation: Logistic growth is characterized by an initial period of rapid growth followed by a slowdown as the population approaches the carrying capacity of the environment.

45. Deforestation Impact

A region experiences significant deforestation for agricultural expansion. What is one major ecological consequence of this action?
A) Increased biodiversity
B) Decreased carbon dioxide levels
C) Disruption of local water cycles
D) Enhanced soil fertility

Answer: C) Disruption of local water cycles
Explanation: Deforestation disrupts local water cycles by reducing transpiration and altering precipitation patterns, leading to changes in the ecosystem.

---

46. Air Pollution Effects

Which of the following is a direct consequence of increased air pollution from greenhouse gases?
A) Decreased global temperatures
B) Enhanced biodiversity
C) Global warming
D) Improved air quality

Answer: C) Global warming
Explanation: Increased greenhouse gases in the atmosphere trap heat, leading to global warming and climate change.

---

47. Water Pollution: Eutrophication

A lake experiences eutrophication due to runoff from fertilizers. What is the primary effect of this process?
A) Increased oxygen levels
B) Decreased plant growth
C) Algal blooms and decreased oxygen levels
D) Improved water clarity

Answer: C) Algal blooms and decreased oxygen levels
Explanation: Eutrophication leads to excessive nutrient input, causing algal blooms that deplete oxygen in the water, harming aquatic life.

---

48. Soil Pollution

Which of the following is a common source of soil pollution?
A) Organic farming practices
B) Pesticide and herbicide use
C) Crop rotation
D) Composting

Answer: B) Pesticide and herbicide use
Explanation: The use of chemical pesticides and herbicides can lead to soil contamination, affecting soil health and biodiversity.

---

49. Climate Change: Rising Sea Levels

What is one major consequence of rising sea levels due to climate change?
A) Increased agricultural productivity
B) Loss of coastal habitats
C) Decreased salinity in oceans
D) Enhanced biodiversity in marine ecosystems

Answer: B) Loss of coastal habitats
Explanation: Rising sea levels can inundate coastal areas, leading to the loss of habitats such as wetlands and mangroves, which are critical for many species.

---

50. Biodiversity: Definition

What does biodiversity refer to in an ecosystem?
A) The number of individuals in a population
B) The variety of life in an ecosystem, including genetic, species, and ecosystem diversity
C) The total biomass of an ecosystem
D) The number of habitats in a region

Answer: B) The variety of life in an ecosystem, including genetic, species, and ecosystem diversity
Explanation: Biodiversity encompasses the variety of life forms, their genetic differences, and the ecosystems they inhabit.

---

51. Threats to Biodiversity

Which of the following is NOT a threat to biodiversity?
A) Habitat destruction
B) Poaching
C) Conservation efforts
D) Invasive species

Answer: C) Conservation efforts
Explanation: Conservation efforts aim to protect and preserve biodiversity, while habitat destruction, poaching, and invasive species are significant threats.

---

52. Endangered Species Conservation

What is one primary goal of the Endangered Species Act (ESA)?
A) To promote hunting of endangered species
B) To protect and recover imperiled species and their habitats
C) To increase urban development in wildlife areas
D) To eliminate invasive species

Answer: B) To protect and recover imperiled species and their habitats
Explanation: The ESA aims to protect endangered and threatened species and their habitats to promote recovery and prevent extinction.

---

53. Renewable Energy Sources

Which of the following is considered a renewable energy source?
A) Natural gas
B) Coal
C) Solar energy
D) Nuclear energy

Answer: C) Solar energy
Explanation: Solar energy is renewable because it is derived from the sun, which is an abundant and inexhaustible resource.

---

54. Sustainable Agriculture Practices

Which of the following practices is an example of sustainable agriculture?
A) Monoculture farming
B) Use of chemical fertilizers
C) Crop rotation
D) Deforestation for farmland

Answer: C) Crop rotation
Explanation: Crop rotation is a sustainable practice that helps maintain soil fertility and reduce pest and disease problems.

---

55. Protected Areas

What is the primary purpose of establishing protected areas, such as national parks and marine reserves?
A) To promote industrial development
B) To conserve biodiversity and protect ecosystems
C) To increase tourism revenue
D) To facilitate urban expansion

Answer: B) To conserve biodiversity and protect ecosystems
Explanation: Protected areas are designated to conserve natural habitats and biodiversity, providing safe spaces for wildlife and ecosystems.

---

56. Climate Agreements

What is the main goal of the Paris Climate Agreement?
A) To promote fossil fuel use
B) To reduce greenhouse gas emissions and limit global warming
C) To increase deforestation
D) To eliminate all forms of energy production

Answer: B) To reduce greenhouse gas emissions and limit global warming
Explanation: The Paris Climate Agreement aims to unite countries in efforts to reduce greenhouse gas emissions and mitigate climate change impacts.

---

57. Invasive Species Impact

How do invasive species typically affect native ecosystems?
A) They enhance biodiversity.
B) They compete with native species for resources.
C) They have no impact on native species.
D) They promote ecosystem stability.

Answer: B) They compete with native species for resources.
Explanation: Invasive species often outcompete native species for food, space, and other resources, leading to declines in native populations.

---

58. Population Density

In a study of a deer population in a forest, researchers find that the population density is 50 deer per square kilometer. What does this measurement indicate?
A) The total number of deer in the forest
B) The number of deer in a specific area
C) The carrying capacity of the forest
D) The reproductive rate of the deer

Answer: B) The number of deer in a specific area
Explanation: Population density refers to the number of individuals of a species per unit area, indicating how crowded the population is in that specific area.

---

59. Limiting Factors: Density-Independent

Which of the following is an example of a density-independent limiting factor affecting population growth?
A) Disease outbreak
B) Competition for food
C) Natural disasters like hurricanes
D) Predation

Answer: C) Natural disasters like hurricanes
Explanation: Density-independent factors affect populations regardless of their density, such as natural disasters that can cause widespread mortality.

---

60. Conservation Strategies

Which of the following strategies is most effective for conserving endangered species?
A) Increasing habitat destruction
B) Establishing wildlife corridors
C) Promoting hunting of endangered species
D) Reducing protected areas

Answer: B) Establishing wildlife corridors
Explanation: Wildlife corridors connect fragmented habitats, allowing for safe movement and genetic exchange between populations, which is crucial for the conservation of endangered species.

Chapter 7: Classification and Diversity of Life

1. Taxonomy and Classification

A biologist discovers a new organism that is unicellular, prokaryotic, and has a peptidoglycan cell wall. To which kingdom does this organism belong?
A) Archaebacteria
B) Eubacteria
C) Protista
D) Fungi

Answer: B) Eubacteria
Explanation: Eubacteria are prokaryotic, unicellular organisms with peptidoglycan cell walls, distinguishing them from Archaebacteria, which are also prokaryotic but have different cell wall compositions.

---

2. Linnaean Classification System

Using the Linnaean classification system, which of the following is the correct order of classification from broadest to most specific?
A) Kingdom → Domain → Phylum → Class → Order → Family → Genus → Species
B) Domain → Kingdom → Phylum → Class → Order → Family → Genus → Species
C) Species → Genus → Family → Order → Class → Phylum → Kingdom → Domain
D) Kingdom → Phylum → Class → Order → Family → Genus → Species → Domain

Answer: B) Domain → Kingdom → Phylum → Class → Order → Family → Genus → Species
Explanation: The correct order of the Linnaean classification system starts with the broadest category (Domain) and narrows down to the most specific (Species).

---

3. Binomial Nomenclature

What is the correct way to write the scientific name for humans using binomial nomenclature?
A) Homo Sapiens
B) homo sapiens
C) Homo sapiens
D) Homo sapiens

Answer: C) Homo sapiens
Explanation: In binomial nomenclature, the genus name is capitalized and the species name is lowercase, both italicized or underlined.

---

4. Three-Domain System

Which of the following domains includes organisms that are primarily extremophiles?
A) Bacteria
B) Archaea
C) Eukarya
D) Protista

Answer: B) Archaea
Explanation: Archaea are known for their ability to thrive in extreme environments, such as hot springs and salt lakes.

5. Six Kingdoms of Life

Which kingdom includes multicellular, autotrophic organisms that perform photosynthesis?
A) Fungi
B) Plantae
C) Animalia
D) Protista

Answer: B) Plantae
Explanation: The Plantae kingdom consists of multicellular, autotrophic organisms that use photosynthesis to produce their own food.

---

6. Viruses vs. Living Organisms

Which of the following characteristics distinguishes viruses from living organisms?
A) Presence of DNA or RNA
B) Ability to reproduce independently
C) Cellular structure
D) Metabolism

Answer: B) Ability to reproduce independently
Explanation: Viruses cannot reproduce independently; they require a host cell to replicate, unlike living organisms that can reproduce on their own.

---

7. Structure of Viruses

What is the primary function of the protein coat (capsid) in a virus?
A) To provide energy for the virus
B) To protect the genetic material
C) To facilitate metabolism
D) To allow the virus to reproduce

Answer: B) To protect the genetic material
Explanation: The capsid serves as a protective layer for the viral genetic material, ensuring its stability and integrity.

---

8. Lytic Cycle

In the lytic cycle of viral replication, what happens after the virus injects its genetic material into the host cell?
A) The virus remains dormant.
B) The host cell is forced to produce viral components.
C) The virus immediately assembles and exits the cell.
D) The host cell undergoes apoptosis.

Answer: B) The host cell is forced to produce viral components.
Explanation: After injection, the virus hijacks the host cell's machinery to replicate its genetic material and produce viral proteins.

---

9. Lysogenic Cycle

In the lysogenic cycle, what happens to the viral DNA after it integrates into the host genome?
A) It immediately causes cell lysis.
B) It remains dormant until triggered.
C) It is destroyed by the host cell.
D) It replicates independently of the host.

Answer: B) It remains dormant until triggered.
Explanation: In the lysogenic cycle, the viral DNA can integrate into the host genome and remain inactive until certain conditions trigger it to enter the lytic cycle.

---

10. Comparison: Viruses vs. Bacteria

Which of the following statements is true regarding the differences between viruses and bacteria?
A) Both have cellular structures.
B) Viruses can reproduce independently, while bacteria cannot.
C) Bacteria have metabolism, while viruses do not.
D) Both can be treated with antibiotics.

Answer: C) Bacteria have metabolism, while viruses do not.
Explanation: Bacteria are living organisms with metabolic processes, while viruses lack metabolism and require a host to replicate.

---

11. Notable Viral Diseases

Which of the following diseases is caused by a virus?
A) Tuberculosis
B) Malaria
C) Influenza
D) Ringworm

Answer: C) Influenza
Explanation: Influenza is caused by the influenza virus, while tuberculosis is caused by bacteria, malaria is caused by a parasite, and ringworm is a fungal infection.

---

12. Taxonomy: Importance

Why is taxonomy important in biology?
A) It eliminates the need for scientific names.
B) It organizes biodiversity and reflects evolutionary relationships.
C) It reduces the number of species in an ecosystem.
D) It promotes the extinction of certain species.

Answer: B) It organizes biodiversity and reflects evolutionary relationships.
Explanation: Taxonomy helps classify organisms based on shared characteristics, aiding in identification and understanding of evolutionary connections.

---

13. Classification Systems

Which of the following is a characteristic of the Linnaean classification system?
A) It uses only common names for organisms.
B) It is based solely on physical characteristics.
C) It includes a hierarchy of categories.
D) It does not reflect evolutionary relationships.

Answer: C) It includes a hierarchy of categories.
Explanation: The Linnaean classification system organizes organisms into a hierarchical structure, from broad categories to specific ones.

---

14. Eukarya Domain

Which of the following organisms belongs to the domain Eukarya?
A) Bacteria
B) Archaea
C) Fungi
D) Eubacteria

Answer: C) Fungi
Explanation: The domain Eukarya includes all eukaryotic organisms, such as fungi, plants, animals, and protists.

---

15. Viruses and Host Cells

What is the primary reason viruses require host cells for replication?
A) They have their own energy sources.
B) They lack the necessary cellular machinery for reproduction.
C) They can metabolize nutrients independently.
D) They can produce their own proteins.

Answer: B) They lack the necessary cellular machinery for reproduction.
Explanation: Viruses do not have the cellular structures needed for metabolism or reproduction, so they must rely on host cells to replicate.

---

16. Biodiversity: Definition

What does biodiversity encompass in an ecosystem?
A) The number of individuals in a population
B) The variety of life forms, including genetic, species, and ecosystem diversity
C) The total biomass of an ecosystem
D) The number of habitats in a region

Answer: B) The variety of life forms, including genetic, species, and ecosystem diversity
Explanation: Biodiversity refers to the variety of life in an ecosystem, including the diversity of species, genetic variations, and the different ecosystems present.

---

17. Threats to Biodiversity

Which of the following is a significant threat to biodiversity?
A) Habitat preservation
B) Sustainable agriculture
C) Pollution
D) Conservation efforts

Answer: C) Pollution
Explanation: Pollution, including air, water, and soil contamination, poses a significant threat to biodiversity by harming organisms and disrupting ecosystems.

---

18. Endangered Species

Which of the following is an example of an endangered species?
A) Common sparrow
B) American bison
C) Giant panda
D) House cat

Answer: C) Giant panda
Explanation: The giant panda is classified as an endangered species due to habitat loss and low reproductive rates.

19. Conservation Efforts

What is one primary goal of conservation biology?
A) To promote urban development
B) To protect and restore biodiversity
C) To increase pollution levels
D) To eliminate all invasive species

Answer: B) To protect and restore biodiversity
Explanation: Conservation biology focuses on protecting and restoring biodiversity to ensure the survival of various species and ecosystems.

---

20. Renewable Energy

Which of the following is considered a renewable energy source?
A) Natural gas
B) Coal
C) Solar energy
D) Nuclear energy

Answer: C) Solar energy
Explanation: Solar energy is renewable because it is derived from the sun, which is an abundant and inexhaustible resource.

---

21. Sustainable Practices

Which of the following practices is an example of sustainable agriculture?
A) Monoculture farming
B) Use of chemical fertilizers
C) Crop rotation
D) Deforestation for farmland

Answer: C) Crop rotation
Explanation: Crop rotation is a sustainable practice that helps maintain soil fertility and reduce pest and disease problems.

---

22. Protected Areas

What is the primary purpose of establishing protected areas, such as national parks and marine reserves?
A) To promote industrial development
B) To conserve biodiversity and protect ecosystems
C) To increase tourism revenue
D) To facilitate urban expansion

Answer: B) To conserve biodiversity and protect ecosystems
Explanation: Protected areas are designated to conserve natural habitats and biodiversity, providing safe spaces for wildlife and ecosystems.

---

23. Climate Agreements

What is the main goal of the Paris Climate Agreement?
A) To promote fossil fuel use
B) To reduce greenhouse gas emissions and limit global warming

C) To increase deforestation
D) To eliminate all forms of energy production

Answer: B) To reduce greenhouse gas emissions and limit global warming
Explanation: The Paris Climate Agreement aims to unite countries in efforts to reduce greenhouse gas emissions and mitigate climate change impacts.

---

24. Invasive Species Impact

How do invasive species typically affect native ecosystems?
A) They enhance biodiversity.
B) They compete with native species for resources.
C) They have no impact on native species.
D) They promote ecosystem stability.

Answer: B) They compete with native species for resources.
Explanation: Invasive species often outcompete native species for food, space, and other resources, leading to declines in native populations.

---

25. Population Density

In a study of a deer population in a forest, researchers find that the population density is 50 deer per square kilometer. What does this measurement indicate?
A) The total number of deer in the forest
B) The number of deer in a specific area
C) The carrying capacity of the forest
D) The reproductive rate of the deer

Answer: B) The number of deer in a specific area
Explanation: Population density refers to the number of individuals of a species per unit area, indicating how crowded the population is in that specific area.

---

26. Limiting Factors: Density-Independent

Which of the following is an example of a density-independent limiting factor affecting population growth?
A) Disease outbreak
B) Competition for food
C) Natural disasters like hurricanes
D) Predation

Answer: C) Natural disasters like hurricanes
Explanation: Density-independent factors affect populations regardless of their density, such as natural disasters that can cause widespread mortality.

---

27. Conservation Strategies

Which of the following strategies is most effective for conserving endangered species?
A) Increasing habitat destruction
B) Establishing wildlife corridors
C) Promoting hunting of endangered species
D) Reducing protected areas

Answer: B) Establishing wildlife corridors
Explanation: Wildlife corridors connect fragmented habitats, allowing for safe movement and genetic exchange between populations, which is crucial for the conservation of endangered species.

28. Biodiversity: Importance

Why is biodiversity important for ecosystem stability?
A) It reduces competition among species.
B) It increases the resilience of ecosystems to disturbances.
C) It eliminates the need for food webs.
D) It decreases the number of species interactions.

Answer: B) It increases the resilience of ecosystems to disturbances.
Explanation: High biodiversity contributes to ecosystem stability and resilience, allowing ecosystems to better withstand and recover from disturbances.

---

29. Human Impact: Urbanization

How does urbanization typically affect local ecosystems?
A) It increases biodiversity.
B) It creates more natural habitats.
C) It leads to habitat fragmentation and loss.
D) It has no impact on ecosystems.

Answer: C) It leads to habitat fragmentation and loss.
Explanation: Urbanization often results in the destruction of natural habitats, leading to fragmentation and loss of biodiversity.

---

30. Climate Change: Effects

Which of the following is a potential effect of climate change on ecosystems?
A) Increased agricultural productivity
B) Loss of biodiversity
C) Decreased frequency of extreme weather events
D) Stabilization of sea levels

Answer: B) Loss of biodiversity
Explanation: Climate change can lead to habitat loss, altered species distributions, and increased extinction rates, resulting in a loss of biodiversity.

---

31. Eutrophication Process

What is the primary cause of eutrophication in aquatic ecosystems?
A) Increased biodiversity
B) Excessive nutrient runoff from fertilizers
C) Decreased water temperature
D) Increased oxygen levels

Answer: B) Excessive nutrient runoff from fertilizers
Explanation: Eutrophication is primarily caused by nutrient runoff, particularly nitrogen and phosphorus from fertilizers, leading to algal blooms and oxygen depletion.

---

32. Soil Conservation

Which of the following practices is most effective for preventing soil erosion?
A) Deforestation
B) Overgrazing

C) Contour plowing
D) Monoculture farming

Answer: C) Contour plowing
Explanation: Contour plowing involves plowing across the slope of the land, which helps reduce soil erosion by following the natural contours of the landscape.

---

33. Endangered Species Act

What is the primary purpose of the Endangered Species Act (ESA)?
A) To promote hunting of endangered species
B) To protect and recover imperiled species and their habitats
C) To increase urban development in wildlife areas
D) To eliminate invasive species

Answer: B) To protect and recover imperiled species and their habitats
Explanation: The ESA aims to protect endangered and threatened species and their habitats to promote recovery and prevent extinction.

---

34. Renewable Energy Benefits

What is one major benefit of using renewable energy sources?
A) They are non-polluting and sustainable.
B) They are always available regardless of weather conditions.
C) They require no initial investment.
D) They produce more greenhouse gases than fossil fuels.

Answer: A) They are non-polluting and sustainable.
Explanation: Renewable energy sources, such as solar and wind, are sustainable and produce little to no pollution compared to fossil fuels.

---

35. Invasive Species Management

What is one effective strategy for managing invasive species?
A) Promoting their spread
B) Ignoring their presence
C) Implementing control measures, such as removal or containment
D) Allowing them to compete with native species

Answer: C) Implementing control measures, such as removal or containment
Explanation: Effective management of invasive species often involves control measures to reduce their populations and limit their impact on native ecosystems.

---

36. Population Growth Models

Which of the following best describes a population that exhibits exponential growth?
A) The population grows slowly and stabilizes at carrying capacity.
B) The population grows rapidly when resources are unlimited.
C) The population experiences regular fluctuations.
D) The population decreases due to limiting factors.

Answer: B) The population grows rapidly when resources are unlimited.
Explanation: Exponential growth occurs when a population increases rapidly in size due to abundant resources and favorable conditions.

37. Climate Change Mitigation

Which of the following actions is most effective for mitigating climate change?
A) Increasing fossil fuel consumption
B) Promoting reforestation and afforestation
C) Expanding urban areas
D) Reducing renewable energy investments

Answer: B) Promoting reforestation and afforestation
Explanation: Reforestation and afforestation help absorb carbon dioxide from the atmosphere, making them effective strategies for mitigating climate change.

---

38. Biodiversity Hotspots

What defines a biodiversity hotspot?
A) An area with low species diversity
B) An area with high levels of endemism and significant habitat loss
C) An area with abundant resources
D) An area with no human impact

Answer: B) An area with high levels of endemism and significant habitat loss
Explanation: Biodiversity hotspots are regions that are rich in endemic species but have experienced significant habitat loss, making them a priority for conservation efforts.

---

39. Conservation Legislation

Which international agreement aims to protect endangered species from over-exploitation through trade?
A) Paris Climate Agreement
B) Convention on Biological Diversity
C) Convention on International Trade in Endangered Species (CITES)
D) Endangered Species Act (ESA)

Answer: C) Convention on International Trade in Endangered Species (CITES)
Explanation: CITES is an international agreement that regulates trade in endangered species to prevent their extinction.

---

40. Ecosystem Services

Which of the following is an example of an ecosystem service provided by forests?
A) Increased urban development
B) Water filtration and carbon sequestration
C) Soil degradation
D) Increased pollution levels

Answer: B) Water filtration and carbon sequestration
Explanation: Forests provide essential ecosystem services, including filtering water and sequestering carbon dioxide, which helps mitigate climate change.

Chapter 8: Human Body Systems and Homeostasis

1. Circulatory System Function

A patient presents with symptoms of fatigue and shortness of breath. Upon examination, the doctor suspects a problem with the circulatory system. Which organ is primarily responsible for pumping blood throughout the body?
A) Lungs
B) Heart
C) Liver
D) Kidneys

Answer: B) Heart
Explanation: The heart is the organ responsible for pumping blood throughout the body, supplying oxygen and nutrients to tissues and removing waste products.

---

2. Blood Components

A laboratory technician analyzes a blood sample and notes a high number of white blood cells. What does this indicate about the patient's health?
A) The patient is dehydrated.
B) The patient has a bacterial infection.
C) The patient has low oxygen levels.
D) The patient is experiencing anemia.

Answer: B) The patient has a bacterial infection.
Explanation: An elevated white blood cell count often indicates an immune response to infection, particularly bacterial infections.

---

3. Respiratory System Gas Exchange

During a physical examination, a doctor assesses a patient's lung function. Which structure in the lungs is primarily responsible for the exchange of oxygen and carbon dioxide?
A) Trachea
B) Bronchi
C) Alveoli
D) Diaphragm

Answer: C) Alveoli
Explanation: Alveoli are tiny air sacs in the lungs where gas exchange occurs, allowing oxygen to enter the blood and carbon dioxide to be removed.

---

4. Digestive System Function

A nutritionist is evaluating a patient's diet and notes that they have difficulty absorbing nutrients. Which part of the digestive system is primarily responsible for nutrient absorption?
A) Stomach
B) Esophagus
C) Small intestine
D) Large intestine

Answer: C) Small intestine
Explanation: The small intestine is the main site for nutrient absorption in the digestive system, where digested food is absorbed into the bloodstream.

---

5. Nervous System Response

A person touches a hot stove and quickly withdraws their hand. What type of response is this an example of?
A) Reflex action
B) Voluntary action
C) Involuntary action
D) Homeostatic regulation

Answer: A) Reflex action
Explanation: A reflex action is an automatic response to a stimulus, allowing for quick reactions to potentially harmful situations.

---

6. Excretory System Function

A patient is diagnosed with kidney disease, which affects their ability to filter blood. What is the primary function of the kidneys in the excretory system?
A) Produce hormones
B) Filter waste from the blood and form urine
C) Regulate body temperature
D) Absorb nutrients

Answer: B) Filter waste from the blood and form urine
Explanation: The kidneys filter waste products from the blood, regulate fluid balance, and produce urine for excretion.

---

7. Immune System Defense

A patient experiences inflammation and fever after an injury. Which part of the immune system is primarily responsible for initiating the inflammatory response?
A) B cells
B) T cells
C) Phagocytes
D) Antibodies

Answer: C) Phagocytes
Explanation: Phagocytes are white blood cells that respond to injury or infection by engulfing pathogens and initiating the inflammatory response.

---

8. Vaccines and Immunity

A child receives a vaccine for measles. What is the primary purpose of this vaccine?
A) To treat an existing infection
B) To stimulate an immune response and create memory cells
C) To provide immediate immunity
D) To eliminate the pathogen from the environment

Answer: B) To stimulate an immune response and create memory cells
Explanation: Vaccines introduce a weakened or inactivated pathogen to stimulate the immune system, leading to the production of memory cells for long-term immunity.

9. Homeostasis Regulation

Which organ system is primarily responsible for maintaining homeostasis by regulating body temperature?
A) Circulatory system
B) Nervous system
C) Endocrine system
D) Respiratory system

Answer: B) Nervous system
Explanation: The nervous system plays a key role in regulating body temperature through mechanisms such as sweating and shivering in response to temperature changes.

---

10. First Line of Defense

What is the first line of defense in the immune system against pathogens?
A) Inflammatory response
B) Skin and mucous membranes
C) Antibodies
D) T cells

Answer: B) Skin and mucous membranes
Explanation: The first line of defense includes physical barriers like skin and mucous membranes that prevent pathogens from entering the body.

---

11. Second Line of Defense

During an infection, a person develops a fever. What is the purpose of this response?
A) To increase blood flow to the site of infection
B) To slow down the growth of pathogens
C) To enhance the production of antibodies
D) To promote tissue repair

Answer: B) To slow down the growth of pathogens
Explanation: A fever raises body temperature, which can inhibit the growth of pathogens and enhance the immune response.

---

12. T Cells Function

What is the primary role of T cells in the immune system?
A) To produce antibodies
B) To attack infected cells directly
C) To engulf pathogens
D) To stimulate B cells

Answer: B) To attack infected cells directly
Explanation: T cells are responsible for directly attacking and destroying infected cells, playing a crucial role in the adaptive immune response.

---

13. Memory Cells

What is the function of memory cells in the immune system?
A) To produce immediate immune responses
B) To remember past infections and respond more quickly upon re-exposure
C) To engulf pathogens
D) To produce antibodies

Answer: B) To remember past infections and respond more quickly upon re-exposure
Explanation: Memory cells are long-lived cells that "remember" previous infections, allowing for a faster and more effective immune response upon re-exposure to the same pathogen.

---

14. Viral Structure

Which of the following components is found in all viruses?
A) Cell wall
B) Nucleus
C) Protein coat (capsid)
D) Mitochondria

Answer: C) Protein coat (capsid)
Explanation: All viruses have a protein coat (capsid) that protects their genetic material, which can be either DNA or RNA.

---

15. Viral Replication

In the lytic cycle, what happens to the host cell after the new viruses are assembled?
A) The host cell remains intact.
B) The host cell undergoes apoptosis.
C) The host cell is lysed (bursts).
D) The host cell enters a dormant state.

Answer: C) The host cell is lysed (bursts).
Explanation: In the lytic cycle, the host cell is forced to produce new viral components, and once assembled, the cell bursts, releasing the new viruses.

---

16. Immune Response to Vaccination

After receiving a vaccine, how does the body develop immunity?
A) By producing more pathogens
B) By creating memory cells that recognize the pathogen
C) By increasing the number of red blood cells
D) By enhancing the inflammatory response

Answer: B) By creating memory cells that recognize the pathogen
Explanation: Vaccination stimulates the immune system to produce memory cells, which provide long-term immunity by recognizing and responding to the pathogen if encountered again.

---

17. Homeostasis and the Excretory System

How does the excretory system contribute to homeostasis?
A) By producing hormones
B) By filtering waste and regulating fluid balance
C) By transporting oxygen
D) By digesting food

Answer: B) By filtering waste and regulating fluid balance
Explanation: The excretory system maintains homeostasis by filtering waste products from the blood and regulating water and electrolyte balance.

---

18. Role of the Liver

What is one of the primary functions of the liver in the digestive system?
A) Absorbing nutrients
B) Producing bile for fat digestion
C) Transporting food to the stomach
D) Breaking down carbohydrates

Answer: B) Producing bile for fat digestion
Explanation: The liver produces bile, which is essential for the emulsification and digestion of fats in the small intestine.

---

19. Immune System and Allergies

What is an allergic reaction?
A) A response to a bacterial infection
B) An overreaction of the immune system to a harmless substance
C) A failure of the immune system
D) A response to a viral infection

Answer: B) An overreaction of the immune system to a harmless substance
Explanation: Allergic reactions occur when the immune system mistakenly identifies a harmless substance as a threat and mounts an exaggerated response.

---

20. Homeostasis and Blood Sugar

Which organ is primarily responsible for regulating blood sugar levels in the body?
A) Liver
B) Heart
C) Pancreas
D) Kidneys

Answer: C) Pancreas
Explanation: The pancreas regulates blood sugar levels by producing insulin and glucagon, which help maintain homeostasis.

---

21. Immune System Components

Which type of white blood cell is primarily responsible for producing antibodies?
A) T cells
B) B cells
C) Phagocytes
D) Neutrophils

Answer: B) B cells
Explanation: B cells are responsible for producing antibodies that target specific pathogens during an immune response.

---

22. Respiratory System Function

What is the primary function of the respiratory system?
A) To transport nutrients
B) To provide oxygen and remove carbon dioxide
C) To regulate body temperature
D) To filter waste from the blood

Answer: B) To provide oxygen and remove carbon dioxide
Explanation: The respiratory system is responsible for gas exchange, supplying oxygen to the body and removing carbon dioxide.

---

23. Circulatory System Components

What is the main function of red blood cells?
A) To fight infection
B) To transport oxygen
C) To aid in blood clotting
D) To produce antibodies

Answer: B) To transport oxygen
Explanation: Red blood cells are specialized for transporting oxygen from the lungs to the body's tissues.

---

24. Immune System and Pathogens

Which of the following is NOT a type of pathogen?
A) Bacteria
B) Virus
C) Antibody
D) Fungus

Answer: C) Antibody
Explanation: Antibodies are proteins produced by the immune system to fight pathogens, while bacteria, viruses, and fungi are types of pathogens that can cause disease.

---

25. Digestive System Role

What is the primary role of the large intestine in the digestive system?
A) Absorbing nutrients
B) Breaking down food
C) Absorbing water and forming waste
D) Producing digestive enzymes

Answer: C) Absorbing water and forming waste
Explanation: The large intestine primarily absorbs water from indigestible food matter and compacts it into waste for excretion.

---

26. Immune System Memory

How do memory cells contribute to the immune response?
A) They produce antibodies immediately.
B) They remember past infections for a faster response.
C) They attack pathogens directly.
D) They enhance the inflammatory response.

Answer: B) They remember past infections for a faster response.
Explanation: Memory cells allow the immune system to respond more quickly and effectively to previously encountered pathogens.

---

27. Homeostasis and Temperature Regulation

Which part of the brain is primarily responsible for regulating body temperature?
A) Cerebellum
B) Hypothalamus
C) Medulla oblongata
D) Cerebrum

Answer: B) Hypothalamus
Explanation: The hypothalamus plays a key role in maintaining homeostasis, including regulating body temperature through mechanisms like sweating and shivering.

---

28. Viral Diseases

Which of the following diseases is caused by a virus?
A) Tuberculosis
B) Influenza
C) Malaria
D) Ringworm

Answer: B) Influenza
Explanation: Influenza is caused by the influenza virus, while tuberculosis is caused by bacteria, malaria is caused by a parasite, and ringworm is a fungal infection.

---

29. Immune System and Vaccination

What is the primary purpose of vaccination?
A) To treat existing infections
B) To stimulate an immune response and create memory cells
C) To eliminate pathogens from the environment
D) To increase the number of white blood cells

Answer: B) To stimulate an immune response and create memory cells
Explanation: Vaccination introduces a harmless form of a pathogen to stimulate the immune system, leading to the production of memory cells for long-term immunity.

---

30. Excretory System and Homeostasis

How does the excretory system help maintain homeostasis?
A) By producing hormones
B) By filtering waste and regulating fluid balance
C) By transporting oxygen
D) By digesting food

Answer: B) By filtering waste and regulating fluid balance
Explanation: The excretory system maintains homeostasis by filtering waste products from the blood and regulating water and electrolyte balance.

---

31. Immune System and Inflammation

What is the role of inflammation in the immune response?
A) To increase blood flow and recruit immune cells to the site of infection
B) To produce antibodies
C) To destroy pathogens directly
D) To regulate body temperature

Answer: A) To increase blood flow and recruit immune cells to the site of infection
Explanation: Inflammation is a protective response that increases blood flow and brings immune cells to the site of infection or injury.

---

32. Digestive System Enzymes

Which organ produces enzymes that aid in the digestion of carbohydrates, proteins, and fats?
A) Stomach
B) Pancreas
C) Liver
D) Small intestine

Answer: B) Pancreas
Explanation: The pancreas produces digestive enzymes that are released into the small intestine to help break down carbohydrates, proteins, and fats.

---

33. Immune System and Allergies

What is an allergic reaction?
A) A response to a bacterial infection
B) An overreaction of the immune system to a harmless substance
C) A failure of the immune system
D) A response to a viral infection

Answer: B) An overreaction of the immune system to a harmless substance
Explanation: Allergic reactions occur when the immune system mistakenly identifies a harmless substance as a threat and mounts an exaggerated response.

---

34. Homeostasis and Blood Sugar Regulation

Which organ is primarily responsible for regulating blood sugar levels in the body?
A) Liver
B) Heart
C) Pancreas
D) Kidneys

Answer: C) Pancreas
Explanation: The pancreas regulates blood sugar levels by producing insulin and glucagon, which help maintain homeostasis.

---

35. Immune System Components

Which type of white blood cell is primarily responsible for producing antibodies?
A) T cells
B) B cells
C) Phagocytes
D) Neutrophils

Answer: B) B cells
Explanation: B cells are responsible for producing antibodies that target specific pathogens during an immune response.

---

36. Respiratory System Function

What is the primary function of the respiratory system?
A) To transport nutrients
B) To provide oxygen and remove carbon dioxide
C) To regulate body temperature
D) To filter waste from the blood

Answer: B) To provide oxygen and remove carbon dioxide
Explanation: The respiratory system is responsible for gas exchange, supplying oxygen to the body and removing carbon dioxide.

---

37. Circulatory System Components

What is the main function of red blood cells?
A) To fight infection
B) To transport oxygen
C) To aid in blood clotting
D) To produce antibodies

Answer: B) To transport oxygen
Explanation: Red blood cells are specialized for transporting oxygen from the lungs to the body's tissues.

---

38. Immune System and Pathogens

Which of the following is NOT a type of pathogen?
A) Bacteria
B) Virus
C) Antibody
D) Fungus

Answer: C) Antibody
Explanation: Antibodies are proteins produced by the immune system to fight pathogens, while bacteria, viruses, and fungi are types of pathogens that can cause disease.

---

39. Digestive System Role

What is the primary role of the large intestine in the digestive system?
A) Absorbing nutrients
B) Breaking down food
C) Absorbing water and forming waste
D) Producing digestive enzymes

Answer: C) Absorbing water and forming waste
Explanation: The large intestine primarily absorbs water from indigestible food matter and compacts it into waste for excretion.

---

40. Immune System Memory

How do memory cells contribute to the immune response?
A) They produce antibodies immediately.
B) They remember past infections for a faster response.
C) They attack pathogens directly.
D) They enhance the inflammatory response.

Answer: B) They remember past infections for a faster response.
Explanation: Memory cells allow the immune system to respond more quickly and effectively to previously encountered pathogens.

Chapter 9: Data Analysis and Scientific Literacy

1. Interpreting Graphs

A researcher presents a line graph showing the increase in average global temperatures over the past century. What type of relationship does this graph likely illustrate?
A) Inverse relationship
B) No relationship
C) Direct relationship
D) Cyclical relationship

Answer: C) Direct relationship
Explanation: A line graph showing an increase in average global temperatures over time typically indicates a direct relationship, where an increase in time correlates with an increase in temperature.

---

2. Data Tables

A data table lists the number of hours studied and corresponding test scores for a group of students. If the data shows that as study hours increase, test scores also increase, what type of relationship is being demonstrated?
A) Inverse relationship
B) No relationship
C) Direct relationship
D) Random relationship

Answer: C) Direct relationship
Explanation: The scenario describes a direct relationship, where an increase in one variable (study hours) leads to an increase in another variable (test scores).

---

3. Analyzing Bar Graphs

A bar graph compares the number of different species of birds observed in various habitats. What is the primary purpose of using a bar graph in this scenario?
A) To show trends over time
B) To represent percentages of a whole
C) To compare different groups or categories
D) To illustrate relationships between two variables

Answer: C) To compare different groups or categories
Explanation: Bar graphs are effective for comparing discrete categories, such as the number of bird species in different habitats.

---

4. Using Averages

A scientist collects data on the growth rates of plants under different light conditions. If the mean growth rate of plants in full sunlight is 15 cm, while the mean growth rate in partial shade is 10 cm, what can be concluded?
A) Plants grow better in partial shade.
B) There is no difference in growth rates.
C) Plants grow better in full sunlight.
D) The data is inconclusive.

Answer: C) Plants grow better in full sunlight.
Explanation: The mean growth rate indicates that plants in full sunlight have a higher average growth rate compared to those in partial shade, suggesting better growth conditions.

5. Scatter Plots

A scatter plot shows the relationship between exercise duration and heart rate in a group of individuals. If the points on the scatter plot form a line that slopes upward, what does this indicate?
A) No relationship
B) Inverse relationship
C) Direct relationship
D) Random relationship

Answer: C) Direct relationship
Explanation: An upward-sloping scatter plot indicates a direct relationship, where an increase in exercise duration correlates with an increase in heart rate.

6. Experimental Design

In an experiment testing the effect of fertilizer on plant growth, the amount of fertilizer used is the independent variable. What is the dependent variable in this experiment?
A) The type of plant used
B) The amount of sunlight received
C) The growth of the plants
D) The type of fertilizer used

Answer: C) The growth of the plants
Explanation: The dependent variable is the factor being measured, which in this case is the growth of the plants in response to different amounts of fertilizer.

7. Control Group vs. Experimental Group

In a study examining the effects of a new drug on blood pressure, the control group receives a placebo while the experimental group receives the drug. What is the purpose of having a control group?
A) To test the drug's effectiveness
B) To provide a baseline for comparison
C) To increase the sample size
D) To eliminate bias

Answer: B) To provide a baseline for comparison
Explanation: The control group serves as a baseline to compare the effects of the drug on the experimental group, helping to determine the drug's effectiveness.

8. Sample Size and Reliability

Why is a larger sample size important in scientific experiments?
A) It reduces the time needed for the experiment.
B) It increases the likelihood of random errors.
C) It improves the reliability and validity of the results.
D) It eliminates the need for a control group.

Answer: C) It improves the reliability and validity of the results.
Explanation: A larger sample size helps ensure that the results are representative of the population, reducing the impact of outliers and increasing the reliability of the findings.

9. Identifying Bias

A researcher conducts a study on a new diet and only includes participants who have previously lost weight on similar diets. What type of bias is present in this study?
A) Selection bias
B) Confirmation bias
C) Publication bias
D) Measurement bias

Answer: A) Selection bias
Explanation: Selection bias occurs when the sample is not representative of the population, as the researcher has only included individuals with prior success on similar diets.

---

10. Reducing Bias

Which of the following methods can help reduce bias in scientific research?
A) Using random sampling
B) Allowing researchers to choose participants
C) Ignoring outliers in data
D) Conducting the study without a control group

Answer: A) Using random sampling
Explanation: Random sampling helps ensure that every individual has an equal chance of being selected, reducing bias and increasing the representativeness of the sample.

---

11. Evaluating Scientific Claims

When assessing a scientific claim, which of the following is a key factor to consider?
A) The popularity of the claim
B) The number of social media shares
C) The presence of empirical data and peer review
D) The opinion of a celebrity

Answer: C) The presence of empirical data and peer review
Explanation: Scientific claims should be based on empirical data and undergo peer review to ensure validity and reliability.

---

12. Distinguishing Science from Pseudoscience

Which of the following characteristics is typical of pseudoscience?
A) Reliance on empirical evidence
B) Peer-reviewed studies
C) Anecdotal evidence and lack of testing
D) Repeatable results

Answer: C) Anecdotal evidence and lack of testing
Explanation: Pseudoscience often relies on anecdotal evidence and lacks rigorous testing and validation, distinguishing it from legitimate scientific inquiry.

---

13. Statistical Significance

What does it mean if a study's results are statistically significant?
A) The results are due to random chance.
B) The results show meaningful differences that are unlikely to occur by chance.
C) The results are inconclusive.
D) The results are not reproducible.

Answer: B) The results show meaningful differences that are unlikely to occur by chance.
Explanation: Statistical significance indicates that the observed effects are likely due to the independent variable rather than random variation.

---

14. Correlation vs. Causation

A study finds a correlation between ice cream sales and drowning incidents. What is a critical point to remember about this relationship?
A) Ice cream sales cause drowning incidents.
B) Drowning incidents cause increased ice cream sales.
C) There may be a third variable (e.g., hot weather) influencing both.
D) The correlation is purely coincidental.

Answer: C) There may be a third variable (e.g., hot weather) influencing both.
Explanation: Correlation does not imply causation; a third variable may be affecting both observed phenomena.

---

15. Analyzing Line Graphs

A line graph shows the population growth of a species over several years. If the graph shows a steady increase followed by a plateau, what does the plateau indicate?
A) The population is decreasing.
B) The population has reached its carrying capacity.
C) The population is experiencing exponential growth.
D) The population is extinct.

Answer: B) The population has reached its carrying capacity.
Explanation: A plateau in a population growth graph indicates that the population has stabilized at its carrying capacity, where resources are limited.

---

16. Using Pie Charts

A pie chart illustrates the percentage of different energy sources used in a country. What is the primary advantage of using a pie chart for this data?
A) It shows trends over time.
B) It compares discrete categories.
C) It represents proportions of a whole.
D) It displays relationships between two variables.

Answer: C) It represents proportions of a whole.
Explanation: Pie charts are effective for showing how different categories contribute to a total, making them ideal for representing percentages.

---

17. Data Analysis Techniques

Which of the following statistical measures is used to find the middle value in a data set?
A) Mean
B) Median
C) Mode
D) Range

Answer: B) Median
Explanation: The median is the middle value in a data set when the values are arranged in order, providing a measure of central tendency.

18. Experimental Variables

In an experiment testing the effect of temperature on enzyme activity, what is the independent variable?
A) The enzyme concentration
B) The temperature
C) The reaction time
D) The substrate concentration

Answer: B) The temperature
Explanation: The independent variable is the factor that is manipulated in the experiment, which in this case is the temperature.

---

19. Control Group Importance

Why is it important to have a control group in an experiment?
A) To increase the sample size
B) To provide a baseline for comparison
C) To eliminate all variables
D) To ensure the experiment is double-blind

Answer: B) To provide a baseline for comparison
Explanation: The control group serves as a standard to compare the effects of the independent variable on the experimental group.

---

20. Identifying Trends

A researcher collects data on the growth of two different plant species under varying light conditions. If the data shows that one species consistently grows taller than the other under all conditions, what trend is being observed?
A) No relationship
B) Inverse relationship
C) Direct relationship
D) Consistent superiority

Answer: D) Consistent superiority
Explanation: The trend indicates that one species consistently outperforms the other in growth, regardless of light conditions.

---

21. Correlation Studies

A scatter plot shows a positive correlation between study time and test scores. What can be inferred from this data?
A) Increased study time leads to lower test scores.
B) There is no relationship between study time and test scores.
C) Increased study time is associated with higher test scores.
D) Test scores cause changes in study time.

Answer: C) Increased study time is associated with higher test scores.
Explanation: A positive correlation suggests that as study time increases, test scores also tend to increase.

---

22. Evaluating Scientific Claims

When evaluating a scientific claim, which of the following is most important?
A) The number of people who believe the claim
B) The presence of empirical evidence and peer review
C) The popularity of the claim on social media
D) The opinion of a celebrity

Answer: B) The presence of empirical evidence and peer review
Explanation: Scientific claims should be supported by empirical evidence and undergo peer review to ensure validity and reliability.

---

23. Statistical Analysis

In a study measuring the effect of a new drug on blood pressure, researchers find a p-value of 0.03. What does this indicate?
A) The results are not statistically significant.
B) There is a 3% chance the results are due to random chance.
C) The drug has no effect on blood pressure.
D) The results are highly significant.

Answer: B) There is a 3% chance the results are due to random chance.
Explanation: A p-value of 0.03 indicates that there is a 3% probability that the observed results could occur by random chance, suggesting statistical significance.

---

24. Data Interpretation

A researcher presents data showing a decrease in the population of a species over several years. What type of trend is being observed?
A) Exponential growth
B) Decline
C) Stabilization
D) Fluctuation

Answer: B) Decline
Explanation: A consistent decrease in population over time indicates a declining trend for that species.

---

25. Graphical Representation

Which type of graph would be most appropriate for showing the relationship between two continuous variables, such as temperature and enzyme activity?
A) Bar graph
B) Pie chart
C) Line graph
D) Scatter plot

Answer: C) Line graph
Explanation: A line graph is suitable for displaying trends over time or relationships between two continuous variables.

---

26. Experimental Design Components

In an experiment testing the effect of light intensity on plant growth, which of the following is a controlled variable?
A) The type of plant used
B) The amount of light received
C) The growth rate of the plants
D) The duration of the experiment

Answer: A) The type of plant used
Explanation: The controlled variable is the factor that remains constant throughout the experiment to ensure that the results are valid.

---

27. Identifying Bias in Research

A study funded by a company that produces a new health supplement shows overwhelmingly positive results. What type of bias might be present in this study?
A) Selection bias
B) Confirmation bias
C) Publication bias
D) Funding bias

Answer: D) Funding bias
Explanation: Funding bias occurs when the source of funding influences the results or interpretation of a study, often leading to favorable outcomes for the sponsor.

---

28. Analyzing Data Trends

A researcher analyzes data showing that as pollution levels increase, the population of a certain fish species decreases. What type of relationship is indicated by this data?
A) Direct relationship
B) Inverse relationship
C) No relationship
D) Cyclical relationship

Answer: B) Inverse relationship
Explanation: An inverse relationship is indicated when one variable increases (pollution levels) while the other decreases (fish population).

---

29. Using Percentages

In a survey, 60 out of 100 respondents reported feeling satisfied with a product. What percentage of respondents expressed satisfaction?
A) 50%
B) 60%
C) 70%
D) 80%

Answer: B) 60%
Explanation: The percentage of satisfied respondents is calculated as (60/100) × 100 = 60%.

---

30. Correlation vs. Causation

A study finds a correlation between increased screen time and higher rates of anxiety in teenagers. What is a critical consideration regarding this finding?
A) Screen time causes anxiety.
B) Anxiety causes increased screen time.
C) There may be other factors influencing both variables.
D) The correlation is purely coincidental.

Answer: C) There may be other factors influencing both variables.
Explanation: Correlation does not imply causation; other factors may be affecting both screen time and anxiety levels.

---

31. Evaluating Experimental Results

A scientist conducts an experiment and finds that the results are not reproducible by other researchers. What does this suggest about the original study?
A) The study is valid.

B) The study may have methodological flaws.
C) The results are statistically significant.
D) The study has been peer-reviewed.

Answer: B) The study may have methodological flaws.
Explanation: If results are not reproducible, it suggests potential issues with the experimental design or methodology.

---

32. Data Analysis Techniques

Which statistical measure is used to determine the most frequently occurring value in a data set?
A) Mean
B) Median
C) Mode
D) Range

Answer: C) Mode
Explanation: The mode is the value that appears most frequently in a data set.

---

33. Graphical Data Representation

A researcher uses a pie chart to represent the distribution of different types of energy sources used in a country. What is the primary advantage of using a pie chart?
A) It shows trends over time.
B) It compares discrete categories.
C) It represents proportions of a whole.
D) It displays relationships between two variables.

Answer: C) It represents proportions of a whole.
Explanation: Pie charts are effective for showing how different categories contribute to a total, making them ideal for representing percentages.

---

34. Experimental Design

In an experiment testing the effect of temperature on enzyme activity, which of the following is the dependent variable?
A) The temperature
B) The enzyme concentration
C) The rate of reaction
D) The type of enzyme

Answer: C) The rate of reaction
Explanation: The dependent variable is the factor being measured, which in this case is the rate of reaction of the enzyme at different temperatures.

---

35. Identifying Trends in Data

A researcher collects data on the number of hours students study and their corresponding exam scores. If the data shows a consistent increase in exam scores with more study hours, what trend is being observed?
A) No relationship
B) Inverse relationship
C) Direct relationship
D) Random relationship

Answer: C) Direct relationship
Explanation: The trend indicates a direct relationship, where increased study hours correlate with higher exam scores.

---

36. Statistical Significance

In a clinical trial, a new medication shows a p-value of 0.01. What does this indicate about the results?
A) The results are not statistically significant.
B) There is a 1% chance the results are due to random chance.
C) The results are inconclusive.
D) The results are highly significant.

Answer: B) There is a 1% chance the results are due to random chance.
Explanation: A p-value of 0.01 indicates that there is only a 1% probability that the observed results occurred by random chance, suggesting strong statistical significance.

---

37. Correlation Studies

A scatter plot shows a negative correlation between the amount of sleep and levels of stress in college students. What does this imply?
A) More sleep leads to higher stress levels.
B) Less sleep is associated with higher stress levels.
C) There is no relationship between sleep and stress.
D) Stress levels do not affect sleep patterns.

Answer: B) Less sleep is associated with higher stress levels.
Explanation: A negative correlation indicates that as one variable (sleep) decreases, the other variable (stress) tends to increase.

---

38. Evaluating Scientific Claims

When evaluating a scientific claim, which of the following is most important?
A) The number of people who believe the claim
B) The presence of empirical evidence and peer review
C) The popularity of the claim on social media
D) The opinion of a celebrity

Answer: B) The presence of empirical evidence and peer review
Explanation: Scientific claims should be supported by empirical evidence and undergo peer review to ensure validity and reliability.

---

39. Identifying Bias in Research

A study funded by a company that produces a new health supplement shows overwhelmingly positive results. What type of bias might be present in this study?
A) Selection bias
B) Confirmation bias
C) Publication bias
D) Funding bias

Answer: D) Funding bias
Explanation: Funding bias occurs when the source of funding influences the results or interpretation of a study, often leading to favorable outcomes for the sponsor.

40. Analyzing Data Trends

A researcher analyzes data showing a decrease in the population of a species over several years. What type of trend is being observed?
A) Exponential growth
B) Decline
C) Stabilization
D) Fluctuation

Answer: B) Decline
Explanation: A consistent decrease in population over time indicates a declining trend for that species.

10: Test-Taking Strategies for the Biology EOC

10.1 Understanding the Test Format

I. Types of Questions You Will Encounter

1. **Multiple-Choice Questions (MCQs):**

    o **Format:** A question or statement is followed by **4 answer choices**, with only **one correct answer**.

    o **Tip: Read all options carefully** before selecting an answer, and **eliminate wrong choices** to increase accuracy.

    Example:
    Which organelle is responsible for energy production?
    A) Ribosome
    B) Mitochondrion (correct answer)
    C) Nucleus
    D) Golgi apparatus

2. **Scenario-Based Questions:**

    o **Format:** Presents a **scientific situation, experiment, or problem**.

    o **Purpose:** Requires you to **apply biological concepts** to analyze the scenario.

    o **Tip: Underline key parts** of the scenario and identify what the question is really asking.

    Example:
    A scientist is studying how temperature affects enzyme activity...
    (Followed by questions on variables and outcomes.)

3. **Experimental Design Questions:**
    o **Format:** Focuses on **scientific method and experiments.**
    o **What you may be asked:**

- Identify **independent and dependent variables**.
- Formulate a **hypothesis**.
- Interpret **results from data tables or graphs**.
  - **Tip:** Review the **steps of the scientific method** before the test.

II. Time Management Strategies for Success

Strategy	Why It Helps
Know the test structure	Helps you **mentally prepare** for number of questions and time limits.
Allocate time per question	Prevents spending too long on any one question.
Answer easy questions first	Secures points and boosts confidence.
Monitor time regularly	Ensures you stay on pace and **have time to review**.

Example:
If the exam is **160 minutes for 60 questions**, aim to spend about **2.5 minutes per question**, but move faster on simple ones to leave time for harder ones.

10.2 Review Tips and Study Techniques

I. Creating Effective Study Guides and Flashcards

Technique	How to Use It Effectively
Identify Key Concepts	Focus on **main topics** (e.g., cell structure, genetics, ecosystems).
Organize Information	Group related ideas (e.g., photosynthesis and cellular respiration together).

Technique	How to Use It Effectively
Flashcards for Vocabulary	Write **term** on one side, **definition** on the other; quiz yourself regularly.

Tip: Use color coding for **different topics** to improve memory retention.

II. Using Practice Tests and Sample Questions

Practice Method	Benefit
Official practice tests	Get familiar with the format and difficulty level.
Timed practice	Develop **test-taking stamina and pacing.**
Review mistakes	Learn from incorrect answers to avoid repeating mistakes.

Example: If you miss a question on the carbon cycle, review that topic specifically to **fill gaps in knowledge**.

10.3 Common Pitfalls and How to Avoid Them

I. Avoiding Common Mistakes

Mistake	Tip to Avoid
Misreading questions	**Underline key words**, read carefully.
Overlooking answer choices	**Read all options** before choosing one.
Rushing through difficult questions	**Skip and return later** to avoid wasting time.

II. Understanding Tricky Question Wording

239

Trap to Watch For	What to Do
Absolute words ("always", "never")	Be cautious; **biology often has exceptions.**
Words like "EXCEPT", "NOT", "LEAST"	**Underline these** to remember you are looking for the exception.
Double negatives	Rephrase in your mind to make it positive and clearer.

Example:
"Which of the following is NOT a function of the mitochondria?"
Focus on **what mitochondria DO NOT do**, rather than what they do.

III. Analyzing Complex Scenarios

- **Break it down** into smaller steps:
    a. **Who/what is involved?** (organism, system, experiment)
    b. **What is happening?** (change, process, experiment)
    c. **What is the question asking?** (cause, effect, outcome)

Tip: Take notes in margins or write a quick outline for scenario-based questions.

Conclusion: How to Succeed on the Biology EOC

Step to Take	Why It's Important
Know the format	Reduces anxiety, improves pacing.
Use strategic study methods	Increases retention and understanding of key topics.
Practice under test conditions	Builds confidence and time management.
Avoid common mistakes and traps	Ensures accurate reading and thoughtful answers.
Stay calm and focused on test day	Helps you think clearly and do your best.

"Biology is not just about memorizing facts — it's about understanding how life works. By preparing thoughtfully and practicing smart strategies, you can approach the Biology EOC with confidence. Trust your preparation, read carefully, and remember that every question is a chance to show what you know."

Biology EOC Printable Checklist: Test-Taking Strategies & Study Tips

I. Before the Test: Study Preparation Checklist

Know the Test Format

☐ Review the **types of questions**: Multiple-choice, scenario-based, experimental design.
☐ Understand how much time you'll have (**160 minutes**) and how many questions (approx. **60–66 questions**).
☐ Practice **reading and interpreting data tables and graphs**.

Organize Your Study Materials

☐ Create **study guides** based on Biology EOC standards (cell biology, genetics, evolution, ecology, human systems).
☐ Make **flashcards** for key terms and definitions.
☐ Group related topics together for better understanding (e.g., DNA → RNA → Proteins).

Use Practice Tests

☐ Take **official practice tests** under timed conditions.
☐ Review **wrong answers** to identify weak areas.
☐ Focus on improving those topics before the test.

Review Common Biology Concepts

☐ Cell structure and function.
☐ Photosynthesis and cellular respiration.
☐ DNA, RNA, and protein synthesis.
☐ Mendelian genetics and Punnett squares.

☐ Evolution, natural selection, and adaptation.
☐ Ecosystems, food webs, and energy flow.
☐ Human body systems and homeostasis.

II. Day Before the Test: Final Prep Checklist

☐ **Get a good night's sleep** (7-8 hours recommended).
☐ Prepare your **materials** (ID, pencils, erasers, approved calculator if allowed).
☐ **Eat a healthy meal** to fuel your brain (balanced with protein and carbs).
☐ **Review your flashcards** briefly — don't over-study to avoid burnout.
☐ **Relax and do something calming** (e.g., light exercise, music).

III. During the Test: In-the-Moment Checklist

Before Starting

☐ **Take a deep breath** and stay calm.
☐ **Skim through the test** if allowed to see how it's laid out.

While Answering Questions

☐ **Read each question carefully**, underlining keywords (especially "NOT," "EXCEPT," "LEAST").
☐ **Identify what is being asked** — watch for tricky wording.
☐ **Eliminate obviously wrong answers** to improve your odds.
☐ Be **cautious with answers using absolute terms** like "always" or "never."
☐ **Watch your time** — don't get stuck on one question. Move on and come back if needed.
☐ **Use logic and what you know** — if unsure, make an educated guess.

For Graph/Data Questions

☐ Read **titles and labels** carefully.
☐ Identify **independent and dependent variables**.
☐ Look for **trends, patterns, and outliers** before answering.

IV. After the Test: Self-Reflection Checklist

☐ Review how you felt during the test — What strategies worked? What would you do differently next time?
☐ Celebrate completing the test — reward yourself for your hard work!

V. Bonus: Mindset Reminders to Stay Positive

■ "I have prepared well, and I am ready."
■ "I will read each question carefully and take my time."
■ "If I don't know the answer right away, I will think through what I do know."
■ "I am capable of doing well on this test."

Conclusion

Preparing for the Biology EOC is about more than just memorizing facts — it's about building a strong understanding of biological concepts and learning how to **apply them to real-world situations**. By using **smart study techniques, managing your time effectively, and staying aware of common testing pitfalls**, you can approach the exam with **confidence and clarity**.

Remember, **practice makes progress**. The more you review and engage with the material, the stronger your knowledge and test-taking skills will become. Don't be discouraged by challenging questions — think carefully, apply what you know, and do your best.

Stay calm, trust your preparation, and keep a positive mindset. You've worked hard to get to this point, and with determination and focus, **you can succeed on the Biology EOC.**

Good luck — you've got this!

Made in United States
Orlando, FL
25 April 2025